DATE DUE

JAN 15 1995 SEP 15 1995		DEC 15 1994	
		SEP 15 1995	

PUBLIC OPINION AND
CANADIAN IDENTITY

PUBLIC OPINION
AND
CANADIAN IDENTITY

MILDRED A. SCHWARTZ
Foreword by SEYMOUR MARTIN LIPSET

UNIVERSITY OF CALIFORNIA PRESS

Berkeley and Los Angeles   *1967*

University of California Press
Berkeley and Los Angeles, California

Cambridge University Press
London, England

FOREWORD

Two NATIONS, the United States and Canada, resulted from the American Revolution. The first, representing the victorious revolutionary side, emerged with a national ethos proclaimed in the Declaration of Independence, and subsequently furbished by the successful efforts of various political tendencies to extend the egalitarian aspects of that ethos. The liberal-left groups in the United States have repeatedly laid claim to the national tradition as they fought for universal suffrage, emancipation, state intervention on behalf of weaker and underprivileged groups, and currently equal rights for Negroes. Conservatives in the United States have been at a disadvantage as contrasted with similar tendencies in many European countries since the American national tradition has been identified with anti-elitist and utopian (assumptions about human perfectibility) conceptions. The extent to which this revolutionary tradition still informs the character of American society must be seen in comparative perspective, by contrasting different aspects of U.S. behavior and values with those of nations such as Canada which lack this tradition. Thus it will probably come as a shock to most Americans that the late Harold Innis, Canada's greatest social scientist, writing shortly after World War II, in discussing the emigration of Canadian university graduates to the United States, could present the problem as one involving "the training of our best students for export to countries with a revolutionary tradition." [1] More recently, a British Labor M.P., David Marquand, in reviewing Hofstadter's book, *The Paranoid Style in American Politics*, pointed to the fact that the "U.S. and the Soviet Union are both revolutionary countries, based on a belief in the perfectibility of man" [2] as an explanation of the belief in un-American and anti-Communist plots in both countries.

Innis and a number of other leading Canadian social scientists, such as S. D. Clark, A. R. M. Lower, and Frank Underhill, made the fact that Canada, the North American nation formed from the losing side

[1] Harold Innis, *Essays in Canadian Economic History*, Toronto: University of Toronto Press, 1956, p. 384.
[2] David Marquand, "America's Bad Guys," *The Observer*, November 27, 1966, p. 27.

in the Revolution, has a counter-revolutionary tradition, the principal clue to an understanding of Canadian values.[3] The historic decision which led to nationhood was the rejection of the Declaration of Independence, and republican status. Whereas after the Revolution many supporters of the American cause left behind north of the new international border emigrated south, many thousands of Tories moved north. And from then on, what emerged as a separate Canadian identity has been based on justifying itself as not being American. As S. D. Clark has put it: "Canadian national life can almost be said to take its rise in the negative will to resist absorption in the American Republic."[4]

In rejecting absorption into the revolutionary tradition, Canada chose the losing side from a world-wide ideological perspective. Although it ultimately incorporated most of the changes which everywhere are defined as "progressive" or "liberal"—independence, adult suffrage, welfare-state policies designed to further egalitarian ideals, widespread popular education on all levels—Canada made these adjustments much later than her southern neighbor in most cases. These reforms were rarely made as consequence of the triumph of a liberal egalitarian-oriented party or movement. Rather, as Canadian sociologist John Porter has argued, "their haphazard development has come about more by the 'demonstration effect' of their existence in other countries, than because they have formed the social philosophy of either of the two parties which have been in power at the federal level."[5]

The presence of Quebec in the Canadian Confederation also represents a negative decision designed to counter the growth of liberal ideals. The ecclesiastics of Quebec, the dominant leaders of the French population after the British Conquest in 1763, did not seize the opportunity of the American Revolution to regain freedom from foreign rule. Rather they feared the revolutionary Puritans of New England more than the Anglican Royalists. And after the French Revolution of 1789 resulted in the widespread dispersion of anticlerical and democratic doctrines in their mother country, the French Canadian church leadership sought to cut their people off from the twin sources of intellectual contamination, the United States and

[3] See S. M. Lipset, "Revolution and Counter-Revolution—The United States and Canada," in Thomas R. Ford, ed., *The Revolution-Theme in Contemporary America* (Lexington: University of Kentucky Press), pp. 21–64 for references to the literature dealing with these problems.

[4] S. D. Clark, "The Importance of Anti-Americanism in Canadian National Feeling," in H. F. Angus, ed., *Canada and Her Great Neighbor*, Toronto: The Ryerson Press, 1938, p. 243.

[5] John Porter, *The Vertical Mosaic: An Analysis of Social Class and Power in Canada*, Toronto: University of Toronto Press, 1965, p. 370.

France. Participation in a union with English Canadians under a British monarchy was far more preferable.

The leaders of both English and French Canada found themselves in an independent large federal union after 1867, not because they wanted new nationhood, but because they did not desire links with revolutionary countries, and Great Britain refused to continue various responsibilities for her autonomous North American provinces. The very notion of Canada which had emerged in French Canada and spread to what is now Ontario, was foreign to the people of the Maritimes and British Columbia. For many decades, residents of these provinces continued to speak of going to Canada, meaning the central regions of the country.

This tradition meant that the concept of a Canadian identity had little meaning to most citizens of the country. Until World War II, the term "Canadian" was not even used in Canadian passports. The British flag remained the flag of Canada until the 1960's. Canada's highest court of supreme appeal was the Privy Council of the British House of Lords until recently. Canada's constitution is the British North America Act, passed by the parliament of Great Britain in 1867. Amendments to the Constitution still require *pro forma* ratification by the British parliament. Such symbols of national inferiority which would be outrageous to the citizens of the various new nations of Africa and Asia apparently have bothered few Canadians.

During the decades of the fifties and sixties, Canada has witnessed a weakening of federal power in favor of the provinces. Although her constitution written immediately after the American Civil War, gives to the federal government much more ultimate power over the provinces than is held by the U.S. government with respect to the states, many of these central powers have rarely been used, because of weak national legitimacy. In short, although Canada has been one of the most successful nations on earth from the point of view of economic growth and the provision of a high standard of living to its citizens, it still lacks a strong sense of national pride and identity. It is still not certain what it is, a North American nation, not much different from the United States, which a significant minority thinks ought to join the United States, a British nation with a large French subculture, two nations, one English and the other French, which exist in a loose confederation, or some combination of these and other concepts.

This is some of the background to which Mildred Schwartz has addressed herself in this magnificent effort to bring together the public-opinion data gathered in many years bearing on the problem of Canadian identity. Her analysis indicates that the problem of identity is far from being resolved. Her emphasis on the integrative role of the two major political parties points to processes which analysts of the formation of national identity in other states have also suggested as crucial. For residents of the United States, this book supplies important insights into their own national development. It suggests that the nationalization of political orientations and opinions which have been occurring there are not a simple outcome of increased urbanization, industrialization, and better transportation and communication facilities. All of these which make the environment of most Americans similar presumably contribute to the formation of common reactions to comparable experiences in different parts of the country. But a basic cultural similarity and national ethos are also necessary for the growth of such value consensus. Where either is lacking, one may expect less integration. Even in very small countries such as Switzerland, Belgium, and the Netherlands, cultural disparities in the form of sharp linguistic and religious differences have not resulted in a strong sense of national identity. Switzerland has much more than the others, resulting in part from the fact that, like the United States, its existence is the result of a conscious effort at maintaining its independence.

I do not wish to comment further on the problems raised in this book, since this is properly the task of the author, a task which she has handled well. I would, however, like to note in conclusion that this book is not only important for its substantive findings, but it should be recommended reading to social scientists as an excellent example of the contribution to knowledge which can be made from a secondary analysis of the public-opinion data collected since the 1930's by the various commercial polling organizations. These materials provide a new dimension to historical and social science analysis. It is a commentary on the lack of imagination and training of scholars in these fields that this is the first book published based on such materials dealing with Canadian problems.[6] Mildred Schwartz, therefore, deserves to be congratulated both for her contribution to our understanding of problems of national identity, and for her methodological pioneering.

Seymour Martin Lipset
Harvard University

[6] There is one previous work which uses Canadian opinion data in a comparative treatment of voting behavior in the four major Anglo-American democracies. See Robert Alford, *Party and Society: The Anglo-American Democracies*, Chicago: Rand McNally, 1963.

PREFACE

THE TWENTY-SIXTH parliament of Canada, in an act preceded by acrimonious argument, finally passed legislation giving Canada its own flag, distinct in design from that of any other nation. It was an act that was probably little noticed outside the borders of Canada. As far as Canada itself was concerned, it did nothing to solve pressing economic problems, nor did it contribute to the social welfare of the people. It did not even have much bearing on French-English tensions, except that in some quarters it served to exacerbate these. Where then does the significance of the new flag lie? It points up the anomalies of Canadian nationhood. Ninety-eight years after its formation as a viable state, Canada was only beginning to cope with problems most nations meet (though not necessarily solve) at their birth. Canada's late start in acquiring the symbols of nationhood is indicative of the larger problems it faces as a creation of Britain, a neighbour of the United States, and a nation peopled by groups that somehow had never developed many unifying bonds.

As a Canadian, and one who has also lived in the United States, I had my own ideas about what it meant to live in Canada. At the same time, as a sociologist, I was attracted to the question of what it meant to other Canadians, divided as they were by regional, ethnic, and religious loyalties. From my interest in the role of political parties in a democratic state, I was drawn to the part played by parties in the development of national ties.

I saw these issues in comparative and historical terms, and I tried to obtain data which would permit me to so treat Canada's identity. In this regard I was helped by the availability of twenty years of Canadian Gallup material. But without disparaging these data, which form the basis of all my generalizations, they were after all collected by others to serve other purposes, and they put considerable limits on the kinds of analyses I was able to make or the conclusions I could draw. Whether they still provide valuable insights into Canadian society, I leave to the reader to judge.

Data were obtained through Professor Philip K. Hastings of the Roper Public Opinion Research Center in Williamstown, Massachusetts, and Miss Byrne Hope Sanders of the Canadian Institute for Public Opinion Research, Toronto. Both Professor Hastings and Miss

Sanders and their staff were consistently helpful and prompt in meeting my requests for information.

This book was originally a doctoral dissertation for Columbia University, partly supported by a predoctoral fellowship from the Canada Council. The dissertation was supervised by Juan J. Linz, whose critical comments have contributed immeasurably to the value of this work.

Tabulations and calculations of statistical tests were done through the great generosity of Statistical Reporting and Tabulating Limited, Toronto, and the Computing Center of the University of Alberta, Calgary. I would particularly like to thank Ronald May, Anton Colijn, Philip Hadfield, and Mary Lynn Losie at the Center. An initial preparation of the hundreds of tables upon which this study is based was ably done by Mrs. Mary Engelmann. In preparing this book, however, it seemed unnecessarily cumbersome to include all these tables. For further information or confirmation of discussions in the text, the unpublished dissertation, "Canadian National Identity as Seen Through Public Opinion Polls: 1941–1963," is available on file at Columbia University.

Other research assistance was provided by Moira McIvor, Lois Carrier, and Victor Marshall. The style of this book has hopefully been improved by the discerning editorial comments of Rosemary Plotnick, Timothy Enos, Ann Jacobs, and especially Jean Block.

The topics which I cover touch on a number of disciplines, and in all cases where I required expert advice I was able to call on my former colleagues at the University of Alberta, Calgary. Of the many who aided me, two in particular can never be adequately thanked. They are Frederick C. Engelmann and Eugene Oetting. Professor Engelmann's fund of knowledge about politics was always available to me, and his sage advice was a major source of support. Dr. Oetting brought his creative insight to bear on my methodological problems, and he was always ready to discuss these with me.

Various versions of the first section of this book were discussed with Robert R. Alford, Leonard Binder, James A. Davis, Thelma H. McCormack, Donald L. Spence, Sidney Verba, Douglas Verney. Although I was not always able to use directly the suggestions they made, I benefited in all cases from their critical comments.

Typing of the final manuscript was the work of Masako Oshita, Nella Siefert, Lillian Rochon, and Dolores Farrell of National Opinion Research Center, University of Chicago.

M.A.S.

CONTENTS

xii PUBLIC OPINION AND CANADIAN IDENTITY

PART III. THE RELATION OF POLITICAL
         PARTIES TO A DEVELOPING
         IDENTITY

		Page
VIII	PARTY INFLUENCE ON OPINIONS	127

The Political Problem, 127
Methods of Discerning Opinion Climates, 128
Evidence of Party Influence, 130

  IX BARRIERS TO CONSENSUS   146

Regionalism, 146
Origin and Party, 158
The Consequences of Diversity, 171

   X THE PULL BETWEEN PARTY AND OTHER
      CHARACTERISTICS   172

Social Class and Party, 172
Party and Age, Sex, and Marital Status, 186

  XI THE SIGNIFICANCE OF PARTIES   196

Canadian Party Types, 196
Differences Between Parties, 200
Cross-Party Consensus, 207
Political Consequences, 210

PART IV. CONFRONTATION WITH NATIONAL
         PROBLEMS

 XII THE IMPACT OF NATIONAL PROBLEMS   215

The Meaningfulness of Issues, 215
Indicators of Salience, 217
An Assessment of Saliency, 231

XIII RESPONSES TO THE CHALLENGE
      OF NATIONAL VIABILITY   233

Problems and Solutions: Stability and Change, 233
Defining an Identity, 239
The Case of Canada, 250

INDEX   259

TABLES

FIGURES

PART I
PERSPECTIVES ON IDENTITY

I   THE PUZZLE OF CANADA

AT PRESENT we are witnessing the creation of more new states than at any other period in history. Many of these are faced with serious problems stemming from a low level of industrial development, a high rate of illiteracy, and a burning impatience to bridge the gap between tradition and modernity. Some of them are also characterized by political instability, both as cause and effect of their other difficulties. Yet many of the problems troubling today's new nations were also troublesome to those created generations ago, and, in some instances, continue to plague long-established states. Among the vexing tasks facing new nations (which some older ones have even yet not resolved) is the need to create a sense of unity for disparate member groups. Partly to satisfy these diverse interests, such nations need to overcome gross inequalities of opportunity, raise the general level of existence, and hold up these accomplishments as a source of pride to their citizens. The political organizations are called upon, then, to prove themselves by providing for the satisfaction of wants. It is important too that, wherever appropriate, a marked disassociation from former colonial rulers take place.

What happens to countries in the presence of these tasks is the subject of the growing literature on new nations. We will seek our answer, however, in the example of Canada, a country which in no sense of the term is a new nation or a developing country.[1] Canada, settled by migrants from developed countries, never had to contend with large-scale illiteracy or stultifying tradition, nor has it suffered from serious political upheavals. It possesses a differentiated social structure with all the accoutrements of a modern, industrial nation and an educated, technically skilled population. Yet Canada, although nearly one hundred years old, recapitulates in its daily existence many dilemmas experienced by newly emerging nations. Unity from diversity, the overcoming of gross inequalities, the need for a focus

[1] Canada is found among the first-ranking countries on a technological scale and among the lowest-ranking countries on a demographic scale, indicating a high rate of economic development, with an absence of acute population pressures. Brian J. L. Berry, "Basic Patterns of Economic Development," *Atlas of Economic Development,* ed. by Norton Ginsburg, Chicago: University of Chicago Press, 1961, pp. 110–119.

3

for national pride, contrast with other nations—in short, the essence of the business of politics and the creation of stable nationhood are still prominent political concerns in Canada, as they are in other multi-ethnic states. Statehood of many years duration or status as a developed country do not in themselves guarantee the existence of an unambiguous national identity. The study of Canada then takes on special significance in illuminating the continued existence of problems of identity long after a nation has passed its infancy.

The character of Canadian nationhood appeared as both an enigma and a cause for concern.

That there should be a country called Canada distinct from the United States is a mere accident of history, in fact, a political paradox. Nature has not conferred upon Canada any particular personality of her own. There is no geographical difference to separate her from her great neighbour to the South. It is a problem to determine wherein lies Canada's centre of gravity: politically it is in England, and geographically it is in the United States—in either case outside her own boundaries. Her very existence is connected with this problem; for a purely British Canada could never be anything but a colony, and an American Canada could only be a group of states in the Union.[2]

Although the Fathers of Confederation and notably the first Prime Minister, John A. Macdonald, were gripped by the vision of a great nation emerging from their political efforts, and a later Prime Minister, Sir Wilfrid Laurier, saw the twentieth century as belonging to Canada, national greatness has often seemed just out of reach, and many have been dismayed at their chance of ever obtaining it. Throughout Canada's history, historians, political scientists, economists, and a host of commentators have expressed concern for the chances of Canada's continued existence as an independent country.[3] They tend to view it as either a British colony or an American satellite. Even the less pessimistic recognize the historical developments which have produced the anomalies of Canadian existence.

To begin with, Canada and the other British colonies emerged as "essentially political projections of Great Britain."[4] More recently, the economic influence of the United States has been so great as to help perpetuate Canada's economic development as a resource-pro-

[2] André Siegfried, *Canada: An International Power*, trans. Doris Hemming, 2nd ed.; New York: Duell, Sloan, Pearce, 1947, p. 23.

[3] For a recent book in the pessimistic tradition, see George Grant, *Lament for a Nation, The Defeat of Canadian Nationalism*, Toronto: McClelland and Stewart, 1965.

[4] Alexander Brady, *Democracy in the Dominions*, 3rd ed.; Toronto: University of Toronto Press, 1958, p. 5.

ducing country. Canadians have always had this prosperous and populous neighbour, and, when disappointments have grown too great and
opportunities have seemed much richer across the border, scores of
Canadians have left their homeland. In the 1880's and 1890's
Canadian immigration to the United States was extensive. Again in
the 1920's, with a population of under ten million, Canada lost about
one million residents to the United States. To one economist deeply
concerned with Canada's development, the most realistic solution is
for Canada to accept its limitations and to grow as best it can with
them.

Canadian economic policy has historically been dominated by the ambition
to create a country rival in power to the United States, and so to prove that
the Americans were wrong to revolt from colonial rule in 1776. The ambition to outgrown the United States is a futile one: in spite of the boasting
about Canada's faster growth in the postwar period, it is a fact that the
growth was insufficient to raise the ratio of the Canadian to the American
population to what it was in 1860.[5]

The initial political dependence on Britain and the continued,
growing, and pervasive influence of the United States are only two
problems with which Canada has had to contend. Within Canadian
society major differences exist as a result of settlement by a population heterogeneous in language, origin, and religion. These differences
are accompanied, and in some cases reinforced, by the existence of
physical resources, industries, and economic problems specific to particular regions. All these differences undoubtedly affect the development of national unity, and their nature and consequences will be
elaborated in the analysis that follows.

All mentioned factors have operated to create a puzzling and
ambiguous nation.

. . . we have emerged in a period of modern history when it has been
impossible for the Canadian national unit to grow slowly in the quiet isolation of slowly moving centuries during which such older nationalities as
Britain and France, or India and China worked out their individual way
of life and solidified their national characteristics. A Briton or a Frenchman
does not have to keep torturing himself now in the twentieth century by
asking questions as to the nature of his national identity or as to how he
is to distinguish himself from his national neighbours.[6]

[5] Harry G. Johnson, *Canada in a Changing World Economy*, Toronto: University
of Toronto Press, 1962, p. 62.
[6] Frank H. Underhill, in *The Price of Being Canadian*, ed. by D. L. B. Hamlin,
7th Winter Conference, Canadian Institute of Public Affairs; Toronto: University
of Toronto Press, 1961, p. 5.

At first glance Canada to the outsider appears almost indistinguishable from the United States. D. W. Brogan writes,

I can remember my first visit to Canada, one of a few hours nearly thirty years ago. To my then untutored eye, the only visible differences were the red coats of the police, the royal monograms and the advertisements for English chocolates. I know better now; but that first impression was not totally false. And there is, consequently, for an outsider like myself a permanent shock arising from the fact that Canada is so like the United States and another from the fact that being so alike she is not identical.[7]

Nationalism has been shaped by many loyalties and has often been expressed with uneasiness and ambivalence.[8] As a further consequence, some commentators believe the state itself has been accorded only minimal legitimacy. Despite major problems of external relations and internal cleavages Canada, nevertheless, continues to exist.

The statements of experts and intellectuals on Canadian history give an elitist conception of the difficulties of existence. It is of even greater relevance to ask how Canadians generally, as residents of an apparently viable nation, see their country. Although intellectual elites undoubtedly serve as spokesmen for various interests in the population and reflect common concerns, they also, because of differences in social background and position, often express views at variance with those of the people at large. Information on nontechnical matters seen only through the perspective of experts can thus be misleading. As the historian Planck writes:

The great obstacle to ascertaining the values of a period lies in the paucity of information concerning the great masses of people as contrasted with the articulate few. What starts out as an attempt to portray the climate of opinion of an age turns out frequently to be a description of its intellectual leadership or of some other limited group. It has been suggested, for example, that the characterization of the Middle Ages as predominantly spiritual in its

[7] D. W. Brogan, "An Outsider Looking In," in *Canada's Tomorrow*, ed. by G. P. Gilmour, Toronto: Macmillan, 1954, p. 273.

[8] For example, a pilot study conducted among 107 respondents in the spring of 1960 in the Toronto area on attitudes toward "Canadian products and practices" found the following results to this question.

> "Some people go too far in making
> an issue of their pride in Canada."

	Percent
Strongly agree	7
Agree	36
Uncertain	12
Disagree	37
Strongly disagree	8

values may have come about because the major primary sources for the period are the products of the clerical pen and mind, and that if a larger number of extant sources about medieval attitudes had been written or compiled by non-ecclesiastics our modern conceptions might well be open to modification.[9]

To overcome these limitations and consider more effectively the nature of Canada as it is perceived by the Canadian population generally, it is necessary to rely on public-opinion polls.[10] Such polls covering two decades provide the main sources for this study.

The use of public-opinion polls for the study of national identity can give us the views of a cross-section of Canadians, but it cannot provide a comprehensive definition of national identity, nor of the forces which have shaped its development. We have deliberately eschewed certain data in order to keep the present study within manageable limits and, more important, to point up the way in which national identity, as an end product of social and political forces not specifically examined here, is reflected in the opinions of Canadians. This technique allows us to answer such questions as how Canada can be described socially and politically, what areas of agreement and disagreement exist on this definition, which social groups are associated with particular viewpoints, and how opinions change over time. These questions are discussed from Part II onward.

The remainder of this Part I is concerned with more general problems. Chapter II deals with the concept of national identity, presenting it in detail so that our subsequent analysis of empirical data may be pegged to significant social and political issues. Chapter III, a resume of Canadian development, illustrates the various aspects detailed in our conceptualization of national identity, filling in some of the gaps left by the public-opinion data. Part I, then, deals with the conceptual tools and the historical context and should be regarded as a prologue to the examination of survey data on the unfolding of Canada's public image in Chapters IV to XII. The concluding chapter returns to the general scheme set out in Part I and relates the empirical findings to it. Results of public-opinion polling are then assessed in terms of a more holistic view of Canadian society.

[9] Russell E. Planck, "Public Opinion in France After the Liberation, 1944–1949" in *Common Frontiers of the Social Sciences*, ed. by Mirra Komarovsky, Glencoe: Free Press and Falcon's Wing, 1957, p. 214.

[10] On the values of public-opinion polls to historians, see Paul F. Lazarsfeld, "The Historian and the Pollster," *ibid.*, pp. 242–262.

II THE ADOLESCENCE OF NATIONHOOD

THE MEANING OF IDENTITY

THE CONCEPT of identity has been introduced to the social-science community from the psychoanalytic literature. Identity was first used by Freud in reference to the process by which infants discriminate among social objects and then internalize the appropriate object and associated values. Identity formation at this stage is largely a response to frustration. The concepts of self which emerge from initial familial experiences are elemental ones of boy, girl, son, daughter, sister, brother.

Acting out the familial drama does not resolve the stream of crises associated with the definition of selfhood. Identity formation proceeds through adulthood, with problems coming to a head especially in adolescence. In adolescence, the individual moves out from the confines of the family to experiences with peers, the school, then to the work world, and the larger community. In this more complex social setting, the search for a consistent self-definition is often experienced with the turmoil we have grown to associate with that peculiar stage of development. For the adolescent, what he is and where he is going are critical matters. Although he enjoys many freedoms and privileges, some experiences are still closed to him; yet many of the moves he makes now will have major implications for those adult roles he will be able to play and those from which he has already shut himself off.[1]

At the level of the individual, the concept of identity is not easy to understand or to use consistently. It is not a physical attribute, it cannot be quantified, and there is no simple means for obtaining empirical referents of it. It becomes especially important, then, that anyone using the concept give enough flesh to his discussion so that those with whom he communicates can grasp the social dimensions of identity. He needs, moreover, to avoid communicating any mystical aura to identity, although the temptation may be great for those so inclined to indulge in flights of fancy about the "spirit of selfhood."

[1] The major intellectual debt on the study of identity is to Erik Erikson. His pertinent works are *Childhood and Society,* New York: Norton, 1950; *Young Man Luther,* New York: Norton, 1958; "Youth: Fidelity and Diversity," *Daedalus,* 91, Winter, 1962, pp. 5–27.

Transferring the concept of identity from the individual to the nation presents even greater difficulties on this score. To speak of the identity of a nation is to engage in metaphor, and whoever then goes on to accept the metaphor as reality sinks into the morass of group-mind fallacies. But if identity in this context is viewed only as metaphor, then it can be a useful research tool. Indeed, it becomes possible to obtain empirical indicators of its nature, allowing description of the nation's identity to take the most prosaic form. The manner in which the public-opinion data are used in the following chapters should provide proof not only of the usefulness of the concept but also of the nonmystical perspective employed. There is no thought given to how survey data might describe a national *Geist,* assuming there ever was such a thing.

National identity is of course not solely metaphor. It is used less abstractly to refer to one of the components of personal identity, that as a member of a particular nation. In this respect, everyone has a national identity. What is variable, however, is the extent to which this aspect of personal identity is relevant. In stable societies, it may only be under such unusual circumstances as travel to a foreign country that the individual is confronted with the question of who he is. Otherwise his identity in this regard may simply be taken for granted. But under conditions of external threats and major internal changes, political or not, the issue of personal identity as a member of a nation may become problematic.

Hence, while the identity of the nation has no independent existence outside of the shared understandings which people have about its nature, it does enter into the formation of collective identities as Canadians, Americans, or Nigerians. Out of the interaction of historical events, actions of governments, activities, personalities, and ideologies of leaders, and conflicts and accommodations between interests, a nation emerges, and in so doing, acquires a distinctive character. This image of the nation then provides the focus for the personal identities of its members, sometimes lying dormant and other times becoming mobilized in the self-definitions of citizens.

One person who has been especially concerned with translating identity from the personal to the national realm is Lucian Pye. From his interest in Erikson and his work in Burma, Pye arrives at a view of national identity as both a component and a counterpart of personal identity.

The quest for nationhood, the awe of politics, and the widespread ambivalences of personal identity are clearly related phenomena, but it is not clear by what logic they are related. At the least, a circuitous pattern is present:

the search for individual identity hinges on the existence of a national identity, and the latter calls for a coherent and consensus-bound political process; but people cannot fundamentally respect their political spokesmen when they are not sure that they can respect themselves, and so back to the issue of personal integrity and identity. A dilemma is framed: the need for self-identity produces the need for a nation-state, and the need for reassurance of individual worth produces the need for a politics of status —and yet such a politics is inconsistent with the requirements of nation-building.[2]

While using some imagery different from that which we employ, Pye's analysis of Burmese society illustrates the interplay between personal identity, the image of the nation, and the collective identities emergent from this interplay. Several contrasts exist, however, between our interests and Pye's. For one thing, he is directly concerned with the way in which personal identities emerge in Burma as a result of the historical context and the patterns of socialization within the family. He also looks at the life histories of political leaders, searching for clues to the development of ideologies which can provide a touchstone for the formation of collective identities for the population generally. In this fashion he is able to tackle much more directly than will be possible in this book the subjective meaning of being a member of Burmese society. But although we lack information on the Canadians' sense of identification with their nation, we are able, unlike Pye, to delineate more sharply the nature of the country itself as it is seen by its citizens.

Pye explicitly pictures issues of identity, at both the individual and collective level, as of pressing concern in transitional societies. In terms of the analogy we are employing, these might parallel the identity crises of childhood. But one of the dilemmas of today's newly emerging nations is that their current crises adumbrate those of adolescence to such an extent that the initial problems do not have sufficient opportunity to be worked out. It is as if a child were faced, at the same time as he was establishing his primary identity vis-à-vis his parents and siblings, with defining himself in terms of more mature heterosexual relations. Thus the uncertainty, anxiety, and vacillation between urgent searching and passivity which Pye describes as characteristic of such nations[3] derives in part from the difficulty of answering *under pressure* "What am I?" "What is Burma?" and "What am I as a Burmese?" Demands for improving the life of the

[2] Lucian W. Pye, *Politics, Personality, and Nation Building: Burma's Search for Identity*, New Haven: Yale University Press, 1962, pp. 4–5.

[3] *Ibid.*, p. 124.

people are so vast and so pressing, and contrast with other, more successful nations is so acute, that not enough time is available for resolving problems stemming from ineffectual leadership, political organs either embryonic or not fully adaptive to current concerns, and a social structure itself out of step with the search for modernity. While such circumstances certainly contribute to the fascination of issues of identity in countries like Burma, at the same time they suggest that other, less harassed, societies might provide more efficient arenas for the study of national identity at the stage of emerging nationhood.

In response to the painful struggles of new states to assume the identity of nations, Lipset has turned to an examination of the early history of the United States as the "first new nation." He traces the tentative steps, the trials and errors in the activities of leaders and particularly of George Washington; in the emergence of political parties, and especially the legitimacy of political opposition; and in the evolution of the system of government in forging a nation: "It was from this crucible of confusion and conflict that values and goals became defined, issues carved out, positions taken, in short *an identity established*. For countries, like people, are not handed identities at birth, but acquire them through the arduous process of growing up, a process which is a notoriously painful affair." [4] As a result of his formulation of the emergence of identity as a slow and painful process, he is more sanguine than Pye about the potentialities of today's new nations to achieve stable governments and even democratic ones. Pye's pessimism is probably well taken, however, because of the distinction implicit in the work of both writers. That is, employing our imagery again, while the beginnings of the United States may properly be seen as the identity struggles of infancy, those of Burma are confounded by the problems of premature adolescence. This is obviously not the sole source of difference between the two countries. It may well be that the contrast in resources, population, values, and experiences are at the root of the differing lines of development as much as the particular problems they faced or the timing of these problems. Although it may be, then, that emerging nations at present can find little that is instructive in the beginnings of the United States, the student of politics in contrast does find it rewarding to isolate a "purer" instance of identity formation than is provided by today's new nations.

Another of Lipset's contributions is that he goes on from his consideration of the early years of United States nationhood to deal with

[4] S. M. Lipset, *The First New Nation,* New York: Basic Books, 1963, p. 16.

later history, even to the current scene. He no longer speaks explicitly of the formation of identity, but it is not inappropriate to continue with this terminology in assessing later historical developments. For example, we can extrapolate that the definition of identity current in the mid-1800's was neither sufficiently unambiguous nor widely enough shared to prevent the Civil War and the threatened dissolution of the Union. The existing identity was, however, helpful in aiding in the absorption of masses of immigrants and in the expansion of the nation westward. While the crises of identity, one hundred years after the thirteen colonies broke away from England, could be seen as those of adolescence, Lipset does not leave us at that point either. Although we can only view the United States as a mature, developed nation, there are still major strains in the society. These strains are perhaps not best conceptualized as crises of identity, yet they do represent instances in which the stable identity of the nation is confronted with searing problems, problems sufficient to shake even the mature identity. Problems, then, such as the struggle of Negroes for equal rights, illustrate the continuing usefulness of focusing on identity at periods later than a nation's formative years.

In the course of *The First New Nation*, Lipset uses the nature of the value system as his primary perspective on American society. In other words, it is mainly through values that he is defining the identity of the nation, even though, in the statements quoted, values appear as only one aspect of identity. Still, the usefulness of this approach is attested to by the success of his book.

In the case of this study, the focus differs from the writers we have considered. Although there is a close relation both to the work of Pye and Lipset, this study differs from the former in not emphasizing the content of subjective identifications and from the latter in not emphasizing values. Our approach instead will be to concentrate on national problems. The selection of problems as the focus for this study of identity has been at least partly determined by the data available, but it is also based on other, more theoretically relevant, considerations. Our desire was to describe how citizens perceive their nation. This raised the necessity of having a simple means of classifying the public-opinion data which was both meaningful in the context of Canadian history and, in keeping with our comparative perspective, could be used for other nations. For this purpose we were able to derive generic problems common to all societies with differentiated political institutions. These basic political problems are of three types: external, internal, and symbolic. The external problems are those of maintaining national integrity—militarily, economically, and politically. Internal problems concern the maintenance of order, as this involves regulating the allocation of resources and rewards of both a political and a more general nature. Symbolic problems imply the provision of unifying, emotion-laden ideas and objects which can serve as a focus for group loyalty.

One advantage of stating the problems in this general form was that they could be used to subsume the concerns of nations at any stage in their development. At the same time, the particular form which the problems take do reflect differences in national status. For example, both the United States and Nigeria face external problems in defining, and maintaining the definition of, their identity. Yet the character of the external problems and the ways these are met are quite different. The United States, already in a position of hegemony, strives to anticipate and counter any threats to its dominance, whether in Viet Nam, the Dominican Republic, or Berlin. For a country such as Nigeria, although the external problems are equally important for its integrity, the cards are played in a less important game. For Nigeria, redefining its role in relation to Britain and acquiring new roles in the British Commonwealth and the African continent are the uppermost concerns.

A further advantage which derives from focusing on problems is their analogy to the crises of identity at the individual level. Thus, in the preceding example, external problems for the United States are crises of maturity; for Nigeria, they are crises of childhood approaching the new-found independence of adolescence.

Canada is older than Nigeria and younger than the United States. In response to the general problems, it has manifested the shift from childhood to adolescence, and in some instances to full maturity. We will go on to describe in detail how, in facing external problems, Canada has moved out from dependence on Great Britain to that on the United States, and how, in keeping with its more mature status, this new dependence has been more rankling. Internally, initial problems of self-definition were achieved with the emergence of a federal system of government and a system of political parties, but the solutions were not appropriate for later developments, and serious strains are now experienced as a result of the demands from Quebec for greater autonomy. Finally, although the national symbols adopted in the early years were adequate for that period, they have not kept pace with historical developments either. The nature of symbols in fact suggests that these, like primal sex-linked identities, need to be defined early in the emergence of nationhood to provide a continuing focus for group loyalties.

The ways in which different societies meet their problems vary greatly. These variations have been conceptualized in ways which emphasize the generic nature of the solutions. For example, Spiro uses political style to refer to the different arguments which are offered as rationalizations for ways of handling problems common to constitutional governments,[5] and Almond speaks of political culture as the patterned orientations to politics developed in each political system.[6] Other terms, such as democracy, authoritarianism, or dictatorship, might also be considered as wholesale descriptions of the manner in which a country may meet its problems. In our usage, however, solutions may cover a wide range, from procedures for the conduct of government, the rights of citizens, and other basic understandings about the political process, to specific choices of governmental policy concerning internal relations among groups or relations with foreign powers. Not all solutions, nor all aspects of problems, need be either of critical concern to a particular country or sources of dissension. But, because we are dealing with the public definition of a country, opinions which happen to be surveyed are often about only those problems or solutions which are troublesome to a nation. This approach may therefore tend to exaggerate the lack of consensus, especially on those fundamentals present in most stable democracies; but this is an unavoidable difficulty.

From problems underlying the formation of national identity, we turn to the influences affecting its definition. These influences can be thought of as operating at any level in the interplay between subjective identifications with the nation, the public image of the nation, and the collective identities of its members. In keeping with our interests in the public perceptions of the nation, our treatment of influences has been geared to emphasize their potential impact on the shaping of opinions.

Influences on the definition of national identity are manifold and include, with societal and temporal variations, the following: (1) social groupings, organized or not, with special reference to intellectual elites and the military; (2) political parties, both as organizations and as aggregates of voters; (3) circumstantial factors including historical

[5] Herbert J. Spiro, *Government by Constitution*, Englewood Cliffs: Prentice-Hall, 1959, pp. 175–177.

[6] Gabriel A. Almond, "Comparative Political Systems," in *Political Behavior*, ed., by Heinz Eulau, Samuel J. Eldersveld, and Morris Janowitz, Glencoe: Free Press, 1956, p. 36. See also Gabriel A. Almond and Sidney Verba, *The Civic Culture*, Princeton: Princeton University Press, 1963. Pye considers the definition of identity to be part of the political culture. Pye, *op. cit.*, p. 124. However, sometimes it is more useful to view the political culture as a component of identity, particularly with reference to the identity of the nation.

events and governmental action; (4) the mass media; and (5) the nature of education.

Social Groupings

It has been long observed that opinions are affected by position in the social structure. Social position affects the range of opportunities and experiences available; common conditions of life are highly correlated with common patterns of behaviour. Shared opportunities lead to the development of common attitudes and values.[7] More recently, the literature on reference groups and relative deprivation has combined the two ideas of objective position and subjective evaluation of that position. In a society with a heterogeneous population, then, different social groups are apt to define the national problems in different ways.[8] This differential evaluation has a high conflict potential, yet can be contained by the ties which surmount group boundaries, for example, through cross-cutting loyalties produced by identification with a number of groups simultaneously. In addition, groups may be dedicated to particularistic views on national identity, but the impact of these views can be restricted by the differential commitment of their members. Consensus may emerge, despite heterogeneity, through the existence of wider loyalties, so that, for example, being a German is more important than being a Berliner, or being a law-abiding citizen more important than being a segregationist. It is also significant that in a plural society only a small number of values require relatively widespread agreement in order to avoid major breakdowns in the political system. Social cleavages, then, are significant in affecting the development of national identity because of their capacity, at least potential, for leading to disparate views on national problems or their solutions. Yet these opinion differences can also be contained by the mechanisms suggested. In every social setting, then, there exists the empirical problem of ascertaining the relationship

[7] According to Marx, for example, although the objective conditions for distinguishing between classes might exist, a class *an sich* did not become a class *für sich* until the class members recognized their identity of interests and the need for working in concert. See the discussion by R. K. Merton, *Social Theory and Social Structure*, rev. ed.; Glencoe: Free Press, 1957, pp. 462–463, 476–479.

[8] Which group memberships or identifications are most significant in affecting points of view varies with the society in question. Political cleavages generally are related to class, including occupation, trade-union affiliation, education, income, and subjective evaluation of position; origin, which refers to birthplace, language, religion, race, and cultural group; age; sex; marital status; community size, and region. For a summary, see S. M. Lipset, *Political Man*, Garden City: Doubleday, 1960, pp. 179–282.

between social groups and specific points of view, and the implications
that this has for national identity.

The intellectual elite.—One group which merits special attention
is the intellectual elite. Intellectuals act as innovators and promul-
gators of values and ideas. It is they who first acquire a national
culture, which is then communicated to the more parochial elements
in the society who are less inclined to recognize common national
bonds. Yet intellectuals may be restricted in their contribution to
formulating a collective identity for a number of reasons. Since their
ideas may derive from foreign sources, they are often troubled by
ambivalent feelings toward their own and the foreign culture, especially where the foreign culture accents the apparent inferiority of the
native. By training and disposition the intellectual may accentuate
his position as critic in opposition to politicians and men of action;
he may then end up taking little positive part in influencing the
development of a collective identity. Even when he lacks such a
negative outlook he may be hindered in his activity by resistance from
traditional sectors in the society. Such resistance is most likely to arise
when new ideas threaten the old value system. Despite these difficulties,
the intellectual elite continues to play a historic role in providing a
secular ideology with which to promote national unity.

The military.—In the recent emergence of new states, the military
has played a prominent role. While often lacking in political skills,
it seems important in transitional societies because it provides a centre
of stability. Existing social, cultural, and personality systems, and the
political structure of transitional societies strengthen the hand of the
military at the same time that they prevent the emergence of strong
political and intellectual elites which could help unify these nations.
Yet even when the army is not in political control, militarism may
contribute to a definition of identity by providing a focus for national
pride, offering at least the threat of solution to problems, and, where
there is a citizens' army, serving to integrate different groups into
the nation.

National Political Parties

Wherever they exist, national political parties contribute appreciably
in answering the primarily political questions raised by the study of
identity. Parties play this role by offering solutions to the central
problems, and by their ability to transcend other group loyalties. Yet,
even more visibly than other social divisions, party divisions are
directly concerned with the generation and public awareness of con-

troversy. In this capacity, parties, by overcoming other centrifugal tendencies, may establish a highly coherent internal consensus. In states with more than one party this may mean that party cleavages become the critical ones, and, as a result, prevent the creation of a national consensus on the nation's image. In cases where one political party is most instrumental in accomplishing the move to modern nationhood, regardless of whether this required a revolutionary struggle, or where it has some traditional claim to the legitimacy of its leadership, the coincidence of party and national consensus may be a critical handicap to the emergence of legitimate opposition parties. But in those countries where democracy and multiple parties have become institutionalized, political parties, even while agents of controversy, have at least the ability to "nurture consensus." [9] This is facilitated by those mechanisms within the political structure which mitigate party polarization, but which do not exist for other group cleavages. These mitigants include the desire of all parties to get elected, after election to govern all citizens including their opponents, and to be recognized in this capacity as the rightful rulers. The contribution of political parties to the shaping of national identity is thus not confined to single-party systems. Multi-party systems would indeed appear to allow a greater degree of peaceful controversy, to provide the mechanisms for resolving it, and to offer the potential for achieving agreement on basic essentials, particularly on the legitimacy of the political system. But even specific issues, although beginning as matters of partisan controversy, so far as they are attractive to the general voter, may also ultimately become part of the general consensus.

The nature of parties.—Parties, in translating issues of national identity into the political arena, do so mainly in relation to three dimensions. The first of these is organizational, and refers basically to the parties' membership structure. At issue here are the distinctions similar to the ones made by Duverger with respect to mass and cadre parties[10] and by Neumann regarding parties of individual representation and social integration.[11] For the sake of convenience, we will use Duverger's terminology even though our usage does not exactly coincide with his. For our purposes we will consider the cadre party

[9] See Austin Ranney and Willmoore Kendall, *Democracy and the American Party System,* New York: Harcourt Brace, 1956, pp. 508–511, for an elaboration of this ability in a two-party system.

[10] Maurice Duverger, *Political Parties,* London: Methuen, 1954, pp. 63–71.

[11] Sigmund Neumann, "Toward a Comparative Study of Political Parties," in *Modern Political Parties,* ed. by S. Neumann, Chicago: University of Chicago Press, 1956, p. 404.

as having as its nucleus a relatively small group of experts and influential persons who control the policy-making decisions. The cadre party is thus organizationally an exclusive body of notables. Activities of the bulk of supporters are confined primarily to elections. In contrast, the mass party relies on the active participation of a large body of recruits without specialized talents. These supporters are expected to be relatively permanent, dues-paying members who are involved in the life of the party in their day-to-day existence.

The second dimension is that of the social base from which the political parties draw support. The character of this support may be broad, so that all major groups in the population are represented, at least in a minority. The base, on the contrary, may instead be restricted to only selected social groups.

The third dimension of party type is its focus of appeal. Here the difference is between those parties oriented to principles based on special interests, issues, groups, or ideology, and those primarily oriented to electoral success, where principle is secondary to getting elected.

The interaction of these three dimensions has implications for the development both of intraparty consensus and national consensus on problems of identity. The organizational dimension makes its contribution only to intraparty consensus. Our assumption here is that mass parties are characterized by a greater degree of mutual agreement than cadre parties, because the former involve the commitment and participation of larger numbers of supporters. The focus of appeal is significant in that those appeals based on principle, by explicitly soliciting support for some policy, have greater implications for consensus than those based on electoral success. Parties obtaining support from many groups would make some contribution to the development of national consensus, but intraparty consensus is likely to be higher in parties with a restricted social base. However, when this is taken in relation with the dimension of appeal, then broad-based parties of principle aid in the development of both intraparty and national consensus (see Figure 1).

Party types and national identity.—A clearer conception of this typology should follow from a description of the eight party types derived. The broad-based mass party of principle is one which, by enlisting widespread participation and support aimed at specific goals, results in high intraparty and high national consensus. Illustrations of this type of party are the nationalistic, anti-colonial parties such as those found in West Africa. Examples of another sort are the Nazi and Communist parties, which, on assuming control, have be-

FIGURE 1

THE RELATION OF PARTY TYPES TO CONSENSUS

Party types			Effects on consensus	
Organization	Base	Appeal	Intraparty	National
mass	broad	principle	high	high
cadre	broad	principle	high	high
mass	narrow	principle	high	low
cadre	narrow	principle	high	low
mass	broad	success	low	high
cadre	broad	success	low	high
mass	narrow	success	low	low
cadre	narrow	success	low	low

come parties of "total integration." By making the party almost synonymous with the nation, integration of outlook is achieved, but at the cost of destroying deviance. Thus the party's definition of national identity is *the* national identity. As a solution to problems of identity this definition is one inimicable to democratic principles. The comprehensive, nationalistic party may, however, be grafted on to a democratic ideology, as has occurred in India. But the position of such parties in a system that includes a legitimate opposition tends to be unstable. Their original strength lies in the ability to attract support from diverse interests for a principle which could command wide loyalty. But if the principle loses some of its strength, as in the case of anticolonial parties when independence is achieved, the parties then tend to become fragmented. The continuity of the Indian National Congress, for example, has been accomplished only by some shift in the character of its supporters and the nature of its appeal.

The broad-based cadre party of principle is perhaps less consensus-inducing than the first type, since decision-making is by an elite, yet appeal is also widespread, largely because of the principle propounded, which, too, is likely to be of a nationalistic nature. A good example is the UNR (Union pour la Nouvelle République), the Gaullist party of the Fifth Republic. Again there are elements of instability in such parties due partly to their organizational structure, which, while attracting a large and varied base of support, concentrates power in the hands of a relatively unresponsive minority. These parties also exemplify that a principle, although important in providing a rallying point for supporters, can be the focus for internal dissension, as has been the case in the UNR and its predecessor. The Liberation Rally of Egypt, founded by Premier Nasser in 1953, was also essentially a party of this type. Although there was an attempt to alter its organizational form by enlisting mass support, the principles it stood for appeared to be too diffuse for a meaningful appeal, and consequently was unsuccessful as a party.

Still making a large contribution to intraparty consensus, but unable to overcome national cleavages, are mass parties of principle with a restricted base. Traditional Marxist parties resemble this type, as does the Swedish Agrarian party.

The narrow-based, cadre parties of principle are even less able to promote national consensus than the previously described types. Here both decision makers and supporters come from special groups working toward specific goals. Hence they may resemble interest groups more than genuine parties. We would place in this category the pre-independence Indian National Congress, the Australian Country party, the Poujadists, and Latin-American Church-oriented parties when such parties do not play a dominant role in the political life of the country.

The broad-based, mass party of electoral success is relatively low on intraparty consensus because of its lack of principle, yet by drawing on wide participation and support, it makes some contribution to overcoming national cleavages. This seems to be the case of the National party of New Zealand since 1949 and, to some extent, of the Swedish Liberal party.

Broad-based, cadre parties of electoral success stress compromise and containment of the interests represented. Intraparty consensus may then not be high, but social divisions at the national level are held in check. This tends to be true of the national Republican and Democratic parties in the United States.

The situation of the narrow-based mass party of electoral success is likely to be unstable and to represent a transitional type. As such, internal consensus can be expected to be low and the contribution which such a party makes to a broadly appealing definition of national identity will also be relatively minor. The position of the British Labour party in recent years has some relation to this party type. Certainly the party has possessed significant principles. But a major movement under the leadership of Hugh Gaitskill downgraded these principles which had apparently become repellent to a large body of voters.[12] Principle was thus being sacrificed to the hope of electoral

[12] For a discussion of voter attitudes see Mark Abrams and Richard Rose, *Must Labour Lose*, Harmondsworth, Middlesex: Penguin Books, 1960.

success. At the same time the retreat from traditional principles was a major source of dissension within the party. But it appears that the British Labour party under Harold Wilson is continuing to adapt itself to the demands of greater voter appeal. This is a further illustration of the potential of party principle for promoting dissension as well as consensus.

Even more unstable than the preceding party type is the narrow-based cadre party of electoral success. This party is similar to Latin American *ad hoc* parties which spring up, generally around a strong leader, before an election and quickly disappear thereafter. Such parties are more likely to emerge during times of political instability. At such periods they appeal to those caught up by confused and confusing circumstances. The United States of the 1840's and 1850's saw the emergence of the Know Nothing party out of the decline of the Whigs and the disruption of the Democrats during a time of major social changes. While the Know Nothings were basically nativist, there were great variations from one state to another in what the party stood for, so that it can hardly be said to have possessed a unifying principle. The result was that the divisive elements in American life were played up at the expense of the unifying ones.

The classification of parties along these three dimensions distinguishes the impacts of parties on national identity in terms of their programs and policies and their ability to establish both intraparty and national consensus. It should be apparent from this scheme that in a true party system, that is, a system with more than one party, a high degree of unanimity in national outlook would be represented by a considerable measure of interparty consensus despite partisan differentiation. The existence of a broad consensus on the identity of the nation and the subsequent emergence of collective identities qua nationals, then, is partly dependent on the ability of parties in the same political system to come to terms on central issues. Where they cannot do this, a lack of consensus may be more characteristic than its presence.

The typology presented here has been intended to provide some guidelines in considering the relation between political parties and national identity. The actual parties cited in the discussion were used to illustrate this relationship. It is possible that this typology will have its greatest usefulness in the comparative study of parties, since it is not likely that any one country will possess all eight party types. Yet so far as political parties have a major bearing on the development of national identity, the absence of some party types also has implications for the character of a country's identity and the self-conceptions of its citizens. Parties are a major factor influencing national identity and provide the primary focus of our subsequent analysis.

Other Influences

Some additional influences remain to be discussed. Among these are historical circumstances, including deliberate efforts of governments to shape events bearing on the central problems of the state. Specification of these events cannot be made at this time since they are closely linked with the national problems and take shape only as these problems are defined. Hence, the perception of the nation's identity acquires its full meaning when it is treated in conjunction with past and current circumstances.

Mass media.—The significance of the mass media in influencing political opinions and behaviour was first seriously challenged by *The People's Choice*.[13] At the same time, the authors of this study noted that the media served important functions as reinforcers of opinions and as influences on opinion leaders. Later studies have elaborated on the political impact of the mass media extending beyond election campaigns: "Not only during the campaigns but also in the periods between, the mass media provide perspectives, shape images of candidates and parties, and define the unique atmosphere and areas of sensitivity which mark any particular campaign." [14] This tends to be obscured in industrialized societies, but the development of mass communication media serves as a precondition for the emergence of nationalism, and as a critical influence in societies undergoing major social change. Because of the political consequences of the mass media, it is not surprising that many societies have been concerned with controlling the content and reception of the communication. The place of the mass media in the study of national identity is thus of undoubted significance.

The educational system.—The final influence, the educational system, makes its contribution to the definition of national identity by deciding, or accepting decisions made elsewhere, what should be taught and who should be educated. With respect to the former, one important decision pertains to the language of teaching. Whether this is the language of a foreign power, the indigenous population,

[13] Paul F. Lazarsfeld, Bernard R. Berelson, and Hazel Gaudet, *The People's Choice*, 2nd ed.; New York: Columbia University Press, 1948, p. 102.

[14] Kurt and Gladys Engel Lang, "The Mass Media and Voting," in *American Voting Behavior*, ed. by Eugene Burdick and Arthur Brodbeck, Glencoe: Free Press, 1959, p. 226.

a majority group, or all the linguistic groups in the society has an important bearing on the availability of an instrument for communicating national unity. The most common procedure

has been and is the urgent insistence on the single national language as one of the central cores of the national being. Nationalist movements have with regularity been accompanied by a flurry of philological activity. As the Communists found the Russians to be the inventors and discoverers of all good things, so the nationalist must seek to derive his language solely from its own native roots without the intrusion of terms and constructions which have an alien flavor.[15]

The perpetuation of a language is not solely the task of the schools, but is the schools which can do this most readily and effectively.

Of all the subjects taught, history, including what is known in some parts of North America as "social studies," is probably the one subject with greatest implications for national identity.

At the opening of the [nineteenth] century history began to be definitely enlisted in the service of patriotism, and attention turned in consequence distinctly to national history. The patriotic conception was by no means novel. It had been suggested by Wimpheling in his textbook of 1505. It had moved the English Privy Council to the action of 1582. It had been in the minds of Comenius and Rolland. It had inspired the French proposals of 1793. "Especially the history of the Fatherland" had again and again appeared in school programs for history.[16]

The manner in which schools teach their native history, if in fact they are permitted to do so, is an additional element in the definition of national objectives. The educational milieu is of course not confined to specific subjects, but also encompasses more general attitudes and values, and these too have a bearing on the manner in which the nation is perceived.

In determining who shall be educated, a decision is also made as to which social cleavages will be perpetuated, and which the educational systems can at least attempt to overcome. Even when no group is formally excluded, values upheld by the educational system may serve to disqualify some from full competitive ability. The system of education in itself and the values upon which it is based thus deserve special attention as factors affecting national identity.

[15] Rupert Emerson, *From Empire to Nation,* Cambridge: Harvard University Press, 1960, pp. 135–136.

[16] Henry Johnson, *Teaching of History in Elementary and Secondary Schools,* New York: Macmillan, 1916, p. 96. This usage of history continues to play an important role, especially with the emergence of new states.

IDENTITY AND CONSENSUS

Central to our discussion of national identity is the existence of a degree of consensus, the degree to be, for the moment at least, left undefined. Such consensus is implied in defining national problems and solutions and in establishing shared outlooks and experiences as members of a single nation.

Consensus is always to be understood in relative terms, as referring to some degree of agreement among particular social groupings with respect to their opinions on specific issues. Even though our subsequent discussion may sound at times as though we meant complete agreement when we speak of consensus, in fact it should always be understood in these relativistic terms.

The extent of opinion agreement, its relative presence among different population groups and on different issues are all questions subject to empirical examination. By such an examination we can begin to evaluate the state of a nation's identity. For example, do we find widely shared beliefs and opinions? Do significant population groups hold similar distributions of opinion? Is there a single, related set of opinions which is highly dominant? If the answers to these questions are yes, then we have indications of common bonds between people, a united nation, and a clear-cut identity for the nation. In this way then we should be able to identify the major consensual elements which go to making up the nation's identity and the collective identities of its citizens.

With the perspectives on national identity provided by the psychoanalytic literature and the writings of political scientists and sociologists, particularly Pye and Lipset, we were able to evolve our conception of national identity, differentiating between personal identity, the image of the nation, and collective identities. Out of this conceptualization we focused on the problems underlying the definition of nationhood and considered some of the influences affecting this definition. Among these influences, most attention was paid to political parties. It is now possible, with this as background, to turn our attention to Canada.

III CANADA: PROMISE
AND DISAPPOINTMENT

NATIONAL PROBLEMS

THE PROBLEMS common to all political systems are manifested in Canada, in some cases in a unique fashion, with external problems of independence and foreign commitments, internal problems of internal cleavages and the role of government, and symbolic problems. The elaboration of these should indicate both the general and the unique natures of the problems.

Independence

Independence has become basic to Canada's identity as a result of several historical factors. In the modern world the attainment of full citizenship has come about either by revolutionary breaks with past governments or by the development of self-government within a colonial empire. For countries which have followed the latter course, the empire has gone through a major transformation in character. At the present this is the development which is most prevalent as Britain continues to divest itself of its colonial domains, but when Canada attained self-government it was the first of the British possessions to follow this course. It set an example for the states and dominions that have followed, but its problems have also been unique: "Canada had not only to achieve autonomy inside the British Empire, but also to maintain a separate existence on a continent dominated by the United States. She thus has to come to terms with two imperialisms, real or potential." [1]

Dependence on Britain.—Canada is, first of all, a political creation of Britain, brought into being by an act of the British parliament and, until 1967, still dependent on that country for constitutional amendments concerning the federal structure. Since Confederation, Canada has had almost complete control over all local affairs except for appointments of the Governor-General; suggestion, and hence

[1] Donald G. Creighton, "Nationalism in Canadian History," *Conservative Concepts*, 2, Spring, 1960, p. 6.

really appointment of, the Governor-General became the prerogative of the Canadian government in 1926. Except for some Canadian participation in discussions, initially Britain alone formulated foreign policy, and in this way some leaders saw Canada committed to the Boer War. This was the first occasion on which Canadians, particularly those of French origin, could complain about "entanglement in British imperialist wars." [2] British initiative again brought Canada into World War I, although, with the formation of the Imperial War Cabinet in 1917, the Dominion prime ministers were permitted to participate directly in policy-making. But this war also produced bitter feelings, and, in 1917, when the Conscription Act was passed, those French-Canadian Liberals who were opposed to it formed a splinter group of the party while the remaining Liberals joined Robert Borden and his Union government. With the Statute of Westminster of 1931, the self-governing dominions attained full autonomy if they wanted to exercise it. When war came in 1939, some dominions felt that Britain's declaration included them, but Canada waited seven days before declaring war. Again the Canadian government had to come to terms with the heritage of previous wars. In this instance, however, Prime Minister MacKenzie King was able to adopt a number of alternatives which avoided the breakdown in relations between French and English that had occurred in 1917.

Although for the American colonists British trade policies were a major source of grievance, since that time Britain's economic relations with her possessions have often appeared advantageous to the latter. The importance of trade with Britain is so crucial to some Commonwealth members that British politicians have had second thoughts about the value of joining the European Common Market. The Canadian government played a leading role in criticizing Britain's proposed membership in E.C.M. in the early 1960's, since, as a leading trading nation, Canada was greatly disturbed by the prospect of losing traditional markets.

Among Canada's ties with Britain are those of population, and this has undoubtedly contributed to the continued development of Canada as an English-speaking country within the British Commonwealth. The largest group of Canadian citizens born outside the country come from Britain. Since the end of World War II about two million immigrants have been admitted, of whom about one-third are of

[2] Frank H. Underhill, *The British Commonwealth*, published for the Duke University Commonwealth Studies Center; Durham: Duke University Press, 1956, p. 32. See also W. L. Morton, *The Canadian Identity*, Madison: University of Wisconsin Press, 1961, p. 49.

British origin. While British immigrants have not been faced with the same discriminatory legislation passed at various times to curtail immigrants from other countries, a certain amount of ill feeling has been expressed against them. Unlike the objection against those from continental European countries, the objection against the British can never be made that they cannot speak the language or understand the basic political institutions. Opposition is less defined, expressing itself in feelings that British immigrants treat Canadians like colonials, or are always commenting on better ways of doing things.

Dependence on the United States.—If relations with Britain, particularly those involving dependency, have been crucial in shaping Canada's existence, then those with the United States are at least equally important. Politically, the United States was an important example to the Fathers of Confederation in developing a system of federal government; in other respects, however, it served as an anti-model.

Federation was not the child of an aggressive democratic impulse or a powerful mass pressure. The colonial leaders, although they championed self-government, shrank from anything like a leveling democratic polity. They were Whigs or contemporary British Liberals rather than Jacksonian democrats. "In our federation," remarked Sir Georges Cartier, "the monarchical principle would form the leading feature, while on the other side of the line, judging by past history and present conditions of the country, the ruling power was the will of the mob, the rule of the populace." [3]

Despite a famous unguarded boundary, fear of an invading army was an important impetus in bringing about Confederation in 1867, and attack seemed imminent as late as 1895.[4] In boundary disputes before Canada attained dominion status the disadvantages of being a small, powerless nation were consistently proved, for even Britain was not willing to antagonize the Americans. Since World War II, as new power arrangements have emerged, Canada and the United States have come to work together more closely in defence plans, to the resentment of some Canadians.

The reason why we in Canada become so neurotic as we brood upon our relations with our North American neighbour is that since the revolution of 1940 we have been going through a difficult period of adjustment to new conditions in the North American triangle. For 100 years before 1940

[3] Alexander Brady, *Democracy in the Dominions*, 3rd ed.; Toronto: University of Toronto Press, 1958, p. 42. The speech of Sir Georges Cartier is quoted from *Confederation Debates*, 59.

[4] This was related to the Venezuela boundary dispute with Great Britain, which President Cleveland saw as an infringement of the Monroe Doctrine.

after Lord Durham's Report in 1839 we enjoyed living in the British century, we took British leadership for granted in everything that concerned our participation in world affairs. Since the Ogdensburg agreement of 1940 we have passed into the American century of our history: we now have to adjust ourselves to American leadership.[5]

Materially and artistically, the United States has always served as a basis of comparison, and Americans have usually been the style setters. Robert Barr, a Canadian journalist who moved to the United States at the turn of the century, told his fellow writers to "get over the border as soon as you can. . . . Shake the dust of Canada from your feet, get out of the land that is willing to pay money for whiskey, but wants its literature free in the shape of Ayer's almanac." [6] Large numbers of Canadians study in the United States, and many of these, as well as others who have taken advanced training in Canada, often decide that opportunities are greater in the neighbouring country.

Immigration contributed about 47,000 professional workers to the supply during the first ten postwar years. Much of this gain, however, was offset by the emigration of about 31,000 professionals to the United States. In the first five years, the outflow of professional workers to the United States was actually greater than the gain from immigration. In the next five years, when immigration reached a much higher level, the number of professional workers among immigrants outnumbered professionals emigrating to the United States by about 18,000.[7]

In the 1940's, the government appointed a royal commission to investigate the ways in which the United States was influencing Canada's cultural development, with a view to presenting proposals for confining some of these. Government agencies specifically designed to confine American cultural influences include the National Film Board, Canadian Broadcasting Corporation, Canada Council, and National Research Council, most of which existed even before the Royal Commission made its recommendations. Despite these measures, Canadians receive most of their news, television programs, movies, and magazines from the United States.[8]

[5] Frank Underhill, "Canadian and American Foreign Policies," in *Text of Addresses Delivered at the 25th Annual Couchiching Conference*, Geneva Park, Lake Couchiching, Ontario: August 4–11, 1956, p. 117. See also Mason Wade, "New Relations of the United States with Canada," in *The United States and the World Today*, ed. by Clyde F. Kohn, Chicago: Rand McNally, 1957, p. 38.

[6] Quoted in Brady, *op. cit.*, p. 37.

[7] Economics and Research Branch, Department of Labour of Canada, *Skilled and Professional Manpower in Canada, 1945–55*, Royal Commission on Canada's Economic Prospects, Ottawa: July, 1957, p. 67.

[8] For evidence on the penetration of American mass media in Canada, see H. F. Angus, *Canada and Her Great Neighbor*, Toronto: Ryerson, 1938, pp. 124–172;

Canada, rich in natural resources but always with a limited population, has depended on the nationals of other countries for its economic development. Resources have been developed mainly with
foreign money. In some cases, particularly that of the United States,
subsidiary manufacturing companies have been set up in Canada.
Since 1939, the United States and Great Britain between them have
made about 90 percent of the total direct investment in Canada, with
the share of the former much greater than that of the latter.[9] Among
the difficulties stemming from this extensive United States investment
in Canada are those related to American foreign policy. Restrictions
on trade with mainland China have been extended, for example, to
Canadian subsidiaries who have been prevented from shipping auto-
mobile parts to China. While this incident aroused considerable resentment, particularly because of the size of the economic loss entailed,
Canada's continued trade with Cuba after the United States broke
with the Castro government did not appear to have an economic
motivation, since trade never achieved a great volume, but rather
an emotional appeal, as a way for Canada to show its defiance of
American policy.

Canada has always been concerned with the nature of its trade
relations with the United States. As early as 1891 the federal election
campaign centred on reciprocal trade with the United States, but,
through the strength of nationalist appeals, the pro-reciprocity Liberals were defeated. Another movement for reciprocity, this time
under American auspices, emerged in 1911, and again this issue contributed to the defeat of the Liberals who were now in power. Since
about 1936, more amicable trade agreements have been worked out
between Canada and the United States, but the issue of trade con-

Report of the Royal Commission on Publications, Ottawa: Queen's Printer, 1961.
Other countries too receive much of the content of their mass media from the United
States. But what has been especially troublesome for the Canadian mass-communica-
tion industry is the geographic closeness of the competition, the sameness of language, the apparent technical superiority of the finished product coming from the
United States, and the economic advantages of Americans in competing for the
same markets. The results have been, for example, that 92 of the 96 periodicals
in Canada which sell more than 10,000 copies per month are American, that there
are no nationally recognized newspaper columnists, and that almost the only
Canadian films which have won international recognition are those produced by
the government-sponsored National Film Board. John A. Irving, "The Problems of
the Mass Media," in *Mass Media in Canada,* ed. by John A. Irving, Toronto:
Ryerson, 1962, pp. 221–235.

[9] J. Grant Glassco, *Certain Aspects of Taxation Relating to Investment in Canada
by Non-residents,* Royal Commission on Canada's Economic Prospects, Ottawa:
February, 1956. This has been a continuing trend, which the present administration
is attempting to limit.

tinues to be a source of dissatisfaction. With each passing year, the amount of American ownership of Canadian industry and resources grows, and, with it, the extent of Canadian resentment seems also to grow. But no matter how concerned Canadians may be about the economic influences of the United States, there are limitations to the amount of ill-feeling that can be expressed or the kinds of reprisals which may be taken: "Owing to the facts of North American civilization, Canadians who set store by material development—and most do—must inevitably be nationalists of a qualified type." [10]

Links with the Commonwealth.—Another traditional tie is that with the British Commonwealth. The new Commonwealth which has emerged since World War II is neither a significant export market nor a major source of immigrants for Canada. But it is perhaps in less tangible ways that the Commonwealth has attained great importance in recent years. Herbert Spiro notes how present-day African nationalism differs from European nationalism of preceding generations in its "internationalist" character. Emerging African nations often seem more concerned with developing pan-Africanism than with uniquely national identities.[11]

There may be an analogy to this in the relations between the Commonwealth and Canada. At the same time that the United States has become an increasingly powerful neighbour, Britain has lost much of its power on the international scene. Meanwhile politicians of many countries have been concerned with the development of a third force that could somehow mediate between the United States and Russia. The Commonwealth has then appeared as one such alternative, where membership is a way of acquiring a greater voice in world affairs.

Other foreign commitments.—In other international commitments Canada has tried even harder to establish for itself a unique role internationally. One of the primary facts of modern life is the division of the world into two main ideological camps. Nations then have the choice of identifying with one or the other of these blocs. (This identification is of course not always voluntary.) Another alternative is to stay aloof from political struggles and attempt to retain friends

[10] Alexander Brady, "Nationalism and Democracy in the British Commonwealth: Some General Trends," *American Political Science Review*, 47, December, 1953, p. 1030. An economist who strongly argues against nationalistic economic measures such as protectionist tariffs and "forced insertion of Canadians into the ownership and management of American enterprises in Canada" is Harry G. Johnson, in "Problems of Canadian Nationalism," *International Journal*, 16, Summer, 1961, pp. 238–249.

[11] Herbert J. Spiro, *Politics in Africa*, Englewood Cliffs: Prentice-Hall, Spectrum Books, 1962, pp. 12–23.

in both camps. For Canada, remaining apart from international conflicts and commitments has always been difficult. Canadian governments have never believed that such isolation is possible, and this is reflected in the views of the Canadian people. Canadians have always had economic, political, and emotional ties with Great Britain, the Commonwealth, and to a more limited extent with France, and there has always been the pervasive evidence of American influence and proximity. In the context of present international realities and the historic and economic ties which involve countries in each other's affairs, what can a country such as Canada do to establish its identity on the international scene? The solution that has become increasingly prominent is participation in international bodies. Through membership in such bodies single nations, by themselves of limited influence and importance, can attain support for national policies and enhance their status on the international scene. For example, the United Nations, through its formal commitment to values of nondiscrimination and self-government, the opportunities it provides as a world meeting place and forum, and its involvement in trusteeship territories, has become an important focus for the new African states eager to acquire stature and throw off colonial ties. In the same way Canada, through its international involvements, has attempted to control and mitigate the influence of the United States on its own affairs.

Canada has taken an active part in the United Nations and its specialized agencies from the inception of the parent body. But participation in international organizations does not necessarily contribute to a characteristic identity unless Canada at the same time pursues some distinctive policies. In particular there should be divergence, at least some of the time, from positions taken by the United States and Britain. Such differences have occurred in Canada's commitments to NATO, the concept of the role Canada should play in North American defence, its lack of participation in the Pan American Union, and reactions to British involvement in Suez. But in many cases Canadian international activities have been guided or at least influenced by the perceived interests of traditional allies. For example, while Canada trades with mainland China and has some cultural exchanges with that country, governments up to the time of writing have never pressed for United Nations recognition of the Chinese Communist government in the face of American opposition, although the British government has officially recognized that country. Up until about 1960 Canadian activities in the United Nations with respect to issues of colonialism were limited and relatively insignificant partly because of the lack of colonial experience and the limited popular appeal of this issue within the country. At the same time Canada's ties with countries which do have colonial and trustee-ship experiences probably contributed to the minor role which Canada has played.

Internal Cleavages

The social and economic diversity within Canada presents major problems both for political stability and for identifying an unam-biguously Canadian nation.

Unequal distribution of people and resources.—Among the major internal differences is the unequal distribution of resources, both human and economic, and of allied rewards. Although Canada covers a land mass of more than three and a half million square miles, settlement has been concentrated only in certain areas, spreading along the southern border; the northern hinterland has few perma-nent residents. The centres of population have always been in the central provinces of Ontario and Quebec, but, since Confederation, other population centres have shifted from the Maritimes to the west (see Table 1). There is also a considerable difference in the extent to which different areas of the country have become urbanized. The most highly urbanized provinces are Ontario, British Columbia, and Quebec; the least urbanized are New Brunswick, Saskatchewan, and

TABLE 1

PERCENTAGE DISTRIBUTION OF POPULATION BY REGION, 1881-1961

Year	Atlantic[a]	Quebec	Ontario	Prairies	British Columbia
1881	20	31	45	1	1
1891	18	31	44	3	2
1901	16	31	41	8	3
1911	13	28	35	18	5
1921	11	27	33	22	6
1931	10	28	33	23	7
1941	10	29	33	21	7
1951	12	29	33	18	8
1961	10	29	34	17	9

[a] Newfoundland is not included in the Atlantic provinces until 1951. Percentage' do not add to 100 because of rounding and the exclusion of the Yukon and North-Wes Territories.

SOURCES: Canada, Dominion Bureau of Statistics, *Ninth Census of Canada*, Ottawa: King's Printer, 1951; and *1961 Census of Canada*, Ottawa: Queen's Printer, 1962.

Prince Edward Island, in the order given. The proportion of those living in cities in the three highly urbanized provinces is about twice as large as the proportion living in the least urbanized.

A limited number of staple products have always had overriding importance in the Canadian economy. Beginning with furs, the major wealth of Canada has also been derived from fish, lumber, pulp and paper, grain, and mineral resources. These products are related to particular regions, and provinces vary in their resource wealth. For example, the major part of the pulp and paper industry is concentrated in northern Ontario and Quebec, whereas the prairie provinces have become the main granaries for the world. At the same time provinces differ in their economic dependence on these staple products. In the trend toward modernization and mechanization throughout the world, increasingly smaller proportions of labour are required in agriculture. In recent years expansion has been in the tertiary sector of the economy, as the primary and secondary sectors become more highly automated; Ontario is the most modern, with less than 15 percent of the male labour force engaged in agriculture and more than 40 percent in tertiary industry. Ontario is followed in this respect by British Columbia. Prince Edward Island and Saskatchewan emerge as dramatic contrasts, with more than half of the male labour force still engaged in primary industry. There are even differences in the rewards received for similar types of work. For example, the highest median earnings in manufacturing are to be obtained in Ontario and British Columbia, those in the Atlantic provinces are considerably less. (See Table 2 for total provincial differences.) As a consequence, each region has a different standard of living. (See Table 3 for some examples.)

Regional differences in ethnic and religious groups.—The second important internal cleavage derives from the marked difference in social composition of the population in various regions. For example, Quebec has a heavy concentration of people of French origin; they also make up a sizable proportion of the population of New Brunswick, while all the other provinces have some representatives of French origin but in lesser proportions. At the time of the first census in 1871, people of European origin who were neither British nor French made up 7 percent of the total population. At the 1961 census the same group constituted 26 percent. Since the last decades of the nineteenth century, continental Europeans have been important in the settlement of the prairie provinces and in recent years their numerical significance has grown in Ontario (see Table 4).

The great diversity in settlement patterns of ethnic groups has

TABLE 2

PER CAPITA PERSONAL DISPOSABLE INCOME,
FOR CANADA AND PROVINCES, 1961,

Provinces	Canadian dollars
Canada	1,400
Newfoundland	860
Prince Edward Island	920
Nova Scotia	1,130
New Brunswick	990
Quebec	1,230
Ontario	1,640
Manitoba	1,340
Saskatchewan	1,080
Alberta	1,460
British Columbia	1,640

SOURCE: Financial Post, *1962 Survey of Markets and Business Year Book*, Toronto: Maclean-Hunter, 1963, p. 19.

TABLE 3

INDICATORS OF DIFFERENCES IN LIVING CONDITIONS BY REGION, 1941–1961

Region	Percentage of labour force unemployed			Infant mortality per 1,000 live births		
	1951–1955	1956–1960	1961	1941	1951	1961
Canada	3.3	5.7	7.2	61	39	27
Atlantic[a]	5.5	9.7	11.1	71	45	31
Quebec	4.5	7.4	9.3	76	48	31
Ontario	2.7	4.2	5.5	46	31	23
Prairies	2.2	3.3	4.6	52	32	26
British Columbia	4.0	6.4	8.5	37	30	24

[a] Newfoundland has been included in the Atlantic provinces for all years.

SOURCES: Percentage of labour force unemployed: Canada, Dominion Bureau of Statistics, *Unemployment in Canada*, Bulletin 71-503; Ottawa: April, 1962. Infant mortality: Canada, Dominion Bureau of Statistics, *Vital Statistics*, Ottawa: 1963.

TABLE 4

PERCENTAGE DISTRIBUTION OF POPULATION
OF NON-BRITISH ORIGIN, BY REGION, 1961

Region	Non-British and Non-French	French
Canada	26	30
Atlantic	9	19
Quebec	9	81
Ontario	30	10
Prairies	50	7
British Columbia	37	4

SOURCE: *Census of Canada*, 1961.

been accompanied by a diversity in religious groups. As would be expected, Roman Catholics are dominant in Quebec because of their connections with the French, but they have also become an increasingly important denomination throughout Canada, making up, for example, the largest single group in Ontario. Fundamentalist groups are concentrated in the prairie provinces.

Related to origin and religion is the distribution of foreign-born Canadians. Since Canada has always been a country of immigration, the foreign-born have naturally contributed significant numbers to the population. Here again settlement has been unevenly distributed throughout the provinces. Since the postwar years Canada has accepted more than two million immigrants, and a sizable proportion, possibly half of these, have settled in Ontario, with major consequences for the composition of the population.

Effects of this diversity on the Canadian political system.—The wide range of interest groups represented in the country and their unequal geographical dispersion present a politically volatile situation. If there is a complete coincidence between social and economic interests, and these are concentrated in particular geographic regions, the likelihood becomes great that they will find an outlet in united political action of a highly divisive sort. When Confederation was still in the planning stages, those concerned with creating a unified nation had already to contend with the varied character of Canada's resources and population. The existence of a French minority was an obvious problem. The Fathers of Confederation also had to come to terms with the prior existence of colonial legislatures. There were some who favoured a unitary system of government, as in Britain. But a more realistic policy had to take into account a French minority, which needed guarantees for its continued existence before it would give its loyalty to the new nation, and sectional interests which were represented by the existing legislatures. Already there was some rudimentary manufacturing industry in Ontario, and those engaged in these enterprises were anxious to have protection. This was the beginning of a conflict that would continue between the manufacturing interests in the central provinces, and those, first in the Maritimes and later in the prairie provinces, whose prime source of income depended on trade in unfinished resources, and who therefore benefited from the free movement of products. The solution to the problem of accommodating all these divergent interests was in a federal system of government.

The Canadian political system which has developed has therefore incorporated several devices to protect sectional interests. These include representation in the House of Commons and Senate, the continued existence of provincial governments, and judicial interpretations on the distribution of powers between provincial and federal governments. Another means of insuring sectional interests has come about through the development of Cabinet government. Although there is no official recognition in the British North America Act of a party system or a Cabinet, tradition, following that employed in the British parliament, has given Canada two or more political parties, a Prime Minister, and a Cabinet normally appointed from members sitting in the House of Commons and responsible to it. The desire for the representation of various interest groups in the Cabinet has grown as the Senate, the body originally intended to reflect regional interests, has shown itself less effective politically. It has become customary for an effective Cabinet to take into account the proportionate size of each province, special regions within the provinces, and various ethnic and religious groups in the country. The existence of major sectional, ethnic, and economic cleavages and the distribution of power, both actual and desirable, which should exist among interest groups based on these cleavages, become then other important determinants of Canada's identity and of the identities of its citizens.

The Role of Government

The role of government is important in affecting the definition of national identity because what government does is an important way of characterizing nations; government activities in the economic sphere have been significant instruments in nation-building; and government activities in the realm of ideas have aided in the development of national cultures.

One of the primary ways of characterizing modern nations is by the amount and kind of governmental participation. Whether they have socialist or free-enterprise systems is thought to have implications, not just for the economy, but for many critical social institutions. There are those who contend that issues pertaining to government activities are no longer significant today. But even if, as Dahl and Lindblom remark, "it has become increasingly difficult for thoughtful men to find meaningful alternatives posed in the traditional choices between socialism and capitalism," [12] these choices refer to decisions between government policies and not to the ideological tone associated with particular forms of government. It is this tone rather than the concrete policies with which we are concerned here as a determinant, in part, of a country's internal character and thus its identity.

Related to this ideological content, the role of government has further relevance because of its connection with class-based appeals. For example, survey material from the United States reveals that those who identify with the working class tend to favour government action in the areas of social welfare, public ownership, and the regulation of economic activities.[13] Attitudes toward the role of government should then serve as an extension of the preceding discussion on cleavages by giving content to class-based appeals in Canada.

Secondly, and more important, however, is the fact that government economic activities have often been a conscious tool used to develop the nation. Part of the "national policy" of the first Prime Minister was the building of a transcontinental railway. Although this railway, the Canadian Pacific, has never been publicly owned, the government's generous assistance in funds and land grants has kept it in an enviable financial position to this day. The publicly owned Canadian National Railways have not fared as well financially, but they "are not to be judged merely by the test of profitable returns on investment, since, like other lines, they have been an instrument of nation-building, drawing together widely-scattered communities and making possible the exploitation of natural resources remote from the industrial heart of Canada." [14] The impetus for government economic activity and regulation has often come, not from organized labour,

[12] Robert A. Dahl and Charles E. Lindblom, *Politics, Economics, and Welfare,* New York: Harper, 1953, p. 3.

[13] Heinz Eulau, *Class and Party in the Eisenhower Years,* New York: Free Press, 1962, p. 64.

[14] Brady, "The State and Economic Life," in *Canada,* ed. by George W. Brown, Toronto: Toronto University Press, 1950, p. 357.

but from the business community. Thus, public regulation of hydro-electric power in Ontario was encouraged by manufacturers and merchants. For these groups in Ontario and elsewhere, government help was needed to protect business interests from American competition or domination. "The concept of Canadian nationality has lent coherence to the numerous claims of these interests for protection, and in public debate has given such claims a more attractive complexion." [15] The tradition of cooperation between private business and government has been an important aspect of the economic life of Canada since 1867, and indications remain that this will continue to be the dominant policy. In a statement made in 1958 a prominent Canadian businessman, R. M. Fowler, president of the Canadian Pulp and Paper Association, said that "the businessman does not, or should not, want to escape from public regulation of business practices and that such regulation is a proper and necessary function of the modern democratic state. Indeed, you will probably think—with some accuracy —that I am suggesting better control and regulation in the national interest than business has had under the present misconceived and misdirected effort." [16] The acquiescence of business interests to government regulation continues to be strongly motivated by a concern with countering American influences.

As a consequence of the way government is seen in Canada—as promoting the development of the nation and controlling competition from the United States—it has been a major participant in economic endeavors. Such varied activities as scientific research, communications, air and rail transport, development of products and resources such as synthetics and atomic energy, have all come under the aegis of government. While the federal government continues to play an important part in economic affairs, its concern in recent years has been more with social-welfare services. Welfare measures include unemployment insurance, family allowances, old-age pensions, and a hospital plan shared with the provinces. At this time the government's efforts at nation-building have been directed toward reducing economic inequalities.

Thirdly, the federal government has attempted to promote the distinctive character of Canada not only through its activities in the economic and social fields, but also in the realm of ideas.

[15] *Ibid.*, p. 354.
[16] R. M. Fowler, "The Future of Competition in Canada: A Businessman's View," in *The Canadian Economy: Selected Readings,* ed. by J. Deutsch, B. S. Keirstead, K. Levitt, and R. M. Will, Toronto: Macmillan, 1961, p. 69. His derogatory reference was to the Conservative government of John Diefenbaker.

Protection . . . has extended beyond the sphere of material interests. The establishment of the Canadian Broadcasting Corporation (1936), patterned in the main upon the British, was designed to afford protection and encouragement to many elements of cultural life. It has ambitiously but quietly sought to foster in the populace some sense of a national community and a national culture, both of which have seemed menaced by the power and success of the private broadcasting companies in the neighbouring country.[17]

Mention has already been made of the creation of government cultural agencies. Since the time of Confederation, cultural domination from outside the country appears to have grown into an increasingly critical issue for many Canadian intellectuals and, through them, the government. For example, in the *Report of the Royal Commission on National Development in the Arts, Letters and Sciences,* the conclusions drawn were that something must be done to develop a unique and rich cultural life in Canada. The best course to follow appeared to be the provision of funds by the three levels of government, although recommendations concerned only federal expenditures.[18] Even in the newspaper and magazine fields, where the participation of government could be viewed as an infringement on freedom of the press, government protection is still seen as a critical necessity. The recent Royal Commission on Publications thought it necessary, in order to have specifically Canadian publications, that the government take steps to enforce economic discrimination against American publications in terms of advertising and postage rates. In their report to the government the Commissioners stated in their introduction that,

only a truly Canadian printing press, one with a "feel" of Canada and directly responsible to Canada, can give us the critical analysis, the informed discourse and the dialogue which are indispensable in a sovereign society.

The view of the Commission is that in an area as vital and sensitive as that of the press, whatever is done should be positive rather than negative, with the goal the promotion of the Canadian periodical, not the suppression of the foreign.[19]

[17] Brady, "The State and Economic Life" (n. 14, above), p. 354.
[18] *Report of the Royal Commission on National Development in the Arts, Letters and Sciences, 1949–1951,* Ottawa: King's Printer, 1951, p. 272. See also the recommendations for government expenditures on pp. 276–382. See also Hugh MacLennan, in *The Price of Being Canadian,* ed. by D. L. B. Hamlin, 7th Winter Conference, Canadian Institute of Public Affairs; Toronto: University of Toronto Press, 1961, pp. 27–35.
[19] *Report of the Royal Commission on Publications,* p. 2.

In a report on the state of scholarly research in the humanities and social sciences in Canada, the author concluded that the only effective solution to the development of these fields in competition with those of the United States was through massive doses of government investment in universities and specifically in research opportunities.[20]

Political Symbols

Before looking at such Canadian symbols as flags, anthems, leaders, rules of government, and historical heroes and events, we must consider their nature and significance in general. The minimal attribute of political symbols is that they are easily recognizable communicative devices. More noteworthy is their peculiarly emotional content. Symbols also have some roots in the traditions of the people they represent, whether these nations are new or have existed for centuries. By their appeal to history symbols can help to enforce respect for authority and for existing institutions.[21] Through this link with the past, symbols also serve to legitimate new laws and practices. They acquire additional importance as they become the basis of some ideological elaboration. In this way, the American Constitution may be regarded as the basis of a relatively consistent system of beliefs in which particular events are always judged in terms of their constitutionality, regardless of the utilitarian value of such judgements. Monarchical institutions also take on this ideological character. A further characteristic of political symbols is their potential for serving as either unifying or divisive rallying points for the residents of a country. For example, in the United States, the refusal of Jehovah's Witnesses children to salute the flag brought forth a historic decision by the Supreme Court which stated in effect that certain aspects of national unity were more important than other constitutional guarantees such as freedom of religion.

The ultimate foundation of a free society is the binding tie of cohesive spirit. Such a sentiment is fostered by all of those agencies of the mind and the spirit which may serve to gather up the traditions of a people, trans-

---

[20] Bernard Ostry, *Research in the Humanities and in the Social Sciences in Canada*, published for the Humanities Research Council of Canada and the Social Science Research Council of Canada; Ottawa: 1962.

[21] Herbert J. Spiro, *Government by Constitution*, New York: Random House, 1959, p. 377. In relation to the British monarchy see Edward Shils and Michael Young, "The Meaning of the Coronation," *Sociological Review*, 1, December, 1953, pp. 63–81. The unifying potential of the monarchy is questioned by N. Birnbaum, "Monarchs and Sociologists: A Reply to Professor Shils and Mr. Young," *Sociological Review*, 3, July, 1955, pp. 5–23.

mit them from generation to generation and thereby create that continuity of a treasured common life which constitutes a civilization. "We live by symbols." The flag is the symbol of our national unity, transcending all internal differences, however large, within the framework of the Constitution.[22]

In Nigeria the use by the British of legal forms and terminology linked with the Crown helped to mobilize national sentiments of Nigerians against British policies. Even before Bismarck added red to the black and white Prussian flag, the political and national aspirations of Germans were divided by loyalties symbolized by different flags. There are religious groups in both Turkey and Israel which do not accept some of the national heroes and which express their opposition in a variety of ways.

By enumerating the attributes of symbols in addition to merely communicative ones, attention is drawn to their political consequences. One view is that at least some of these symbols, notably national rituals and holidays, represent a "major test of legitimacy" [23] for the nation. Examples cited where symbols had divisive effects would be taken to indicate that some proportion of the population does not accord legitimacy to the state. This raises an empirical question of how critical this is for political stability. In the view of the Justices who ruled in the case of *Minersville School District* v. *Gobitis*, the uniform acceptance of symbols was essential for national unity, but the later ruling acknowledged that this was not in keeping with other values of the United States: "Freedom to differ is not limited to things that do not matter much. That would be a mere shadow of freedom. The test of its substance is the right to differ as to things that touch the heart of the existing order." [24]

But in countries such as Germany and South Africa, lack of approval of political symbols has been highly divisive. A major difference between these countries and the United States is that symbols in the former have served as focal points for public advocacy. Jehovah's Witnesses make up a small proportion of the American population, and their activities are primarily centred in the religious sphere, with only secondary implications for the polity. If, however, they should

[22] *Minersville School District* v. *Gobitis*, 310 U.S. 586, 60 S. Ct. 1010, 84 L. Ed. 1375 (1940). Three years later this ruling was reversed.

[23] S. M. Lipset, *Political Man*, Garden City: Doubleday, 1960, p. 80. For an interesting discussion on the use of ritual in legitimating the identity of Yankee City, see W. Lloyd Warner, *The Family of God*, New Haven: Yale University Press, 1961, pp. 89–154.

[24] *West Virginia State Board of Education* v. *Barnette*, 319 U.S. 624, 63 S. Ct. 1178, 87 L. Ed. 1628 (1943).

increase greatly in number and extend their activities to opposing other aspects of the state, then the danger to political stability could indeed be great. In Germany and South Africa differences in attitudes towards political symbols have been mainly related to political matters and have become associated with specific parties. Agitation then has been conducted principally in the political sphere, with important consequences for national unity.

In Canada, the provision of either unambiguous or unifying symbols has been singularly lacking. At Confederation Canada was given permission to fly the Red Ensign, the flag of the British Merchant Navy. By 1891, the Commonwealth dominions were permitted to use either the Red or Blue Ensign with the addition of their coat-of-arms. Prime Minister MacKenzie King in 1925 attempted to introduce a new flag but dropped the idea in the face of strong opposition. A parliamentary committee met in the fall of 1945 to consider more than two thousand designs and select a new flag. Although the committee made a choice, the government failed to act on it because, for one thing, it feared that the continued inclusion of the Union Jack would be offensive to French-speaking Canadians. A uniquely Canadian flag was adopted in 1965, but not until great controversy had been generated about the design which most appropriately represented Canadian origins and loyalties.

The official national anthem of Canada is generally recognized to be "God Save the Queen," and it is this song which is most often played at public assemblies. After Confederation many felt that Canada needed a national song of its own. At that time English-speaking Canadians were singing "The Maple Leaf Forever," which Alexander Muir wrote in 1867. In it reference is made to the British victory at Quebec and it has never been acceptable to French Canadians.[25] In 1880 Calixa Lavallée wrote "O Canada," and although this has not yet been acknowledged as an official anthem, it is the most widely accepted national song in English and French-speaking Canada today.

Canada is a constitutional monarchy, and the Queen does not share in any governmental activities except ceremonial ones. When she is absent from the country her representative, the Governor-General, carries out these activities. Many outsiders still believe that Canadians support the royal family through direct taxation. This is not the case, but it is understandable how such a misconception may persist in

[25] At the 1963 meeting of the Canadian Authors' Association, it was agreed that a contest be held to obtain new words for the music of "The Maple Leaf Forever," words which would be acceptable to all Canadians.

view of the widespread display of the Queen's picture on Canadian money and postage and in public places generally. Canadians apparently feel a real bond of affection for the royal family, as witnessed by the widely read magazine and newspaper articles about it and the warm welcome that accompanies its visits. Some commentators have considered this the Canadian equivalent to attitudes toward Hollywood stars, but the significance of the Queen as a unifying symbol for all Canadians is a topic which has never been publicly discussed.[26] The hostile reception which the Queen received during her 1964 visit to Quebec may then have come as a shock to many Canadians.

The Governor-General, like the monarch, has, over the years, evolved into a symbolic rather than an actual head. Appointment of the Governor-General as the Queen's representative had been interpreted by the British parliament as lying within their purview. After the Imperial Conference of 1926, the Governor-General was appointed only after consultation with the Canadian Cabinet, which meant in effect that the Canadian Cabinet decided on whom it wanted. In 1952, the first Canadian, Vincent Massey, was appointed. It has been questioned whether the Governor-General can ever attain the same emotional appeal as the monarch. Since he is nominated by the Canadian government and holds office for a relatively short period of time, it does not seem likely that he can build up the same prestige or inspire the same loyalty. But now, as a Canadian, his unifying potential is conceivably greater.

The British North America Act, though drawn up by Canadians from two major political parties and presenting a number of points of view, was never ratified by the Canadian people. Instead it was passed as an ordinary Act of the British parliament. In contrast, the Australian Constitution, which was drafted somewhat later, was passed by a direct vote of the people as well as by the British parliament. The British North America Act does not provide for amendment by Canadian authorities and full responsibility for this has yet to be settled. Many written constitutions contain formal guarantees of basic rights. The Canadian one has never had this, and it was not until 1960 that a Bill of Rights was passed by parliament. This is in striking

---

[26] For the Queen's possible impact on non-British, non-French immigrants, see Mildred A. Schwartz, "Political Behaviour and Ethnic Origin," in *Papers on the 1962 Election*, ed. by John Meisel, Toronto: University of Toronto Press, 1964, p. 258. A Canadian TV star, now resident in the United States, raised an outcry from some segments of the public when she appeared on the Jack Paar show before a royal visit and said that most Canadians were "indifferent" to the Queen. Reference is made to this event in one of the polls discussed in Chapter VII.

contrast with the American Constitution in which the drama of the Bill of Rights and the preamble to the Constitution provide foci to which people can pay homage.

In the neighbouring republic, the constitution as a single written document has been from the outset an arch of the covenant, the sign and seal of the state, whereby civil and political order is preserved. Its very creation was a break with the past, and it has been cherished as the major symbol of the nation. But in Canada the constitution has never been viewed in such a light, because in many significant features it is much older than the British North America Act. It is grounded deep in British law, precedent, and convention, and has assimiliated miscellaneous elements of the British constitution.[27]

Although Canadian history seems short, it is certainly lengthy enough to have acquired historical heroes and dates of important events. But, lacking a revolutionary tradition, Canada has none of the dramatic heroes or historical occasions that are commemorated by other peoples. Politicians in Canada, because of the requirement of knitting together so many divergent strains, have been, where successful, experts at compromise, and as such they are often considered rather colourless individuals. National heroes inherited from earlier periods are marked by their divisive potential. If the English Canadians have General Wolfe, the French Canadians have General Montcalm. History has been taught in French Canada with an emphasis on past glory rather than on present conditions. But Canadian history often seems even more remote to English-speaking Canadians.[28]

Perhaps the most fitting summary of the state of Canadian symbols is contained in a verse by F. R. Scott,

> The Canadian Centenary Council
> Meeting in Le Reine Elizabeth
> To seek those symbols
> Which will explain ourselves to ourselves
> Evoke unlimited responses
> And prove that something called Canada
> Really exists in the hearts of all

[27] Brady, *Democracy in the Dominions* (n. 3, above), p. 63. Brady suggests here that the Canadian constitution does not have the emotional appeal that the American does because of the former's deep roots in British precedent and its close connection with British law-making.

[20] A Toronto newspaper reported how a group of children made elaborate preparations to enact the American Civil War. Questioned on the appropriateness of this battle rather than one more closely related to Canada, the children's teenaged adviser answered, "We thought about that, but we seem to know so very little of our own history. The kids see Civil War scenes on television, and this is more interesting to them." *Toronto Star*, August 23, 1962.

Handed out to every delegate
At the start of proceedings
A portfolio of documents
On the cover of which appeared
In gold letters

not

A Mari Usque Ad Mare

not

E Pluribus Unum

not

Dieu et Mon Droit

but

COURTESY OF COCA-COLA LIMITED.[29]

INFLUENCES ON NATIONAL IDENTITY

Political Party

The political party plays a major role in influencing the character of the nation and the identities of its members. (See Figure 2.) Political party is defined here as made up of respondents who have indicated that they would vote for that party in a forthcoming election.[30] To suggest that party identification alone influences opinion would be to take an absurd position. It is rather the intention of this study to examine the *degree* to which parties have an impact on their supporters.

This may be taken as a further attempt to grapple with Lazarsfeld's statement that "a person thinks, politically, as he is, socially" as an explanation of political attitudes.

Before proceeding, some comments are in order about the nature of the Canadian party structure. Despite some changes in name, the national scene has been dominated by two parties, the Liberal and the Conservative (see Table 5). Along with this two-party dominance

[29] F. R. Scott, "National Identity," *Maclean's*, June 1, 1963, p. 2.

[30] In referring to party supporters it should be understood that the main unit and its constituent parts are only relative terms since many supporters will not vote and some may change their allegiance in a coming election. But the important thing is that at the time of each survey respondents were willing to identify themselves as party sympathizers. It might increase the significance of this study if it were possible to discover how strongly partisan supporters were, but this information is not available. Still, as the subsequent analysis will indicate, this conception of parties is a useful device as long as it is recalled that parties are loosely organized and allow considerable shifts in composition over time. Even if we were concerned with party membership we would still find major definitional problems. See Maurice Duverger, *Political Parties*, London: Methuen, 1954, pp. 61–64.

FIGURE 2

CANADIAN IDENTITY: UNDERLYING PROBLEMS AND CRITICAL INFLUENCES

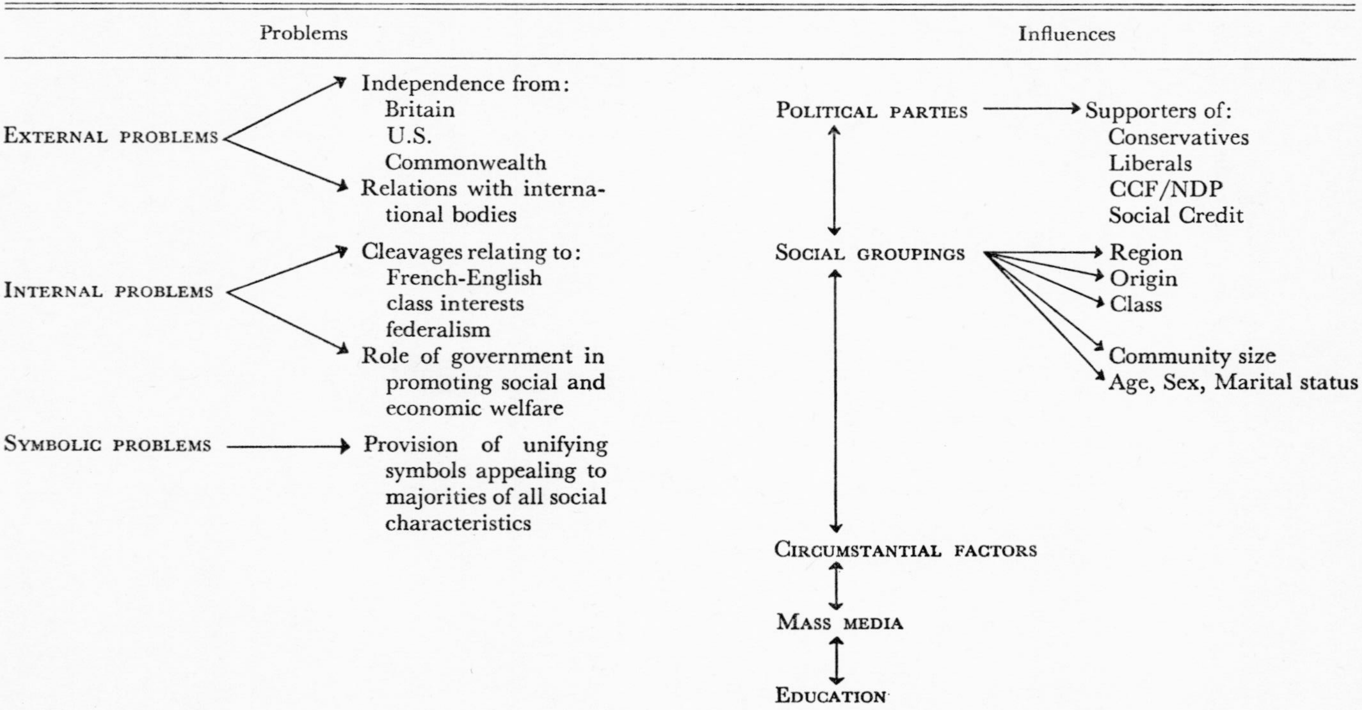

Problems		Influences

POLITICAL PARTIES ⟷ —→ Supporters of:
Conservatives
Liberals
CCF/NDP
Social Credit

SOCIAL GROUPINGS ⟷ Region
Origin
Class
Community size
Age, Sex, Marital status

CIRCUMSTANTIAL FACTORS

MASS MEDIA ⟷

EDUCATION ⟷

EXTERNAL PROBLEMS —→ Independence from:
Britain
U.S.
Commonwealth
Relations with international bodies

INTERNAL PROBLEMS —→ Cleavages relating to:
French-English
class interests
federalism
Role of government in promoting social and economic welfare

SYMBOLIC PROBLEMS —→ Provision of unifying symbols appealing to majorities of all social characteristics

TABLE 5

Canadian General Election Results, 1940–1963

Year	Percent popular vote[a]				Percent seats in House of Commons[a]			
	Conservative	Liberals	CCF/NDP	Social credit	Conservative	Liberals	CCF/NDP	Social credit
1940	31	51	8	3	16	74	3	4
1945	27	41	16	4	27	51	11	5
1949	30	49	13	4	16	74	5	4
1953	31	49	11	5	19	64	9	6
1957	39	41	11	7	42	40	9	7
1958	54	34	9	3	79	18	3	0
1962	37	37	14	12	44	37	7	12
1963	33	42	13	12	36	49	6	9

[a] Votes and seats for other parties and independent candidates have not been included in this table.

sources: H. A. Scarrow, *Canada Votes*, New Orleans: Hauser, 1962; *Canadian Parliamentary Guide*, Ottawa: Queen's Printer, 1963, and supplement.

there have always been some splinter groups. New alignments assumed importance in four federal elections: in 1917 as the result of the conscription crisis in Quebec, in 1925 during a period of agrarian protest, 1935 because of the depression, and in 1945 when conscription again became an issue in Quebec. In most cases dissident groups have been reabsorbed into the two-party structure. The election of 1935, however, resulted in some lasting changes. It was then that the Co-operative Commonwealth Federation (CCF) and Social Credit parties first appeared on the federal scene. These two parties both have their roots in the depressed conditions of western farmers, but they took different directions. The CCF began and has continued as a party of democratic socialism. In 1961 the party was reorganized, and its name changed to the New Democratic party (NDP) in order to broaden its base from agrarian support to that of organized labor. The Social Credit party was founded on the economic theories of Major Douglas, but with the passage of time these theories have been played down, and it has emerged as a second conservative party. While neither of these parties has attained a significant number of seats in the federal House of Commons, they both have had experience governing in the provinces, the CCF in Saskatchewan and the Social Credit in Alberta and British Columbia. In speaking of parties and party support in Canada the subsequent analysis is confined to these four parties.[31]

The public image of Canada can be further elaborated by taking into account the views of those whose social characteristics have been commonly found to have a bearing on political opinions. These are social groupings associated with region, origin, social class including trade union affiliation, community size, age, sex, and marital status. In Part III, each of these groupings is discussed more fully and compared with party support in influencing opinions.

Since this is primarily a study of public opinion derived from national polls, other influences on national identity cannot be derived from these same sources. The activities of elites, the military, the mass media, and educational institutions and organizations cannot be extensively treated, but their consequences are at least partly manifested in the opinions of party supporters and other social groups. To ex-

---

[31] In June 1963, two months after a general election, thirteen of the twenty Quebec Social Credit members of parliament broke away from the national party, and formed a new party, Le Ralliement des Créditistes, under the erstwhile deputy leader of the Social Credit, Réal Caouette. But since we are concerned with party supporters, and the electorate had not yet had the opportunity to vote for this party, it is not necessary for our analysis that we distinguish between the two factions.

pand our understanding of the Canadian setting, then, at least some brief description of these otherwise omitted agents for building national unity is necessary.

The Intellectual Elite

In speaking of elite groups and their role in the promotion of a distinct identity, we have confined ourselves to intellectual elites. When they have become self-consciously nationalistic, English-speaking Canadian intellectuals have often forcefully rejected American culture. In some instances they have preferred to look to Britain as a model. Some French-speaking intellectuals too have looked outside the boundaries of their society for a standard of comparison. For some, a completely separate identity for Quebec has become the favoured alternative.[32] But for many writers, artists, educators, and others concerned with the creation and dissemination of ideas, survival as Canadians is a crucial problem. The conditions of working in a country that has not as yet completely outlived its frontier tradition, where most things are judged by their instrumental utility, and where both official languages are used in more populous countries with richer cultural heritages have made Canadian intellectuals outspokenly nationalistic. In seeking to formulate a national identity both for themselves and for others they have often looked to government to protect their indigenous market from outside competition. How successful these people have been in influencing the development of Canadian identity is not the task of this study to evaluate. For our purposes it is sufficient to say that the intellectual elite as a group is both concerned with the state of Canada's identity and often desirous of defining it as distinctly different from any other country.

Because of our major concern with the role of political parties, some brief comments are in order on the role of intellectuals in parties. Considering in this category educators, journalists, writers, scientists, economists, political scientists, and artists, these were represented to varying degrees among the candidates of the four parties in the 1963 general election. Of the four parties, the New Democratic party

[32] According to a survey conducted for the Canadian Broadcasting Corporation and Maclean's magazine, 29 percent of those interviewed who had technical training beyond the secondary level and 26 percent of those with classical college or university education were in favour of separation of Quebec from the rest of Canada. This compared with 11 percent for those with either elementary- or secondary-school education. Unpublished tables on separatism, Le Groupe de Recherche Sociale, Montreal, September, 1963.

had the largest proportion of intellectuals (25 percent) among its candidates. The Liberal and Social Credit parties were similar with 12 and 11 percent respectively, and the Conservatives had fewest intellectuals (5 percent).[33] Yet, according to popular feeling at least, the parties differ considerably in their use of intellectuals as candidates and as contributors to policy-making. These differences, however, are based mainly on hearsay, and we have little empirical evidence. On such grounds, at least, the Liberals and CCF/NDP are considered to command allegiance of the majority of politically minded intellectuals and to use their training and ideas within the parties. For example, the Liberals held a successful Study Conference on National Problems in Kingston, Ontario, in September, 1960, to which a wide representation of liberally minded persons from business, the professions, universities, trade unions, and the mass media were invited. According to the chairman, Mitchell Sharp, who was to become Minister of Trade and Commerce, the purpose of the conference was not to criticize the administration, nor to write a party platform for the Liberals, but rather to provide a relatively nonpartisan forum where serious-minded people could discuss what should be done about national problems. The long-range implications presumably were that the Liberals would make use of the papers prepared for the conference and the discussions which followed in order to plan policies in anticipation of the time when they would again take office. Support of intellectuals for the CCF/NDP is exemplified in the scholarly publication *Social Purpose for Canada*.[34] In fulfilling the needs for specialized talent, the Conservatives as well undoubtedly make considerable use of Canadian intellectuals. Yet they acknowledge some difficulty in attracting such supporters. For example, an official of the Progressive Conservative party, on a cross-country tour of university campuses during the fall of 1963, complained of the relative lack of interest of university students in the Conservative party, and appeared to be searching for ways to make the party more attractive to these potential leaders. No information is available on the Social Credit party at the national level. However, in the two western provinces where Social Credit forms the provincial governments, the universities have suffered from some governmental interference. This, coupled with a general suspicion of the effects of academic freedom, has contributed to an

[33] Source: Canada, Chief Electoral Officer, *Report, 26th General Election, 1963*, Ottawa: Queen's Printer, 1963.

[34] Michael Oliver, *Social Purpose for Canada*, Toronto: University of Toronto Press, 1961. This book was not sponsored by either party, but represents the thinking of many prominent Canadian scholars who have been in one sense or another attracted by democratic socialism.

anti-intellectual image for the Social Credit party.[35] Undoubtedly, then, intellectuals make a prominent contribution to the definition of Canada's identity. The extent of their influence on political parties is not clear but it is probably greatest within the Liberal party and CCF/NDP.

The Military

The military probably plays a relatively minor part in the formation of an identity in a country such as Canada. Canada, lacking a revolutionary tradition, gives even less significance to the military than the United States. Still, veterans' organizations such as the Canadian Legion may be important as pressure groups and do in fact present annual briefs to the Prime Minister and Cabinet, but little is known about their operation. The Canadian Legion was one organization, however, which came out openly for the adoption of the Red Ensign as Canada's official flag.

Mass Media

The mass media, as we have already indicated, have often been perceived as conscious tools for the formation and continuation of a national consciousness. This is true whether or not the media are controlled by the government. Despite efforts to provide a unifying system of national communication through the Canadian Broadcasting Corporation, regional sentiments may actually be strengthened because

[35] In the 1963 municipal election in Edmonton, Alberta, the man elected as mayor had previously been charged with "gross misconduct" while holding that office. At that time he had resigned as mayor and paid the city $100,000 plus legal costs in a consent judgment after the city had brought a civil suit against him. Despite this record, gained in 1959, he was once more allowed to become mayor. Later, when four University of Alberta staff members attempted to read a protest statement at the inaugural meeting of City Council, they were arrested and charged with unlawfully disturbing the meeting. Considerable public controversy was aroused, and among those who made public statements were the Provincial Treasurer, who said that since the university was supported by public funds, staff members must restrain their teachings to remain in keeping with what the public was willing to accept. Speaking before the Social Credit Women's Auxiliary, Premier Manning went on to condemn what he considered abuses of freedom of expression by the public press and people he termed "intellectual perverts" who "debunk the Scriptures, moral values and conventions developed over the years." The press quickly came to the defence of the freedoms being threatened. "There are many, many non-Social Crediters in Alberta who vote Social Credit because, on the whole, it has given reasonably efficient government. The same people feel their souls shrivel when Social Credit occasionally reveals its deep-down strains of anti-intellectualism, anti-professionalism, even anti-Semitism and the kind of hill-billy fundamentalism which cringes and runs in the face of new thought and criticism. Especially criticism." Editorial, *The Calgary Herald*, November 20, 1963.

broadcasting is done in both English and French, allowing Canadians of either language to minimize contact with the other. But if the development of the broadcasting media has been guided by the need to establish some basis for national unity despite the limitations imposed by two official languages, this has been much less true of the printed media. The poor competitive position of Canadian magazines provided the major impetus for the Royal Commission on Publications.

The desperate situation of the magazines . . . is due almost entirely to the tremendous competition of the so-called Canadian editions of American publications. *Time* and *Reader's Digest*, the two largest of these, dump their editorial material into Canada and then solicit advertising to keep the news pages apart. Since their editorial costs have already been paid in the United States, they can run a highly efficient and well staffed advertising department, and can offer combination deals to big international advertisers.[36]

At present at least, newspapers remain Canadian-owned, although Roy Thomson, the owner of one newspaper chain, lost his Canadian citizenship when he appeared on the 1964 Queen's Honours List. But, due to a number of factors, including the lack of a single national newspaper, the uneven dispersion of population, and the relative cheapness of syndicated services provided from the United States and Great Britain, a content analysis of major Canadian newspapers reveals that they tend to be filled with local news of a most restricted nature, and supplemented by national and international news and columns, often of foreign origin. According to Donald Gordon, political scientist and formerly London correspondent for the Canadian Broadcasting Corporation,

I put it to you that our Canadian newspapers—those paragons who are doing all the shouting about Canadian identity these days—are in fact selling out on that very goal.

For all their pretensions, they are actually—albeit partly unintentionally— the spotters for the barrage of American and British brain-washing that we have such cause to worry about right now. Through a sustained, substantial and significant pattern of coverage, they are managing to condition us daily to abandon our own real culture in favour of a blurred carbon of the two giants at our elbows.

The basis of this indictment is straight forward: the *source* of most— around 80 per cent—foreign news reaching us is basically American and British. An editing screen is maintained by the Canadian wire services (Canadian editors selecting and adjusting copies before relay), but this can-

[36] Arnold Edinborough, "The Press," in Irving, *op. cit.* (in n. 8), p. 27.

not make up for the fact that alien eyes actually see and evaluate events as they occur.[37]

A great potential for national image-building lies with the mass media. While their actual effectiveness appears to be seriously hampered, we must keep in mind both their intentions and the conditions under which they operate as factors in the formation of opinions on national problems.

Education

The place of education in furthering national consensus is no doubt hindered by the constitutional provision that the provincial govern- ments be responsible for education. Since each province may establish its own system of education and curricula, differences are found in emphasis on historical events and heroes and even on general social values. Integrative possibilities are further hampered by evidence of regional inequalities in educational opportunities. In addition, the operation of the educational system has helped to perpetuate social- class differences to an extent probably greater than might be imagined by those who see Canada as an approximation of the more equali- tarian United States. That Canadian education is so bound up with social class is not in itself damaging to national unity. For example, in avowedly class-based countries mechanisms may exist whereby talented individuals of all social classes can be incorporated into the elite. Alternatively, and this is probably more characteristic of Canada where social class in itself is not a particularly salient characteristic, the perpetuation of class cleavages through the educational system is usually not perceived as a cause for resentment or disunity. Yet ob- jectively the system of education does not provide the foundation for integration across lines of social class, region, or official language.

The preceding summary, brief though it is, of those factors, outside the scope of this study, but nevertheless influencing the development of national identity should contribute to extend our understanding of Canadian society and the conditions affecting public opinion. The remaining influence, that of events, is treated sequentially in reference to the specific questions which were asked of the public.

SOURCE MATERIAL

The study proceeds from a secondary analysis of Gallup Poll data col- lected in Canada for the past twenty years. In that time span, the

[37] "Moulding the Canadian Mind Without Really Trying," *Saturday Night,* January, 1964, p. 17.

Canadian Institute of Public Opinion, the Canadian affiliate of the
Gallup organization, asked more than two hundred relevant questions.
But because of the physical setup of the poll, almost two-thirds of the
IBM cards for surveys conducted before 1949 were not kept; of those
that remain, many were stored by the Roper Public Opinion Research
Center at Williamstown. Fortunately the newspaper releases of this
earlier period are available, and some of these were recorded in the
Cantril compendium of public-opinion polls.[38] All available releases
were used for the study, supplemented by a sampling of questions from
the surveys for which IBM cards existed. Selection of the latter questions was based on the need to give adequate coverage to the several
areas of national problems and the time spanned.

The values of a secondary analysis of this sort are many. It is not
always possible for the researcher to gather his own material, and
even when it is, he is usually restricted in the time span he can cover.
Access to data such as those provided by Gallup Poll surveys provides
materials for a longitudinal analysis of some of the factors making
for stability and change, and helps avoid the possible selection of an
atypical year or survey.

A major reason for wishing to look at trends in opinions is the
increased understanding that should result. As the authors of *Voting*
have noted, issues should be thought of as having certain typical life
histories. Issues change from the time when there is little crystallization of opinion on them, to when they become matters of partisan
disagreement, after which they enter into the field of cross-party consensus. Dealing with only one phase in time, it is possible to select
issues at any stage in their life history. For example, if issues are
selected after they have become subjects of consensus among parties,
we might be led into believing that parties have little influence on
opinion. Focusing on the American party system, Key sees the problems this way: "If the time dimension is ignored, emphasis on consensus in the interpretation of American politics may convey a conception of a static politics and lead to the inference that the party
battle is meaningless. If a differentiation is made between levels or
types of consensus and if the party process is viewed through time, additional aspects of the working of party dualism may be identified." [39]

One example of such an opinion shift is the attitudes of businessmen toward New Deal legislation, evidenced from a content analysis

[38] Hadley Cantril, *Public Opinion, 1935–1946*, Princeton: Princeton University
Press, 1951.

[39] V. O. Key, Jr., *Politics, Parties and Pressure Groups*, 4th ed.; New York: Crowell,
1958, p. 243. See also V. O. Key, Jr., *Public Opinion and American Democracy*,
New York: Knopf, 1961, p. 443.

of the official publication of the Manufacturers' Association of Connecticut. A comparison of the content of articles from 1934 to 1940 and from 1946 to 1948, showed a long-term decline in the amount of anti-government feeling. This does not necessarily mean that there had been an increase in favourable attitudes toward government regulation, but rather that a relative acquiescence to the legislation had been achieved.[40] Government regulation was apparently no longer a highly controversial matter for businessmen, although these data do not indicate whether a parallel change occurred in partisan attitudes.

The study of trends, in addition to providing information about the life cycle of issues, also places these issues in the perspective of an ongoing political system. This would not be true if only questions central to specific election campaigns were dealt with. While campaign periods may accentuate divisions in opinion, the opposite can also occur. During an election the majority of voters may hold opinions, but these may be only imperfectly aligned with party policies. Between election years less crystallization of views is likely, but at the same time the views of those who hold opinions may be more polarized. Such a situation could occur because of differing demands made on parties during and between elections. For example in terms of party propaganda, "some distinction should perhaps be made between the propaganda put out by a party at election time and its actions when in office: the former is relatively moderate in order to win over the 'floating' voters situated at the Centre, the latter is less so in order to satisfy the militant who are more extremist." [41]

A study of trends also allows the consideration of political generations and the differential impact the issues considered herein may have for them, because of the needs and requirements of people in different stages of the life cycle and the particular historical circumstances in which they find themselves. Finally, an analysis of trends allows examination of the differential impact of questions not only on political generations, but also on other groups in the population.

Although there are advantages in the study of trends which a secondary analysis of data permits, there may also be disadvantages due to sampling, interviewing, or the choice of questions. Depending on the purpose of the analysis, whatever deficiencies do exist may be either negligible or may vitiate the findings. Personal experience with the Canadian Institute of Public Opinion, however, has proved interviewing techniques to be, at the very least, adequate. Sample sizes

[40] Robert E. Lane, *The Regulation of Businessmen*, New Haven: Yale University Press, 1954, pp. 54–55.

[41] Duverger, *op. cit.* (in n. 30), p. 388.

range from 3,000 to 700 respondents; the more usual size is around 1,600 before 1958, and 700 after. Respondents are usually selected by quota samples designed to obtain a cross-section of the population with respect to location, age, occupation, origin, and similar attributes. Quota samples cannot be projected to a larger universe with a known statistical margin of error, but the record of the Canadian Institute of Public Opinion in predicting election results has been good. It was only in the election of 1957, when the Institute underestimated the Conservative share of the popular vote by 5 percent, that its figures differed appreciably from the results. For the purpose of this study this type of error was not too serious since the concern of the study was not with prediction. It was rather with trends in opinions and the association of these trends with particular groups in the population. Whatever bias has been introduced by the method of sampling has probably remained the same from one survey to the next, allowing comparisons between similar groups. Actual question-wording has been discussed in those few instances where the manner in which the question was framed may have had some untoward effect on the results.

Ideally, an examination of public opinion should treat opinions on issues, their distribution over time, and the influences presumably affecting these simultaneously. However, because of the state of the data—trends were ascertained mainly from newspaper releases and influences were deduced from a selection of surveys conducted over the last twelve years—we were forced to separate these different aspects of our analysis. Thus Part II discusses trends in consensus on national problems and takes account of the reasons for their occurrence. Part III gives only limited attention to the development of trends, concentrating instead on a description and examination of selected influences on consensual development.

PART II

DOMINANT OPINIONS
AND THEIR TRENDS

IV   EXTERNAL PROBLEMS

INTRODUCTION

IN CONSIDERING ways of describing Canada's identity we took note of historical circumstances and present conditions as they have contributed to the present state of Canada's nationhood. The creation of a clear-cut image as the basis of a collective identity has been hampered by weaknesses and problems both external and internal. The most important issue underlying national identity, the issue of independence, has brought about the loosening of ties with Britain and a growing dependence on the United States. This realignment of traditional bonds has aroused concern and resentment in some circles. Meanwhile, the Commonwealth has grown as a more attractive affiliation for Canada. Relations with other international bodies have also increased in importance as Canadian governments have continued to follow a nonisolationist policy and have sought to attain a greater voice for Canada in world affairs. Internally, the country is marked by great regional diversity. Although some divergent strains are protected by the political system, the potential for conflict remains great as social and economic groups, especially with a geographic locus, seek to sustain and enhance their positions. Consequently, internal cleavages are likely to be a source of weakness in the development of a distinct identity. Governments of whatever political label, however, have taken an active role in fostering the development of the nation through protecting it from outside influences and attempting to equalize opportunities for all citizens. Finally, most countries have found political symbols an effective focus for national sentiment, yet these symbols are relatively absent in Canada.

Our concern now is with testing the accuracy of our summary description insofar as it agrees with public perceptions of these issues. By focusing on public opinion, we necessarily disregard a number of factors which are admittedly crucial to a full understanding of national identity, especially in relation to the formative influences on opinions and to the nature of subjective identifications. We are also limited by the coverage provided by the polls to specific issues about which opinions are surveyed. Hence, at times, we are frustrated in our attempts to generalize about areas of interest and about population groups because of gaps in our information. Nevertheless, the following description and analysis should document the utility of approaching national identity in this manner.

Of the number of ways in which public opinion may be examined, this study has considered only dominant views and the direction of trends since 1941. For this analysis all available Gallup Polls were used. These were derived mainly from newspaper releases, but in about one-fifth of the cases it was possible to examine the data in their original form. At times the newspaper releases included the distribution of opinions by different groups in the population. In contrast, those questions for which the surveys were available could be analysed by a variety of characteristics. In attempting to isolate trends, then, it was often difficult to say conclusively what were the reactions of specific groups. For this reason, there may be some tendency to err on the side of caution in attaching opinions to groups.

Data are presented in detail in the tables accompanying the text. Those tables giving the initial overview of dominant views also paraphrase the actual content of the questions. Each table gives the proportion of respondents expressing the dominant viewpoint, although some tables also indicate other responses. No sample sizes have been shown in these tables because they were not known for data obtained from newspaper releases. To distinguish between data obtained from newspaper releases and those directly from the IBM cards, the latter data have been marked with an asterisk.

Once more we need to emphasize that the data presented here are used to show general patterns. Since the wording of questions has frequently been altered, it is not possible to trace smooth trend lines over time. Yet we can still, in many cases, speak of trends with some assurance.

VIEWS ON INDEPENDENCE

Relations with Britain

Financial assistance.—Relations with Britain, especially since World War II, have often involved nonmilitary assistance. From 1942 to 1952 there was a decided increase in satisfaction with the kind of help Canada had offered Britain (see Table 6). This could have indicated a growing reluctance on the part of Canadians to overextend themselves in the assistance they offered to Britain. This interpretation is suggested by the contrast between the views of Quebec residents and those of other Canadians. In 1947, 44 percent of respondents from

TABLE 6

OPINIONS ON AID TO BRITAIN, 1942–1952

Date	Question	Percent
4/3/42	Approve of sending war supplies and food to Britain free	53
27/12/47	Satisfied with what country is doing to help Britain	59
24/9/52	Canada has done what she should to help Britain in financial crisis	74

Quebec were satisfied with the help being given to Britain, compared to 65 percent of the remainder. The larger number of dissatisfied Quebec respondents felt that assistance was excessive. In a 1952 survey the Gallup Poll reported that 89 percent of Quebec residents felt that Canada had done enough to aid Britain in her financial crisis, while only 60 percent of residents in the prairie provinces felt this way. The large amount of satisfaction found in 1952 then is likely related to a lessening concern with Britain's problems.

Trade.—Questions on trade with Britain asked between 1947 and 1963 found from one-fifth to one-half of the sampled population unaware of the subject or without an opinion.[1] Among those who did express an opinion, views were relatively stable, with a moderately larger proportion approving trade policies favourable to Britain than opposed to them (see Table 7). In particular the largest proportion of Canadians have remained in favour of buying fewer goods from the United States and more from Britain and the Commonwealth. However, the campaign efforts of the Conservatives in the 1957 election to convince voters of the desirability of diverting trade from the United States to Britain did not raise appreciably the proportion of those who approved of this course. The one exception to favourable attitudes toward trade relations with Britain concerns that toward food agreements made during the war years. By 1951 twice as many people felt that Canada had lost in these arrangements than those who felt it had gained. The most recent development in this area concerns Britain's avowed intention of joining the European Common Market. Canada's Conservative government voiced strong objections to this plan. In 1961, when asked about the government's opposition to Britain's prospective membership in the European Common Market (E.C.M.), two-thirds of those sampled had no opinion, mainly because they had heard nothing about this new economic community. Of the

[1] The significance of "no opinions" will be discussed fully in Chapter XII.

TABLE 7

OPINIONS ON TRADE RELATIONS WITH BRITAIN, 1947–1963

Date	Question	Percent
21/5/47	Favour Empire Preference if duties and tariffs reduced in all countries	23
24/5/50	Make effort to buy fewer goods from U.S. and more from Britain	43
2/5/51	Canada lost from food agreements made with Britain after the war	38
16/1/52	Make effort to buy fewer goods from U.S. and more from Britain	38
9/57[a]	Make effort to buy fewer goods from U.S. and more from Commonwealth	42
10/57[a]	Approve developing free-trade area between Britain and Canada	44
7/61[a]	Disapprove government opposition to Britain joining Common Market	20
21/4/62	Development of European Common Market will be a good thing for Canada	46
23/1/63	British entry into Common Market will be a good thing for Canada	39

[a] The complete survey is available for these questions, in which the month during which interviewing took place is given, rather than the newspaper-release date.

remainder, about two-thirds were opposed to the government's disapproval and one-third approved of its stand. Approval of government opposition could be basically a pro-British position where objection is being made to any weakening of Commonwealth ties, even if these are instigated by the mother country. On the other hand, it could be that those who disapproved of the government's stand were more pro-British in their desire not to deter Britain from following those policies most beneficial to her. But either opinion might also be based on anti-British attitudes. Thus approval could stem from a concern that Canadian trade arrangements were being jeopardized, and, therefore, no matter what happened to Britain, Canada should come first. Disapproval might also be motivated by anti-British feelings in the sense of indifference to Britain. It is difficult then to interpret these findings, although two later surveys indicate that a majority did at least not feel threatened by the E.C.M. In 1962 nearly one-half of the sample felt the development of the E.C.M. would be a good thing for Canada. In the following year the view of the largest group, while proportionately smaller, was still that British entry into the E.C.M. would be good for Canada. It is possible then that disapproval of the government stand stemmed from at least mildly pro-British feelings.

Although the Conservative election platform in 1957 was concerned with strengthening trade relations between Canada and Britain, in the two surveys taken that year, the major difference was between Liberal and CCF supporters. Only one-third of Liberal supporters wanted closer trade ties with Britain, as compared with almost two-thirds of CCF supporters. Conservatives and Social Crediters were more like the national average. Because of the large number who had no opinion about the Common Market, particularly among minor-party supporters, and because this was a partisan issue, it is difficult to interpret these results clearly. Considering only those who expressed an opinion, 83 percent of NDP supporters, 69 percent of the Liberals, and 57 percent of the Conservatives disapproved of the government's stand against British entry into the E.C.M. If we discount the Conservatives, since they were in a situation of conflict between supporting Britain and supporting their own party in office, we again find the NDP more favourable toward Britain and the Liberals less so.

Region also affected opinions about this issue. In 1950, 1952, and 1957 Quebec was much less favourable to British-Canadian trade arrangements than the rest of the country, although this unfavourable attitude seems to have declined somewhat over time. In 1957 greatest approval for free trade was to be found among western Canadians, particularly those living in British Columbia. It is difficult to say whether this was related to greater affinities with Britain, or to more dependence on primary products aimed for an export market. The latter contention tends to be supported by the fact that 56 percent of farm households approved of free trade. Other occupational groups were more like the national total. Yet there is undoubtedly an ethnic component in the regional differences since, in the same survey, only 27 percent of French-speaking respondents approved of free trade.

Involvement as part of the British Empire in military crises.—In the dark days of 1942, approximately two-thirds of those interviewed said Canada would be fighting even if she were completely independent and not a part of the British Empire. In fact, about 43 percent saw Canada as an independent country and not still dependent on Great Britain. Even so, most were satisfied that the Canadian air force remain part of the RAF rather than be formed into a separate Canadian force. At this time it is likely that the majority saw strong ties with Britain in a favourable light. Since then the largest proportion of every sample has given a favourable evaluation of Britain. An exception occurred in 1957, immediately after the Suez crisis, when 42 percent of respondents said that Britain was losing friends through her foreign policy, as compared with 41 percent who said she was not. In the preceding year only 28 percent felt Britain was losing friends, compared with 44 percent with the opposite view (see Table 8).

TABLE 8

EVALUATION OF BRITAIN, 1942–1963

Date	Question	Percent
27/6/42	Canadian airmen should fight as part of RAF rather than as separate force	48[a]
19/8/42	Canada would be fighting if she were completely independent and not a part of the British Empire	65[a]
19/8/42	Canada is independent country, not dependent on Britain.	43[a]
9/5/51	Britain has done a good job in dealing with world problems since the war	42
10/56[b]	Britain is not losing friends through foreign policy	44
26/1/57	Britain is losing friends through foreign policy	42
15/6/63	Britain's status as world power is not finished	47

[a] Approximately.
[b] Month of interviewing rather than newspaper-release date.

Here again the major contrast in opinions is between Quebec and the rest of the country. In 1942 only 20 percent of respondents in Quebec as compared with 62 percent of the other Canadians wanted Canadian airmen to be part of the RAF. This regional difference in evaluating Britain has remained constant from 1942 until 1963.

Since differences are largely between Quebec and the remaining provinces, it semes likely that they are related to ethnic origin rather than region. This tends to be supported by those Gallup Poll releases which contrast French-speaking with English-speaking Canadians (see Table 9). If we can regard these varied questions as having primarily a pro- and anti-British dimension, then it is reasonable to say that anti-British feeling was strongest in French Canada in 1942. But French-English differences continued at least up until 1956. The survey done in that year is available in its complete form, and it provides additional evidence of ethnic differences. Thus, 42 percent of the Canadian-born felt Britain was not losing friends compared with 53

TABLE 9

EVALUATION OF BRITAIN, BY OFFICIAL LANGUAGE, 1942–1956

Date	Question	English (percent)	French (percent)	Both languages (percent)
19/8/42	Canada would fight if completely independent	81	33	...
19/8/42	Canada is an independent country	52	25	...
9/5/51	Britain has done a good job in dealing with world	...	37	...
10/56[a]	Britain is not losing friends through foreign policy	51	26	34

[a] Month of interviewing rather than newspaper-release date.

percent of the foreign-born.[2] Fifty-two percent of the Protestants and 34 percent of the Roman Catholics gave this response.

Relations with the United States

Joint air defense, the range and destructiveness of modern weapons, and the expense and constant technological innovations demanded in order to achieve military preparedness, have all contributed to closer ties between the United States and Canada. For example, the Distant Early Warning Line (DEW Line) was established in 1956 and the North American Air Defense (NORAD) in 1958, the latter having served on an interim basis since 1957. By 1959 one-half of the Canadians interviewed felt that Canada was becoming more and more dependent on the United States for air defense, one-quarter disagreed, and one-quarter had no opinion. At the same time a majority approved of an air-defense merger, and this approval grew to 68 percent of the sample in 1961. The disapprovers have remained stable at 22 percent, but the number of those with no opinion has decreased. But along with these basically realistic attitudes toward North American defense, no desire for complete dependence on the United States seems to exist. In 1959, 71 percent of those interviewed felt that both countries should develop and pay for DEW Line bases (see Table 10). With this degree of consensus it is hard to distinguish differences between

[2] There is good reason to believe, on the basis of sampling procedures, that the foreign-born come disproportionately from the British Isles.

TABLE 10

OPINIONS ON MILITARY RELATIONS WITH THE UNITED STATES, 1959–1961

Date	Question	Percent
28/1/59	Canada is becoming more and more dependent on the U.S. for air defence	50
28/1/59	Would approve if Canada's air defence becomes merged more and more with that of the U.S.	59
3/59[a]	Both U.S. and Canada should develop and pay for DEW Line bases	71
9/12/61	Would approve if Canada's air defence becomes merged with that of the U.S.	68

[a] Month of interviewing rather than newspaper-release date.

groups. However, residents of Quebec were more in favour of both countries participating in the DEW Line endeavour, and 36 percent had no opinion, compared with 18 percent of the national total with no opinion. Of British Columbia residents, 14 percent felt that the United States should look after the DEW Line by itself, in contrast to only 5 percent of the total sample. There was also a difference between Protestant and Roman Catholic supporters, with the latter less likely to choose the alternative of joint development, and instead having a high rate of no opinion. The consensus of favourable opinions about relations between Canada and the United States in 1959 might have been altered if surveys had been taken after the Canadian government canceled contracts of the Avro Arrow as a result of the decision of the United States defence department not to purchase these planes.

Economic relations.—Questions on economic relations with the United States when compared with questions on economic relations with Britain generally show a much lower rate of no opinion, usually well under 20 percent. This greater awareness and concern is undoubtedly related to the closer economic ties to the United States. Relatively comparable questions asked in 1943, 1944, 1946, 1953, and 1963 on free trade showed a sharp decline of those in favour from over two-thirds to one-half (see Table 11). Approval was sufficiently strong in 1944 so that 23 percent answered that they would favour free trade, even if it meant a cutback in Canadian production, but 37 percent would favour it only if it did not necessitate such a move. Similar regional breakdowns were not released, but in 1943 the West was considerably more favourable to free trade than the East. In 1953

TABLE 11

OPINIONS ON ECONOMIC RELATIONS WITH THE UNITED STATES, 1943–1957

Date	Question	Percent
2/6/43	Favour free trade with the United States	67
19/2/44	Favour free trade with the United States	70
19/2/44	Favour free trade, but not if it meant cut in Canadian production	37
1946	Canada would be better off if U.S. goods were let in free . . . and Canadian goods allowed into U.S. free	54
27/9/50	Should continue to encourage U.S. capital to help develop natural resources	60
6/6/53	Canada would be better off if U.S. goods were let in free . . . and Canadian goods allowed into U.S. free	49
3/2/54	Should not import Texas gas even if cheaper than Alberta gas	52
18/7/56	Good for Canada that a lot of development has been financed by U.S. money	68
10/57[a]	Favour U.S. investment in Canada	64
10/8/63	Good for Canada that a lot of development has been financed by U.S. money	55
21/8/63	Canada would be better off if U.S. goods were let in free . . . and Canadian goods allowed into U.S. free	50

[a] Month of interviewing rather than newspaper-release date.

it was Ontario which was more favourable than was Quebec, but here the difference was not great (see Table 12).

On the question of United States investment in Canada, approval continued to be high from 1950 to 1957, reaching a peak of 68 percent in 1956, but dropping off sharply in 1963. Curiously, during this time span, when respondents were asked about the development of natural resources by capital from outside the country without specifying the source, only about one-half expressed their approval[3] (see Table 13).

United States investment in Canada received greatest approval from British Columbia and the Maritimes and least from the prairies povinces. By 1963, however, criticism of the United States from politicians and mass media was having an effect on all residents, with

[3] The one specific objection made to American economic contact occurred in response to the question of importing Texas rather than Alberta gas because the former would be cheaper.

regional differences becoming slight (see Table 12). Regional variations occurred also in opinions about foreign capital for resource development, but in this case it was British Columbia alone which
showed high approval, while the other regions were similar. The greatest variation was found among the supporters of the four parties, with
CCF supporters consistently less favourable to American or other foreign investment. There was also some tendency for those in higher
social-class positions to be more favourable to outside investment.

TABLE 12

OPINIONS ON ECONOMIC RELATIONS WITH UNITED STATES, BY REGION, 1943–1957
(in percent)

Date	Question	Mari-times	Quebec	Ontario	Prairies	British Colum-bia
2/6/43	Favour free trade with the United States	...	63		78	
2/6/53	Canada better off if U.S. goods let in free	...	37	44	...	...
3/2/54	Should not import Texas gas even if cheaper	...	...	50	63	...
18/7/56	Good for Canada that development has been U.S.-financed	...	70	68	69	
10/57[a]	Favour U.S. investment in Canada	70	61	64	59	73
10/8/63	Good for Canada that development has been U.S.-financed	...	55	59	54	

[a] Month of interviewing rather than newspaper-release date.

TABLE 13

OPINIONS ON FOREIGN RESOURCE DEVELOPMENT, 1954–1957

Date	Question	Percent
9/54[a]	Development of natural resources by capital from outside the country good for Canada	50
10/57[a]	Development of natural resources by capital from outside the country good for Canada	54

[a] Month of interviewing rather than newspaper-release date.

General dependency on the United States.—A series of questions
have been asked over the past fifteen years about ties with the United
States and a general evaluation of that country. Beginning with those
questions which are comparable, we find that the largest group (43
percent) believe that Canada is becoming more dependent on the
United States than during the ten years previously. In 1957 however,
27 percent of the sample felt that Canada was becoming less dependent
on the United States, 22 percent said more dependent, and 35 percent had no opinion. The other questions asked between 1948 and
1963, however, showed a small increase in the proportion who saw
a greater dependency. In 1963 the result of this dependency was seen
as a good thing for Canada by 48 percent and not a good thing by
44 percent. The rather surprising finding that almost one-half should
find dependency good for Canada suggests that this question is not a
particularly good indicator of an underlying anti-Americanism.

Another question which has been repeated for several years is
whether the Canadian way of life has been influenced too much by
the United States. Between 1951 and 1961 the largest proportion
answered in the negative. The feeling that American influence was not
excessive was greatest in 1956, dropped off somewhat the following
year, and dropped off even more sharply in 1961 (see Table 14).

Evaluation of United States policies and prestige.—Respondents
were also asked to evaluate relations between Canada and the United
States as excellent, good, just fair, or poor. Between 1955 and 1960 the
excellent and good categories dropped off slightly, and the fair or
poor categories increased from 19 to 27 percent. In 1956 the United
States, like Britain, was not thought to be losing friends as a result of
her foreign policy, but by 1958 opinions were quite different. In 1958
only 30 percent felt that American policies were not costing her the
friendship of her allies. If the population interviewed were responding
to events, they had many instances of difficulties between the two
countries from which to choose. In that year the Conservatives were
campaigning on a strong anti-American platform. In particular they
were publicizing the extent of American control over Canadian industry and the hardships resulting from American policies in disposing
of agricultural surplus. At this time also the Canadian subsidiary of
the Ford Motor Company was prevented from selling automobiles to
Communist China because of American government restrictions on
traffic with that country. When President Eisenhower visited Ottawa
that year, his official communiques were dominated by a concern with
smoothing over these issues. The following year a majority said that
their opinion of the United States had remained unchanged, 14 per-

TABLE 14

EVALUATION OF THE UNITED STATES, 1948–1963

Date	Question	Percent
10/3/48	Becoming more dependent on U.S. than ten years ago	42
8/7/51	Canadian way of life is not being influenced too much by U.S.	48
9/5/51	U.S. has done a good job in dealing with world problems since the war	47
7/5/55	Relations between Canada and the U.S. today are, on the whole, good	56
11/7/56	Canadian way of life is not being influenced too much by U.S.	63
10/56[a]	U.S. is not losing friends among Western countries because of her foreign policy	42
3/7/57	Becoming less dependent on U.S. than 10 years ago	27
29/6/57	Canadian way of life is not being influenced too much by U.S.	57
9/57[a]	U.S. T.V. programs better	47
27/8/58	U.S. is losing friends because of her foreign policy	38
17/10/59	Opinion of U.S. is unchanged—has not gone up or down	57[b]
3/9/60	Relations between Canada and the U.S. are, on the whole, good	54
25/1/61	Becoming more dependent on U.S. than 10 years ago	43
13/2/61	In the past year respect for the U.S. has decreased in the country	36
2/12/61	Canadian way of life is not being influenced too much by the U.S.	49
13/3/63	In the last year respect for the U.S. has increased in this country	54
3/7/63	Becoming more dependent on U.S. than 10 years ago	49
6/7/63	Dependence on the U.S. is good for Canada	48

[a] Month of interviewing rather than newspaper-release date.
[b] Approximately.

cent said it had gone up, and the same percentage said it had gone down. In a survey reported early in 1961, although the interviewing for it had been done in November of the preceding year, the evaluation of the United States was again a poor one: 36 percent said their respect for, or the prestige of, the United States in the past year had gone down, compared with 28 percent who said it remained the same, and 20 percent who said it increased. Here response may have been to the deterioration of relations between Cuba and the United States, and the American reaction to Canada's continued trade with Cuba. Similar surveys were also conducted in Britain and the United States. In Britain opinions were almost identical with those in Canada. In the United States, however, an even larger proportion, 45 percent of the sample believed that respect for the United States had decreased. But by 1963 Canadians seemed again impressed by American initiative, and respect for that country had gone up, according to 54 percent of those interviewed.

Among the correlates of attitudes toward the United States is that of region. Since 1961 anti-American sentiments have increased in the western provinces. On the basis of available data this first became apparent in British Columbia in 1956 (see Table 15). Beginning at about the same time, in Quebec feelings became more favourable toward the United States. An early indication of the more positive feelings of Quebec residents was evidenced in a 1951 survey when 58 percent of French-origin respondents answered that the United States was handling world problems well, as compared with 47 percent of the national total. Feelings in the West may be related to the dependence of that part of the country on such products as wheat, oil, and, on the coast, lumber, and the difficulty of marketing these products at times because of American trade restrictions or agricultural policies. Quebec sentiments appear more difficult to account for, particularly during a time of growing nationalist feeling in that province. Yet pressures for provincial autonomy are directed against the central government and English-speaking Canada rather than against control from outside the country. Also, there is evidence that the most extreme sentiments, those in favour of separatism, are confined to a small minority of the Quebec population.

Factors other than region are probably contributing to these attitudes toward the United States, but information on these is not at hand. For example, the 1956 survey on whether the United States was losing friends was available for complete analysis, and it showed that party, in addition to region, was a significant variable. In this case CCF supporters were inclined to be least favourable to the United States, and Social Credit supporters most. However, party is only available for one other survey, that on the comparison of United States and Canadian television. In this case it was the Conservatives who felt American television was best; Liberals were least likely to be of this opinion. Other items of information which may be significant are that in the 1956 survey on American influence, Canadian-born

TABLE 15

EVALUATION OF THE UNITED STATES, BY REGION, 1956–1963
(in percent)

Date	Questions	Maritimes	Quebec	Ontario	Prairies	British Columbia
10/56[a]	U.S. is not losing friends because of foreign policy	41	39	41	54	37
17/10/59	Opinion of U.S. is unchanged	44 (Maritimes–Quebec)		60	68 (Prairies–B.C.)	
3/9/60	Relations between Canada and U.S. are good	53	45	56	60 (Prairies–B.C.)	
25/1/61	Becoming more dependent on U.S.	38	40	45	46 (Prairies–B.C.)	
13/2/61	Respect for U.S. has decreased in this country	28 (Maritimes–Quebec)		40	40 (Prairies–B.C.)	
13/3/63	Respect for U.S. has increased in this country	60 (Maritimes–Quebec)		57	43 (Prairies–B.C.)	
3/7/63	Becoming more dependent on U.S.	41	47	52	50 (Prairies–B.C.)	
6/7/63	Dependence on U.S. is good for Canada	57	65	42	39 (Prairies–B.C.)	

[a] Month of interviewing rather than newspaper-release date.

were less likely to object against too much influence than those born in other countries, and younger people were less likely to object than those forty and over. In 1958 those with higher education were more negative in their evaluation of the United States than those with less education, but in the previous year education had little impact in differentiating between Canadian and American television.

From this conglomeration of questions we can say that pro-American feeling is more widespread than anti-American feeling. There have been fluctuations in the way the United States is evaluated; 1956 and 1963 were particularly good years in terms of a positive evaluation, 1958 and 1961 showed a more negative evaluation. These fluctuations have been related both to international and domestic events.

The Commonwealth

Perhaps the most interesting manifestation of the desire for independence appears in the attitudes of Canadians toward the Commonwealth and the changes that have occurred in these. In 1943, 49 percent of those interviewed wanted Canada to remain in the Commonwealth after the war, 21 percent were in favour of Canada joining the United States, and 24 percent wanted the country to become completely independent. In 1947 and 1950 when this question was repeated, independence had risen in favour from one-quarter to about one-third of the responses, and the other two alternatives had gone down correspondingly. But between 1950 and 1952, a change occurred in the evaluation of the United States as a prospective partner: instead of 18 percent in favour of joining the United States, only 9 percent now responded in this manner, and more than one-half wanted Canada to remain in the Commonwealth. Since that time, approval of Canadian membership in the Commonwealth has remained the favoured alternative for more than one-half of those interviewed. A stable proportion of about 10 percent seems convinced that Canada should join the United States, and another group of under 30 percent continues to believe that Canada should become an independent country. Although this change in attitude may mean an increase in anti-American feelings, it may also reflect anxiety over the implications of close ties with the United States. In 1950 the Korean War broke out, and the tensions of the cold war increased. Canadians may then have come to look to the Commonwealth as a new centre of gravity in the modern world. How effective the Commonwealth might be in dealing with international tensions is open to question, but to the ordinary citizen the Commonwealth has become a more attractive organization

than ever before. This view becomes most apparent in those questions
for which other alternatives were not given. For example, in 1954,
70 percent answered that it was a good thing for Canada to continue
as a member of the Commonwealth. In 1963, 50 percent said that
"the British Commonwealth is a fine example of the way in which
widely different people of all colors, creeds, and social economic levels
can live and work together," and an additional 23 percent said "it is

TABLE 16

OPINIONS ON COMMONWEALTH, 1943–1963

Date	Question	Percent
15/6/43	Remain in Commonwealth after war	49
	Become independent	24
	Join U.S.	21
12/11/47	Continue as member of Commonwealth	44
	Become independent	32
	Join U.S.	18
18/10/50	Continue as member of Commonwealth	44
	Become independent	32
	Join U.S.	18
3/9/52	Continue as member of Commonwealth	53
	Become separate country	31
	Join U.S.	9
11/54[a]	Good thing for Canada to continue as member of Commonwealth	70
14/7/56	Continue as member of Commonwealth	56
	Become independent	29
	Join U.S.	10
7/60[a]	Continue as member of Commonwealth	62
	Become independent	28
	Join U.S.	10
3/62[a]	Continue as member of Commonwealth	55
	Become independent	28
	Join U.S.	10
19/1/63	The British Commonwealth is a fine example of the way in which widely different peoples of all colors, creeds, and social economic levels, can live and work together	50

[a] Month of interviewing rather than newspaper-release date.

nothing very spectacular, but it is worthwhile and we should continue to play our part in it" [4] (see Table 16).

Considerable differences of opinion are found among party supporters. Conservative supporters are most frequently favourable to the Commonwealth, Liberals less so. But it is the minor parties who differ most markedly in their advocacy of an independent course for Canada. Independence was chosen by 35 percent of CCF/NDP supporters in 1947, 37 percent in 1956, 43 percent in 1960, and 38 percent in 1962. Social Credit supporters were similarly forming independence in 1956. In 1960, 30 percent chose this alternative as did a similar percentage of Liberals. But Social Creditors were more likely in that year—26 percent—than other party supporters to advocate joining the United States. In 1962, joining United States dropped off in attractiveness for Social Credit supporters, but independence was felt to be best for Canada by 49 percent.

There are also large regional variations in opinions. Generally, the Maritimes and Ontario are most favourable to the Commonwealth, and Quebec is least so. During the excitement of the Cuban crisis in 1960, approval of the Commonwealth reached its highest level. In that year, except for the particularly high favouring shown by the Maritimers, regional differences leveled off considerably. However, Quebec became less in favour again in 1962. Changes in the attitude of Quebec respondents are best reflected in the large proportion who formerly advocated independence for Canada (see Table 17). These residents did not seem as affected by events in 1950 as the national sample. But in 1960 they were favouring independence even less than prairie and British Columbia respondents. The desire for independence went up again in Quebec in 1962. At the same time support for the Commonwealth seemed to be declining in the West, particularly British Columbia, and independence was looked on with new favour.

Differences of opinion are also related to ethnic origin. Here in-

---

[4] A survey conducted in 1964 by Le Groupe de Recherches Sociales, based on a random sample of Canadians eighteen years of age and older but excluding farm residents, suggests that ties with the United States are even closer than our Gallup Polls indicate. This survey found 12 percent strongly in favour of political union with the United States, and an additional 17 percent favouring union with less intensity. These results could be affected by sampling techniques, particularly the exclusion of farm respondents, although our own findings do not indicate much difference between rural and urban residents. More significant, no doubt, were the questions used. Our own analysis is based on questions which focus on the Commonwealth. In the 1964 survey, no mention was made of the Commonwealth, and respondents were asked only to think in terms of union with the United States. "Who's for Canada—and Who's for the U.S.A.," *Maclean's*, June 6, 1964, pp. 12–13.

TABLE 17

REGIONAL VARIATIONS IN FAVOURING INDEPENDENCE
FROM THE COMMONWEALTH, 1950–1962
(in percent)

Region	1950	1952	1956	1960	1962
Canada	32	31	29	28	28
Quebec	49	56	50	29	39
Maritimes	...	...	21	12	16
Ontario	...	...	21	29	27
Prairie provinces	...	...	} 26	32	23
British Columbia	...	...		38	30

formation is incomplete but, up until 1954, respondents of French origin were considerably less favourable toward the Commonwealth than those of British origin or English-speaking. Religious differences have continued from 1954 to 1962, with Protestants being considerably more pro-Commonwealth than Roman Catholics. For the latter, independence and, to a lesser extent, union with the United States, were relatively more attractive alternatives. These findings can be at least partly accounted for by the coinciding of origin and religion for French-speaking Canadians.

Commonly used indicators of social-class position also show some relation to opinions about the Commonwealth. In general, approval of Canadian membership in the Commonwealth is greatest among those with higher class position, allowing for the different rates of no opinions among lower class respondents. However, in the generally favourable climate of 1960, white-collar workers and those with high-school education had the lowest percentages of those favouring Commonwealth membership. Finally greatest inclination for Commonwealth membership was usually shown by women, those in the oldest age group, and widowed or divorced.

Along with a trend toward greater preference for the Commonwealth goes evidence that groups generally recognized as more conservative are its most frequent supporters: the dominant English-speaking Protestants; residents of the older, settled regions of Canada; older people; and socially more restricted women.

To summarize briefly this diversified material on independence we found first of all, opinions which were favourable toward Britain although not overwhelmingly so, but no discernible trends. Opinions of the United States were more uneven, apparently fluctuating with international conditions, particularly those which might affect U.S.-Canadian relations. On the whole, though, opinions were favourable. Opinions were most distinctively favourable to the Commonwealth, and the trend has been to an increase in this view. Pro-British feelings were expressed most often by English-speaking respondents and by those in the Maritimes. Opinions more favourable to the United States appear to be on the increase in eastern Canada, on the decrease in the West. Supporters of the CCF have been least pro-American. The Commonwealth was favoured most often by Conservatives and least by those of the minor parties. Greatest support for the Commonwealth also came from the traditionally more conservative groups in the population.

CANADA'S ROLE ON THE INTERNATIONAL SCENE

World Organization

In 1945, as Canada went into the last year of World War II, 90 percent of those interviewed expressed a willingness for the Canadian government to join with other countries in forming an international organization. But in the following two years, perhaps disillusioned by the emergence of new power alignments after the war and the extension of Russia's sphere of influence, a majority of those answering were dissatisfied with the progress of the United Nations. In 1946, an equal proportion of Americans, 37 percent, expressed dissatisfaction, slightly fewer than the number of dissatisfied Canadians. But by the following year, American dissatisfaction had risen to 51 percent of the sample, Canadians were dissatisfied in 38 percent of the cases, and another 36 percent had no opinion. Only 16 percent of the Americans, though, were lacking opinions. But as time went on, and the United Nations successfully weathered crises in Korea, Indochina, Suez, Berlin, and Lebanon, the majority of Canadians felt that the United Nations had justified its existence. As a result, in a Gallup release early in 1960, 77 percent were convinced that it was very important for the United Nations to succeed (see Table 18). The same poll was taken in a number of countries, but only in the United States was opinion more favourable toward the United Nations. In that country, 88 percent answered that it was very important that the United Nations succeed, as compared with 63 percent in Britain, and 32 percent in France, while the average world response was 59 percent.[5]

[5] Canadian Institute of Public Opinion release, February 26, 1960.

TABLE 18

Opinions on World Organization, 1945–1960

Date	Question	Percent
6/5/45	If world organization is formed after war to try to keep peace, Canada should join	90
12/6/46	Dissatisfied with progress made to date by U.N.	44
13/7/46	Would be willing to have Canada turn over control of foreign policy to a world parliament, if leading countries did the same	51
14/12/46	Each country should decide by itself what people, and how many, it will take in rather than to have all immigration planned by the U.N.	79
20/9/47	Dissatisfied with progress made to date by U.N.	38
23/7/55	U.N. has justified its existence	62
27/7/55	U.N. should be strengthened to make it a world government with power to control the armed forces of all nations, including Canada	45
19/1/57	U.N. has justified its existence	66
20/2/57	U.N. should be strengthened . . . with power to control the armed forces of all nations, including Canada	53
8/10/58	U.N. has justified its existence	66
10/2/60	It is very important that we try to make the U.N. a success	77

Canadians have been willing to give up some of their national sovereignty to the United Nations. For example, in 1956 they were willing to have Canada turn over control of foreign policy and, in 1955 and 1957, control over armed forces. Support for United Nations control over armed forces rose slightly in 1957, perhaps as a result of favourable experiences in the Suez. However, there was widespread disapproval of permitting the United Nations to make decisions about the number and kinds of immigrants that Canada should admit (see Table 18).

Some information is available on regional differences in favouring United Nations control: Quebec residents saw United Nations control as much less desirable than those in other parts of the country.

Canadian Troops Abroad

Canada has participated on the side of the United Nations in controlling a number of international disputes. Probably the most significant instance followed the Suez crisis. At this time Secretary of State for External Affairs Lester B. Pearson took a leading role in organizing the United Nations peace force to supervise the settlement of the dispute. In general, public opinion has tended to support such activity. Before the war had ended, a large majority of Canadians were in favour of the establishment of an international peace force in which Canada would participate. Specifically, respondents approved sending troops to Western Europe, Korea, the Arab-Israeli disputed area, and Lebanon (see Table 19). Approval, however, was probably less widespread than this table may indicate. For example, in 1950, only those respondents who approved of sending equipment to Korea were asked about troops. Thus, 23 percent were omitted, and if they are added to the 16 percent who disapproved of sending troops and the 15 percent who gave a qualified answer, we have more than half of the respondents who may not have been favourable toward sending troops to Korea. In the Arab-Israeli war, approval was also less because those who were unaware of the dispute were omitted from the calculation.

TABLE 19

Opinions on Canadian Troops Serving Abroad, 1942–1958

Date	Question	Percent
25/2/42	Would approve if Canadian soldiers were sent to Australia to help defend that country from Japanese attack	55
20/11/43	Would like Canada to take an active part in maintaining world peace, even if it meant sending troops to help keep peace in other parts of the world	78
10/1/45	Would approve of Canada sending troops to international armed force maintained at all times to keep the peace	72
3/8/50	Would approve if Canada sent men to fight in Korea	34
2/12/50	Would approve of Canada providing troops for the defence of Western Europe	54
23/7/52	Was not mistake for Canada to send troops to fight in Korea	50
5/54[a]	If trouble in Indochina increases, Canada should stay out of it	59
25/6/56	If U.N. police force set up to patrol Arab-Israel borders, Canada should send troops	46
24/7/58	Canada should participate with either Britain or U.S. in Lebanon	92

[a] Month of interviewing rather than newspaper-release date.

TABLE 20

Opinions on Canadian Troops Serving Abroad by Region, 1943–1954

(in percent)

Date	Question	Quebec	Maritimes	Ontario	Prairies	British Columbia
20/11/43	Would like Canada to take an active part in maintaining world peace, even if it meant sending troops	56		85		
10/1/45	Would approve of Canada sending troops to international armed force	51		85		
2/12/50	Would approve of Canada providing troops for the defence of Western Europe	37		59		
3/8/50	Would approve of Canada sending men to fight in Korea	21		41		
23/7/52	Was not mistake for Canada to send troops to fight in Korea	32	…	59	58	46
5/54[a]	If trouble in Indochina increases, Canada should stay out of it	72	50	54	52	55

[a] Month of interviewing rather than newspaper-release date.

The Lebanon question was only asked as a telephone survey in Toronto, and it is difficult to determine how those with no opinion were treated. Willingness to participate reached a distinct low in 1954, when the majority felt that Canada should stay out of troubles in Indochina. From these data no distinct trends are apparent, although 1954 was a low year for participation. In general, there is a tendency to favour sharing in United Nations activities which supervise the peace, a tendency which is more pronounced, however, when peace in Europe and the Middle East is at stake than when the difficulties are in Asia. Thus, even during the early war years, when asked about sending Canadian troops to Australia to defend that country from Japan, only a relatively small majority favoured this course (see Table 19). Again, compared to the rest of the country, Quebec residents show greater reluctance to take part in such international activities (see Table 20).

Other Commitments

Other international commitments have also had favourable responses (see Table 21). Knowledge of the Pan American Union in 1944 was restricted to only 28 percent of the sample; however, of those, more than 80 percent wanted Canada to join. Fewer than two-fifths had heard of NATO, but when this body's nature and objectives were explained, a large majority approved of Canadian participation in it. By 1960, most Canadians were committed to the belief that Canada was too much influenced by events outside its boundaries to gain anything by attempting dissociation. But along with this goes the feeling that the United States and the Western Nations are doing enough to aid underdeveloped countries financially and technically (see Table 21).

Based on complete information from one survey and two other breakdowns from two additional ones, the following picture emerges of those respondents most favourable to international commitments. They are Conservatives, of higher socioeconomic status, not residents of Quebec or, to a lesser extent, British Columbia, Protestant, male, and in the older age groups. Age, however, does not seem to be a consistent factor, since the younger respondents were less satisfied with aid to underdeveloped countries in 1962, and in 1952 were most inclined to say that it had not been a mistake to send troops to Korea. The clearest indications that these polls give are that participation in international bodies is desirable for Canada, but the heritage of previous wars has left a hard core of isolationism in Quebec.

TABLE 21

OPINIONS ON INTERNATIONAL COMMITMENTS, 1944–1962

Date	Question	Percent
12/1/44	Canada should be a member of the Pan-American Union	24
17/5/52	Approve of Canada taking part in NATO	78
19/3/60	Approve of Canada taking part in NATO	72
7/60[a]	Canada should not become a neutral nation like Switzerland	59
28/2/62	America and the West are doing as much as they should to help underdeveloped countries with financial and technical assistance	53

[a] Month of interviewing, rather than newspaper-release date.

Further interpretation of the results of trends in opinions on external problems will be reserved until trends on internal and symbolic problems have been considered in the following two chapters.

V INTERNAL PROBLEMS

THE DIVERSITY OF SOCIAL INTERESTS

French-English Relations

HISTORICALLY, the most critical question that has arisen out of the complexity of social, political, and economic interests in Canada has concerned the relations between the French and the English. The major problems for the French minority have been their lack of economic opportunities and the preservation of their culture.

Economic opportunities.—Conclusive evidence has been accumulated over the years to show that Canadians of French origin have not achieved the same positions of economic authority as those who are English-speaking.[1] French Canadians interviewed in 1942 about their treatment in the civil service, war industries, the army, and business, said that they were not fairly treated, especially in the civil service (see Table 22). In a survey conducted by *La Presse* of Montreal in 1961 among its readers, 89 percent of the respondents said that French Canadians were not treated fairly in the federal civil service and 96 percent said that business and industry in Canada were dominated by English Canadians.[2] The desire for full participation in the economic life of the province and the country as a whole is much in the forefront of the "quiet revolution" in Quebec. While the appointment of the Royal Commission on Bilingualism and Biculturalism in 1963 did not empower the commissioners to deal specifically with such economic problems as limitations on employment opportunities, the commission's obligation "to recommend what steps should be taken to develop

---

[1] E. C. Hughes, *French Canada in Transition*, Chicago: University of Chicago Press, 1943, pp. 46–64; Bernard R. Blishen, "The Construction and Use of an Occupational Class Scale," *Canadian Journal of Economics and Political Science*, 24, November, 1958, p. 524; John Porter, "The Economic Elite and the Social Structure of Canada," *Canadian Journal of Economics and Political Science*, 23, August, 1957, p. 386; Yves de Jocas and Guy Rocher, "Intergeneration Occupational Mobility in the Province of Quebec," *Canadian Journal of Economics and Political Science*, 23, February, 1957, pp. 57–68.

[2] *La Presse*, March 18, 1961, reported in Marcel Rioux, *Quebec's New Look: An Interpretation*, Canadian Association for Adult Education; Pamphlet No. 15, April, 1961, p. 10.

TABLE 22

OPINIONS ON FRENCH-ENGLISH RELATIONS, 1942–1963

Date	Question	Percent
15/8/42	French-speaking respondents who feel French Canadians are not treated well in the following:	
	Civil service	60
	War industries	54
	Army	55
	Business	53
7/4/43	French should be compulsory in English Canadian public schools	50
7/4/43	English should be compulsory in French Canadian elementary schools (French-speaking respondents)	85
4/8/56	If public school pupils learned both English and French it would lead to better understanding between French- and English-speaking Canadians	67
16/8/61	French should be compulsory in English Canadian public schools	71
16/8/61	English should be compulsory in French Canadian elementary schools (French-speaking respondents)	97
22/5/63	Feelings between English- and French-speaking Canadians are about the same as they were about five years ago	29

the Canadian Confederation on the basis of an equal partnership between the two founding races" has certainly led it to consider these problems.[3]

Bilingualism.—It has been argued that to achieve better understanding between the two dominant language groups it is necessary to extend and increase bilingualism. But the issue of bilingualism has remained complicated. According to some, French should be confined to those settings defined in the British North America Act. Others feel that French should be extended in its use both within parliament and throughout the government. In the survey conducted by *La Presse,* 46 percent wanted obligatory bilingualism in the whole country, and 41 percent wanted obligatory bilingualism for all in Quebec.[4] In the 1961 census only 12 percent of the population gave their official lan-

[3] *A Preliminary Report of the Royal Commission on Bilingualism and Biculturalism,* Ottawa: Queen's Printer, 1965.
[4] Rioux, *op. cit.,* p. 10.

TABLE 23

REGIONAL DISTRIBUTION OF CANADIANS STATING OFFICIAL LANGUAGE
AS BOTH ENGLISH AND FRENCH, 1961

Region	Percent
Canada	12.2
Atlantic provinces	9.0
Quebec	25.5
Ontario	7.9
Prairie provinces	5.3
British Columbia	3.5

SOURCE: Canada, Dominion Bureau of Statistics, *1961 Census of Canada*, Ottawa: Queen's Printer, 1962.

guage as both English and French, and most of these were found in Quebec (see Table 23). (There are, however, undoubtedly many more who are fluent in both languages.) The teaching of French has not been compulsory in any province west of Quebec although the situation is now changing. In interviews with French-speaking Canadians attending the School of English at Queen's University, Kingston, during the summer of 1955, the majority indicated that the failure of English-speaking people to learn French was "the greatest cause of conflict between English and French Canadians." [5] The best remedy for this, they thought, was to have the English learn to speak French. Gallup Poll respondents also have become increasingly convinced of the helpfulness of bilingualism, and the number of those who desired two compulsory languages in the elementary schools increased sharply from 1943 to 1961 (see Table 23). While bilingualism is advocated by more than 90 percent of those in French Canada, it has now also become the choice of a majority of English-speaking Canadians.

With the new growth of French Canadian nationalism in Quebec and the activities of vocal and even violent separatist groups, Canadians are equally divided among those who feel relations between English- and French-speaking Canadians are better, those who feel they are worse, and those who think they have remained the same in the past five years (see Table 24). French-speaking residents of Quebec, perhaps heartened by the new attention which English Canada is giving their problems, are more likely to feel that relations have be-

[5] Jane Stewart and Julian Blackburn, "Tensions Between English-Speaking and French-Speaking Canadians," *Contribution à l'étude des sciences de l'homme*, 3, 1956, p. 148.

TABLE 24

OPINIONS OF CHANGE IN FEELINGS BETWEEN ENGLISH- AND FRENCH-SPEAKING
CANADIANS OVER PAST FIVE YEARS, 1963
(in percent)

Development of relations	National	French Quebec	Remainder
Better	27	37	24
Worse	27	14	30
About the same	29	36	27
Undecided	17	13	19

come better.[6] The rest of Canada, however, is convinced that relations have deteriorated. Yet, at least on the issue of bilingualism, a new identity of interest has begun to emerge.

Population

In the early postwar years, a majority of Canadians, perhaps arguing on the analogy that what is bigger must be better, felt that Canada was in need of a larger population. Although Canada has one of the highest birth rates in the Western World, it is natural to assume that respondents were thinking mainly of immigrants, since Canada has always been settled by foreign peoples. Approval for a larger population was greatest in 1945, with 65 percent in favour. But, as the stream of postwar immigrants began, approval began to decline. After the large influx which began in 1948 and then reached a new peak in 1951, disapproval of increased immigration rose sharply, reaching a high of 67 percent in 1960. Even a humanitarian appeal during World Refugee Year to permit a limited number of refugees from Europe to enter brought almost the same amount of disapproval as approval. In fact, if the issue of colour (which called into question what have become socially approved values among Canadian leaders) had not been raised in 1961, an even larger number of Canadians would probably have recorded their opposition to increased immigration (see Table 25). Disapproval has always been greatest in Quebec but, since 1960 at least, there has also been a high frequency of disapproval in the West,

[6] For example, in a 1963 survey on separatism, 32 percent of French-speaking Montreal respondents replied that the activities of separatists were *improving* French-English relations and only 16 percent of the total sample felt that the result was a deterioration in relations. Groupe de Recherche Sociale, *Opinions sur le separatisme*, unpublished tables, Montreal, 1963, Table 39.

TABLE 25

OPINIONS ON POPULATION SIZE, 1945–1960

Date	Question	Percent
24/2/45	Would like to see Canada have a much larger population	65
26/10/46	Would like to see Canada have a much larger population	63
2/8/47	Canada needs immigrants	51
7/1/48	Would like to see Canada have a much larger population	57
31/5/52	Canada does not need immigrants	55
23/9/59	Canada does not need immigrants	64
7/60[a]	Would disapprove if the Canadian government increased the number of immigrants coming into the country next year	67
9/3/60	Believe that in this World Refugee Year, Canada should relax immigration laws to permit a limited number of refugees from Europe to come to Canada	48
7/61[a]	Canada should continue to restrict the admission of nonwhites	52
19/10/63	Would like to see Canada with a much larger population	49

[a] Month of interviewing rather than newspaper-release date.

unlike the distribution of opinions in 1952. Opinions are also related to social class, with those in higher positions more favourable to immigration. Apparently at stake here are the greater economic vulnerability of those at lower-income levels, the threat to French Canadian culture posed by the entry of large numbers of immigrants who will be assimilated to the English culture, and, possibly—if we recall the growth of anti-Americanism in the West—a reawakened isolationism and fear of strangers in that part of the country.

Together with disapproval of immigration grew disapproval of its effects. Although the proportion of those evaluating these effects as good has remained fairly stable from 1949 to 1961, the proportion who see immigration as relatively deleterious to Canada has grown steadily from 26 percent in 1950 to 42 percent in 1961 (see Table 26). Here again a favourable evaluation is related to a higher social-class position. Regional breakdowns are available only for a survey conducted in 1954; in that year, Quebec once more was most critical of the results of immigration, with only 39 percent approving of the effects of

TABLE 26

EFFECTS OF IMMIGRATION, 1949–1961

Date	Question	Percent
21/5/49	Settlement of thousands of immigrants and displaced persons from Europe since the end of the war	
	has been good for Canada	40
	has not been good	35
2/8/50	Settlement of many people from other countries since the war	
	has been good for Canada	50
	has not been good	26
5/54[a]	Settlement of many people from other countries	
	has been good for Canada	46
	has not been good	37
21/6/61	Settlement of many people from other countries	
	has been good for Canada	49
	has not been good	42

[a] Month of interviewing rather than newspaper-release date.

immigration compared with a national average of 46 percent. A restrictive attitude toward immigration is thus on the increase. It is particularly apparent among those groups in the population who see themselves as economically and culturally threatened by more immigrants.

Economic Differences

We have noted that social cleavages arise from the existence of two official languages and of a small population continuously reinforced by immigration. Other cleavages arise from diverse economic interests. On the question of whether big business or organized labour should influence the government, most Canadians have preferred labour influence, although there has been a slight trend toward favouring business (see Table 27). In 1952, while 39 percent felt both groups should have equal influence, labour alone was chosen by 31 percent compared to 13 percent who chose big business alone. The 1960 survey can be compared with a similar one conducted in the United States, which found labour chosen by 29 percent, business by 14 percent, and both equally by 46 percent.[7] In contrast, Canadians favoured labour 39 percent of the time, big business 20 percent, and both equally 27

[7] American Institute of Public Opinion release, May 13, 1960.

TABLE 27

PREFERRED INFLUENCES ON GOVERNMENT, 1943–1960

Date	Question	Percen
8/12/43	If had to choose, would prefer labour unions to control the government	49
2/3/46	Labour should have most influence on the laws passed in this country	50
12/4/50	Groups which should have most influence on the government at Ottawa:	
	labour unions	22
	farm organizations	21
	none/no opinion	41
26/1/52	Both big business and labour should have most influence on laws passed	38
12/3/60	Labour should have most influence on laws passed	39

percent. The preferences for labour influence on government are greater in Canada than in the United States even when the occupations of the respondents' household heads are taken into account. The legitimacy of labour's claims to influence legislation seems to have increased in Canada between 1952 and 1960 (see Table 28).

Even though it is thought desirable that interest groups, particularly labour, be able to make their views known to the government in office, there is no accompanying feeling that these interest groups should be represented by their own political parties. There has been consistent opposition from 1948 until 1962, reaching a peak of 70 percent in 1959, to having labour unions support their own party (see Table 29). Despite the creation of the New Democratic party in 1962 through overt support from trade unions, this feeling has still not abated. Instead there has been a rise in the proportion of those undecided on the issue. Though questions on farm parties have not been asked as frequently, their formation has been opposed as well. Those in labour households are less disapproving of a labour party, but the majority of those expressing an opinion share the dominant view (see Table 30). Hence, while Canadians interviewed believe that labour and farmers should have an important voice in influencing government decisions, and that this voice should be greater than that enjoyed by big business, they do not agree that having the influence of farm or labour support centred in one party would be desirable for Canadian politics.

TABLE 28

PREFERRED INFLUENCES ON GOVERNMENT, BY OCCUPATION OF HOUSEHOLD HEAD, 1952–1960
(in percent)

Occupation	Canada 1952			Canada 1960			United States 1960		
	Labour	Business	Both	Labour	Business	Both	Labour	Business	Both
Business and professional	18	24	46	29	23	35	16	17	58
White collar	32	17	36	41	21	24	35	11	42
Blue collar	42	7	34	46	17	23	33	12	45
Farmer	26	10	43	32	21	31	36	12	40

SOURCE for United States: American Institute of Public Opinion release, May 13, 1960.

TABLE 29

PARTICIPATION OF ORGANIZED LABOUR AND FARM GROUPS IN POLITICS, 1948–1962

Date	Question	Percent
27/11/48	Bad thing for Canada to have organized labour unions support a particular party at election time	55
1/12/48	Bad thing for Canada if farmers supported a particular party at election time	46
3/12/52	Bad thing . . . if organized labour unions support a particular party	60
6/12/52	Bad thing . . . if farmers support a particular party	55
25/7/56	Bad thing . . . if organized labour unions support a particular party	53
28/7/56	Bad thing . . . if farmers support a particular party	49
4/3/59	Disapprove of suggestion that labour should give its support to one political party	67
28/11/59	Unions should not engage in political activities	70
1/62[a]	Bad thing for Canada to have organized labour unions support a particular party at this time	52

[a] Month of interviewing rather than newspaper-release date.

TABLE 30

OPPOSITION TO ORGANIZED LABOUR AND FARM GROUPS IN POLITICS, BY UNION STATUS OF HOUSEHOLD, 1948–1962
(in percent)

Date	Opposed groups[a]	National sample	Union households	Nonunion households
27/11/48	Labour	55	41	. . .
1/12/48	Farm	46	38	. . .
3/12/52	Labour	60	50	63
25/7/56	Labour	53	44	55
4/3/59	Labour	70	66	72
28/11/59	Labour	67	61	69
1/62[b]	Labour	52	48	54

[a] See Table 29 for content of questions.
[b] Month of interviewing rather than newspaper-release date.

Federalism

The final area to be considered here concerns the allotment of political authority between federal and provincial governments and the evaluation of Confederation. Confederation in itself is not seen as in danger, and, despite recent evidence of strains, a healthy prognosis was given by just under three-quarters of the population in 1963 compared with under two-thirds in 1945 (see Table 31). Yet there have been major shifts in opinions on the benefits of Confederation to individual provinces. In 1948 a large majority were satisfied with the effects of Confederation for all parts of Canada. But by 1949 this was true only for a much smaller group. More than one-third thought all were benefiting equally, 30 percent said some were losing out, and an additional one-third had no opinion. In contrast, 1960 was apparently another year of relative satisfaction. Here the question was whether any province was more powerful than it should be in running the affairs of the country. Where provinces were singled out as becoming too powerful, these were Quebec and Ontario. Most frequent reactions to the influence of Quebec came from other than Liberal party supporters and those in higher-class positions. Attention was focused

TABLE 31

EVALUATION OF CONFEDERATION, 1945–1960

Date	Question	Percent
20/1/45	Believe that differences between various parts of Canada will be solved and Confederation will not break up	63
30/10/48	Do not believe there are any parts of Canada which would have been better off if they had not joined Confederation	63
28/12/49	All the provinces are benefiting equally from being part of the Dominion of Canada	35
7/60[a]	Province more powerful in running Canada than it should be:	
	Quebec	23
	Ontario	14
	none/no opinion	61
4/9/63	Disagree that French-Canadians have not been given their full rights under Confederation	43
18/12/63	Disagree that differences between various parts of Canada are now so great they will never be solved, and that Confederation will break up	72

[a] Month of interviewing rather than newspaper-release date.

directly on Quebec in 1963, when respondents were asked whether French Canadians had been given their full rights under Confederation. All those of French origin are not, it is true, resident in Quebec, but there is evidence from supplementary questions that English-speaking respondents at least did make such an association. The largest group, almost half of the national sample, denied that French-Canadian rights had been limited—in this sample only 6 percent French Canadians, sharply contrasting with 53 percent of the rest of the population. Complainants in 1948, 1949, and 1960 had been mainly in the Maritimes and the West, particularly British Columbia, but 1963 showed growing discontent in Quebec.

Questions suggesting a general increase in federal powers found at least half the population expressing disapproval. Disapproval in fact increased to almost two-thirds in 1960 (see Table 32). In terms

TABLE 32

Opinions on Federal-Provincial Powers, 1943–1960

Date	Question	Percent
13/3/43	Would disapprove if more powers were taken away from the provincial governments and given to the federal government in Ottawa	45
	Would approve	29
6/12/44	After the war, the Dominion government should give back powers which belonged to the provinces	50
	Should keep them	33
17/4/46	Canada would be worse off if all provincial governments were abolished and the whole country governed from Ottawa	50
	Would be better off	25
29/5/48	Would disapprove if more affairs now attended to by the provincial government were transferred to the federal government in Ottawa	47
	Would approve	26
6/4/49	People would be worse off if the Dominion government looked after more of the affairs of this province in place of the provincial government	38[a]
	Would be better off	30[a]
30/7/60	Canada would be worse off if all provincial governments were abolished and the whole country governed from Ottawa	62
	Would be better off	17

[a] Approximately.

of specific areas of responsibility, provincial authority was preferred for schools, as outlined in the British North America Act. Federal control was preferred to provincial for nonresidential building, but municipal control was considered even more desirable. Opinion was relatively equally divided between those who felt highways would be better, worse, or no different if they were under federal control. The right to tax incomes was felt to be best retained by the federal government. More than one-third also felt that the federal government should be responsible for problems of unemployment. In the thirteen-year time lapse between the two surveys which dealt with this last question, the percentage of those who felt that provincial governments should have sole responsibility decreased. This was the only instance in this area of a trend in opinion (see Table 33). Those who supported the

TABLE 33

Opinions on Specific Areas of Responsibility for Federal and Provincial Governments, 1944–1957

Date	Question	Percent
6/5/44	Problem of making plans to provide jobs for everyone after the war should be up to:	
	federal government	38
	both federal and provincial	36
21/3/45	Provincial governments should continue to run most public and high schools	53
20/4/46	The Dominion government in Ottawa should have the right to tax incomes	46
25/1/47	Control over nonresidential building, where there is a great shortage of houses:	
	municipal	43
	federal	28
5/3/47	The Dominion government in Ottawa should have the right to tax incomes	46
16/12/50	Highways and roads would be better if the Dominion government were to take over full responsibility for them	27
11/54[a]	Provincial governments should continue to run most public and high schools	51
12/57[a]	Provincial governments should continue to run most public and high schools	51
12/57[a]	Level of government which should be responsible for the problem of unemployment, of which there is quite a bit at this time:	
	federal government	39
	all three equally	33

[a] Month of interviewing rather than newspaper-release date.

CCF party were also the weakest supporters of provincial rights and most frequently in favour of federal control. Residents of Quebec were most consistently in favour of provincial rights. In some instances, they were matched by residents of the Maritimes and the West, whereas Ontarians seem least interested in the exercise of provincial authority. Other characteristics of respondents did not seem to affect opinions consistently. Thus, English-speaking respondents were much more in favour of federal control of unemployment than were French-speaking, but the differences between language groups were minor on the question of control of education. Those in higher-class positions were more frequently in favour of federal control of unemployment and provincial control of education. In education, this relationship seemed to be affected by the larger number of "no answers" among those in lower-class positions. In total, support for provincial rights continued to be strong, particularly among those from Quebec. The federal government was increasingly favoured, however, in areas requiring large-scale planning and expenditure of money.

The composite picture of Canada which emerges from the responses to these varied questions is born of the distinctions of party, region, origin, and social class which characterize the nation. In this image of Canada the legitimacy of federalism and biculturalism is increasingly recognized. It is felt that interest groups should have a voice in the governing of the country but not to the extent of forming their own political parties. Finally, immigration, at one time considered beneficial and desirable, is no longer so regarded.

THE ROLE GOVERNMENT SHOULD PLAY

Public Ownership and Control

Over the years opposition to public ownership has slightly increased (see Table 34). From 1943 to 1957, questions on the public ownership of specific industries and resources usually found one-third in favour. Approval dropped to 20 percent for banks, farm implements, and a trans-Canada pipeline in 1956. Special mention should be made of the question on the best way of financing the trans-Canada pipeline because of the furor that this issue raised in parliament and its contribution to the downfall of the Liberal government in the following year. Alternatives offered to respondents were private Canadian investment, sole government financing, and combined government and private financing using Canadian and United States sources. The latter was proposed by the government. Thirty-two percent favoured private

TABLE 34

Opinions on Public Ownership, 1943–1957

Date	Question	Percent
27/2/43	Would not be good idea for government to own all industries that handle and distribute certain necessities of life like milk, bread, meat, and fuel and sell them to the people without profit	45
3/5/44	Do not think the government should own and operate all banks in Canada	66
18/3/44	Best plan for operating railroads:	
	have all railroads owned and operated by the government	35
	continue the present system with some owned and operated by the government and some run by private companies	38
9/10/48	Would be best for these concerns to be left in private hands as at present:	
	banks	48
	CPR	47
	iron and steel	51
	farm implements	57
	meat packing	48
23/7/49	The Canadian government should not own and operate the following:	
	banks	49
	CPR	47
	iron and steel	50
	farm implements	54
	meat packing	49
21/12/49	The Dominion government should not own and operate the following:	
	banks	44
	CPR	44
	farm implements	59
	telephone services	43
8/7/50	The Dominion government should not own and operate the following:	
	banks	49
	CPR	50
	farm implements	59
	telephone services	48
24/11/51	The Dominion government should not own and operate the following:	
	banks	53
	CPR	52
	farm implements	57
	telephone services	54

TABLE 34—*Continued*

Date	Question	Percent
3/56[a]	Of three alternatives, best way of financing trans-Canada pipeline is by a pipeline built and run by private Canadian investment	32
10/57[a]	Of two ways in which exploration and development of Canada's natural resources could be carried out, would like to see private companies take all the risks of prospecting and take all the losses or a large share of the profits	43

[a] Month of interviewing rather than newspaper-release date.

Canadian investment, 21 percent government financing, and 12 percent the combination. Although there are many instances in Canada of partnership between government and private enterprise, the fear of American domination, emphasized by opposition political parties, may have hindered respondents from feeling that this was a satisfactory choice. A fairly uniform 20 percent of all groups sampled expressed support for a pipeline developed by the government. The percentage was somewhat higher for CCF and Social Credit supporters and markedly lower for French and bilingual respondents. Even when party preference is controlled, the figures show that French-speaking Canadians did not support government policy. Generally, they were highly indifferent to the issue or, in the case of bilingual respondents, frequently favoured private Canadian investment.[8] Support for private Canadian investment was also greatest from those in higher socioeconomic positions.

Similar party and class factors were also important in the distribution of opinions on government versus private resource development. French-speaking respondents showed less support of private development, but they also had a higher rate of "don't knows." This was also the case when residents of Quebec and Ontario were compared.

From 1941 to 1963 government control over prices was generally accepted. The one exception was in 1959, when almost one-half of

[8] According to Pierre Elliott Trudeau, French Canadian parliamentary correspondents could not see the point of the pipeline debate. "Indeed, had the crisis over the Speaker's office aroused any considerable excitement at all in Quebec, it most surely would have been interpreted as a racial attack on Mr. Louis-René Beaudoin." P. E. Trudeau, "Some Obstacles to Democracy in Quebec," in *Canadian Dualism*, ed. by Mason Wade, Toronto: University of Toronto Press, 1960, pp. 248–249.

the respondents opposed a price and wage freeze. Greatest approval for price control followed the early postwar years (see Table 35). In 1962 a favourable view of a price and wage freeze was most frequent among blue-collar workers and farmers.

TABLE 35

OPINIONS ON GOVERNMENT CONTROL OVER PRICES, 1941–1962

Date	Question	Percent
2/12/41	Approve of price control	76
18/7/42	Favour law which keeps wages and prices from going higher remaining in effect after war	50
18/1/47	Would disapprove of taking price controls off everything but rents after Christmas	66
20/12/47	Agree that government should put price controls on again	76
28/9/49	If it were your job to handle rent control in living quarters in Canada, would:	
	leave as now	37
	make controls stricter	21
	gradually relax	12
4/3/50	Government should control prices of food stuffs in the stores, like eggs, butter, meat, and so on	59
7/10/50	As things are right now, we should have price controls again	75
17/1/51	It has been suggested that both prices and wages should be frozen. . . . This is a good idea	44
7/11/51	It has been suggested that both prices and wages should be frozen. . . . This is a good idea	43
18/2/59	Would oppose laws which would keep both prices and wages at their present level	48
10/11/62	It has been suggested that both prices and wages should be frozen. . . . Would favour this	49

Social Welfare

The most widespread approval for government participation is in social welfare (see Table 36). The issue of family allowances for children is an outstanding example. In 1943, two years before beginning payments, just under half of those interviewed felt that family allowances paid by the federal government were a good thing. Two

TABLE 36

Opinions on Social Welfare Measures, 1942–1962

Date	Question	Percent
8/4/42	Would be willing to pay a small part of income monthly to government-sponsored national health plan to receive medical and hospital care whenever needed	75
22/5/43	Would be willing to pay a small part of income to government-sponsored national health plan	69
17/7/43	If after war income taxes are cut in half, would be willing to pay five cents in every dollar of income in addition to income taxes so government could guarantee every Canadian enough to live on if he were out of a job	65
20/10/43	Would be good idea if government paid family allowance of $9 per child every month to families in the lower income group, instead of raising wages	49
8/4/44	Would be willing to pay a small part of income to government-sponsored national health plan	80
2/9/47	For a year or so now, family allowances have been paid in Canada. This is proving to be a good idea	74
15/5/48	Family allowances are proving to be a good idea	75
25/8/48	Generally speaking, unemployment insurance plan is good	51
13/7/49	Would approve of a national health plan whereby you pay a flat rate each month and are assured of complete medical and hospital care by the Dominion government	80
19/4/50	Would favour a government-sponsored compulsory old-age pension plan to which all wage and salary earners would contribute	67
17/5/50	Family allowances are proving to be a good idea	84
8/51[a]	Approve of every Canadian 70 years of age or over getting a pension of $40 a month, regardless of financial position	81
12/3/55	Generally speaking, family allowances are a good thing	90
3/56[a]	Would favour a government-operated plan whereby any hospital expenses would be paid out of taxes—even if it meant higher taxes	63

TABLE 36—*Continued*

Date	Question	Percent
3/56[a]	Would favour a government-operated plan whereby any doctor bills would be paid out of taxes—even if it meant higher taxes	55
3/57[a]	Old-age pension raise from $40 to $46 a month is too low	78
10/2/62	Generally speaking, unemployment-insurance plan is good	40

[a] Month of interviewing rather than newspaper-release date.

years after payments had begun three-quarters of those sampled expressed approval. The proportion of those favouring federal family allowances rose until, in 1955, 90 percent held this view. This issue is an example of what the authors of *Voting* have termed one that has "passed the gateway" and become part of a general consensus.[9]

A contributory medical plan has also been highly appealing, particularly until 1949. In more recent years, approval of a government-operated medical and hospital plan which would not be contributory but which would come out of taxes has not been as great. Respondents may have been replying to the suggestion that there might be higher taxes if such plans were instituted. Unemployment-insurance plans, although approved by a majority, have received more limited approval. This was particularly true in 1962 when, after a period of large-scale unemployment, there was also some evidence that collections from the Unemployment Insurance Fund were being made by those not interested in obtaining further employment. Federally administered, noncontributory old-age pensions, paid to all persons seventy years of age and older without regard to financial qualifications, are another instance of an issue which received a high proportion of favourable responses. Before the 1957 general election, when the Liberal government raised old-age pensions by four dollars per month and the Gallup Poll interviewed Canadians on their opinions of this raise, 78 percent said it was too low and only about 15 percent felt it was either too high or about right.

Greatest approval of government welfare measures was generally found among those supporting the CCF. However, in 1951, with respect to noncontributory old-age pensions, approval was fairly uniform across party lines. In 1957, when the Liberal party was in power, although supporters of all parties were agreed that the raise in old-

[9] B. Berelson, P. F. Lazarsfeld, and W. McPhee, *Voting*, Chicago: University of Chicago Press, 1954, pp. 209–210.

age pension was not sufficient, the main difference was that Liberal supporters, normally in favour of welfare measures, were less likely to hold this view.[10] Other differences in opinion were related to origin and region. In general, French-speaking respondents, Roman Catholics, those born in Canada, and those resident in the Maritimes and Quebec were somewhat less favourable to social-welfare measures than were others. Because information here is not complete, it is difficult to say how this view is affected by the kind of social-welfare measure in question. Opinions of the foreign-born may be related to their experiences with more extensive welfare measures abroad. The somewhat less favourable views of French Canadians and Catholics may be related to the reluctance of these groups to have the government participate in fields traditionally allocated to the Church.[11] It may be that these differences between French and English and Protestant and Catholic are diminishing, since a study done in Quebec before the 1960 provincial election found a large majority favourable to family allowances and health insurance.[12] But during the time span for which we have information from Gallup Polls, the differences between origin groups probably contributed to the surprising lack of differentiation in opinions between social class levels.

Culture

Opinions on government participation in areas of culture and ideas did not show the same high level of consensus as did those of social welfare (see Table 37). More than one-half approved the continuation of the government-operated CBC, but disapproval had grown concerning the lack of competition from private agencies; and 42 percent

[10] According to a study of teachers' attitudes in seven European countries, the crucial factor in respondents' evaluation of an issue, in this case that of defence, was related to whether they supported the party in power. Rokkan comments that "This finding is of considerable interest since it cuts across any 'left-right' dimensions: the differentiating factor is not ideology as such but the actual power position of the political movement." Stein Rokkan, "Party Preferences and Opinion Patterns in Western Europe: A Comparative Analysis," *International Social Science Bulletin*, 7, 1955, p. 593.

[11] These findings are somewhat surprising in comparison to the United States, where Catholics have been found to be more favourable to social-welfare measures than Protestants, even when a statistical control for social class is introduced. See Gerhard Lenski, *The Religious Factor*, rev. ed.; Garden City: Doubleday Anchor, 1962, pp. 149–157. It may be that the high correlation between Catholicism, French origin, and residence in Quebec has made Canadian respondents more sensitive to federal government welfare activities. That is, the issue of provincial rights is also raised by such activities, and those most concerned with these rights tend also to oppose welfare measures.

[12] Groupe de Recherches Sociales, "Les Électeurs Québécois," Montreal: mimeographed, 1960, pp. 171–173.

TABLE 37

OPINIONS ON GOVERNMENT PARTICIPATION IN FIELDS
OF CULTURE AND IDEAS, 1942–1957

Date	Question	Percent
21/11/42	Satisfied with arrangement, where at the present time the radio stations of the CBC are operated by the government	56
22/11/52	At the present time, the CBC has complete control of television programs and broadcasting in Canada. Private stations should be allowed to broadcast television broadcasts	57
13/3/54	Do not agree that the publicly owned CBC should suspend operations and leave all radio broadcasting to private stations	53
7/55[a]	Agree that artistic things, like symphony orchestras, art galleries, and so on, which are not self-supporting, should be assisted by the government out of tax money	42
3/56[a]	In six of the major cities across Canada— Vancouver, Winnipeg, Toronto, Ottawa, Montreal, Halifax—under present regulations, independent TV stations may not be set up in competition with CBC stations Disapprove of this	63
3/4/57	Approve of plan to establish Canada Council with government funds to give financial encouragement where needed to Canadian arts—things like painting, music, the ballet, and so on	62

[a] Month of interviewing rather than newspaper-release date.

approved of government support of artistic activities, as against 40 percent who disapproved. Yet by 1957, 62 percent approved of the activities of Canada Council after this agency's responsibilities were outlined to them. Regional variations in opinion appeared in 1942 when Westerners were most satisfied with the government-operated CBC, and in 1959, when only Quebec residents showed clear-cut approval for government-supported cultural activities. In the earliest survey, residents of farm communities were most favourable to the CBC. In 1955 and 1956, however, those in small towns of under 10,000 population were least disapproving of lack of competition with the CBC and most approving of government-supported cultural activities. There also appeared to be some variation by origin, with French-speaking and Roman Catholic respondents less disapproving of government activity in this field. Low social class and greater age tended slightly to influence respondents to favour what was at that time the status quo; that is, lack of competition with the CBC and disapproval of government activity in the cultural field. Here, unlike in social welfare, French Canadians seemed more anxious than others to have the government aid them in the protection of their culture. Particularly in the case of the CBC, support also was strongest from those isolated groups which might not obtain services from commercial organizations.

Ideological Orientation

Belief in the desirability of government control over business and industry markedly decreased after the war. The question was last asked in 1947 and, at that time, only 19 percent felt workers would be better off under government-controlled industry, but there was still a widespread feeling that government intervention was needed to ensure sufficient employment opportunities (see Table 38). When the question was asked whether it was the job of government to provide opportunities for one to get ahead on one's own or to guarantee a steady job, these alternatives were chosen fairly equally in 1947 and 1954, 49 percent selecting opportunities and 40 percent a guaranteed job. Government activity in providing jobs was more often desired by CCF supporters, residents of Quebec, and those at a low socioeconomic level.

If the conclusion is drawn from these data that there is a trend toward opposing public ownership but approving social-welfare legislation, and a more limited approval of government support for culture, price control, and the provision of jobs, the question can then be asked if any ideological rationale has been developed in respect to governmental participation in the social and economic life of the country. According to one observer,

it is evident that there are differences of opinion among the various sectors of the Canadian population as to what government should or should not do. However, these divergent preferences have not developed into opposite ideologies. Slogans denouncing the Welfare State or creeping socialism or government controlled by wicked capitalists had to be imported from other countries and were soon found to be unfit for Canadian consumptions.[13]

[13] Maurice Lamontagne, "The Role of Government," in *Canada's Tomorrow*, ed. by G. P. Gilmour, Toronto: Macmillan, 1954, p. 144. See also Lloyd D. Musolf, "Canadian Public Enterprise: A Character Study," *American Political Science Review*, 50, June, 1956, pp. 405–421. American voters display similar tendencies to support specific policies involving government economic and social-welfare activities, but are apt to oppose even more strongly than Canadians anything labeled "socialistic." V. O. Key, Jr., *Public Opinion and American Democracy*, New York: Knopf, 1961, p. 425.

TABLE 38

IDEOLOGICAL ORIENTATION, 1942–1961

Date	Question	Percent
15/8/42	Since the war started, the government has taken a bigger and bigger share in the control of business, industry, and agriculture. Agree that this control should continue after war	45
2/10/43	Since the war started, the government has taken a bigger . . . share in the control of business. . . . Disagree that this should continue after war	45
18/12/43	After the war workers would be better off if left under private management	47
18/10/44	Of three alternatives, feel federal government in Ottawa should take the lead in setting up and carrying out plans to provide postwar employment	49
31/10/45	Workers would be better off if left under private management	64
5/1/46	Business firms will not be able to provide enough jobs for everyone during the next five years and government will have to step in and provide work	70
22/10/47	Workers would be better left under private management	65
27/9/47	The most important job for the government is to guarantee every person a decent steady job	50
16/9/50	Disagree that, because of things like family allowances, and other social security measures, Canada is headed toward socialism	50
30/10/54	Business firms will not be able to provide enough jobs for everyone during the next five years, but government will have to step in and provide work	65
6/11/54	The most important job for the government is to make certain that there are good opportunities for each person to get ahead on his own	49
20/12/61	As you may know, Prime Minister Diefenbaker has said that the next federal election will be fought on free enterprise vs. socialism. . . . If this were the main issue . . . other things being equal, would be most inclined to favour free enterprise	52

This view was apparently justified by a 1950 poll to which only 14 percent answered that Canada was becoming socialistic and another 17 percent said this was true to a limited extent. Before the 1962 general election, Prime Minister Diefenbaker attempted to raise as a central campaign issue the struggle between free enterprise and socialism. At about the time of Mr. Diefenbaker's challenge, the Canadian Chamber of Commerce at its annual convention launched a program in adult education which they termed Operation Freedom. This program was intended to "rouse Canadians from apathy and indifference into action against the growing threat of socialism and communism." [14] It then remained for officials and public relations men in the Chamber of Commerce to convince local autonomous groups of the value of the program. In general, they were faced with indifference, and in some cases, as with the Toronto Board of Trade, Operation Freedom was even publicly denounced. This contrasts with the efforts of a number of business and trade associations in Britain to battle the issue of nationalization before the British general election of 1959. At that time these associations launched a massive advertising campaign against nationalization. The effects are difficult to assess, particularly because the Conservatives would probably have won without it, but it did keep the issue alive and in the forefront and forced the Labour party to consider its stand in future policy-making.[15] In Britain there was obviously large-scale commitment to the values of an antinationalization campaign, but in Canada the placement of political issues in the context of clear-cut distinctions between free enterprise and socialism was unpopular. Canadians interviewed about these issues were unable, in more than one-half of the cases, to define free enterprise or socialism. Asked what they would do if these became the main issues in the election, 52 percent said they would choose free enterprise, 8 percent socialism, and 40 percent could not say. Long-term pressure by those in positions of authority for government participation and actual participation in the social and economic life of the country, has not been followed then by the development of an image of Canada as a socialist state. In 1961, only Westerners and farmers, exposed to the more ideologically oriented minor parties, were slightly more likely than others to choose socialism.

[14] Quoted in "The Future of Operation Freedom: Same Package but a Softer Sell," *Maclean's,* June 16, 1962, p. 1.

[15] D. E. Butler and Richard Rose, *The British General Election of 1959,* London: Macmillan, 1960, pp. 241–255.

VI   PROBLEMS OF SYMBOLIC REPRESENTATION

THE SYMBOLIC representation of Canada takes a number of different forms which should be treated separately, although they may be regarded as parts of a single unit.

THE FLAG

In Chapter III the history and ambiguous legal status of Canada's political symbols were surveyed. Contemporary trends in public opinion show an increasing desire for specifically Canadian symbols. For example, surveys conducted in 1943, 1945, 1946, and 1947 allowed respondents to choose between a new flag and the Union Jack. In the earliest survey, 51 percent favoured a new flag and 42 percent the Union Jack. Since that time there has been a consistent trend downward in approval for the Union Jack, until it has become the choice of a relatively stable 25 percent of those interviewed. Desire for a new flag has risen and, in 1958 when the question was asked whether Canada should have an entirely new flag different from that of any other country, 79 percent were recorded as in favour. But when respondents were permitted to choose between a new flag, the Red Ensign, and the Union Jack, supporters of a new flag were reduced to no more than 46 percent. In surveys where only two choices were given, those who would prefer the Red Ensign apparently aligned themselves with those who wanted an entirely new flag (see Table 39). This seems surprising in a number of ways. For one thing, the Red Ensign has the Union Jack prominently displayed in one corner; for another, the Ensign has been used with varying degrees of official approval since Confederation and therefore can hardly be considered new. What is particularly unexpected is that over this time period the Red Ensign, a traditional Canadian flag, has not acquired more adherents.

Over the years regional differences in opinions about the flag have remained great (see Table 40). Quebec residents are most frequently in favour of a new flag while Maritimers are least so, and other regions fall in between. Greatest support for the Union Jack generally comes from the Maritimes, and, in 1962, the Ensign found most sup-

TABLE 39

CHOICE OF NATIONAL FLAG, 1943–1963

Date	Question	Percent
21/7/43	Canada should have a national flag of its own	51
	Continue to use Union Jack	42
3/11/45	Canada should have a national flag of its own	68
	Continue to use Union Jack	26
20/3/46	Canada should have a national flag of its own	68
	Continue to use Union Jack	28
5/3/52	Canada should design a new national flag of its own	46
	Use Union Jack	30
	Use Red Ensign	14
30/6/53	Canada should design a new national flag of its own	39
	Use Union Jack	35
	Use Red Ensign	15
6/7/55	Canada should have a national flag of its own	64
	Continue to use Union Jack	28
8/58[a]	Approve of Canada having entirely new flag, different from that of any other country	79
3/62[a]	Canada should design a new national flag of its own	46
	Use Union Jack	26
	Use Red Ensign	18
25/5/63	Canada should design a new national flag of its own	45
	Use Union Jack	25
	Use Red Ensign	16

[a] Month of interviewing rather than newspaper-release date.

porters in British Columbia. As we would expect from these regional differences, there is also a distinct cleavage between English and French Canadians on the amount of support given a new flag. Place of origin is not available for respondents in the 1962 survey, but large differences were apparent between Protestants and Roman Catholics which are probably related to French-English differences.

In comparing those surveys where information is available on respondents' party preferences, the most marked change has been in the lessened desire of Conservatives for the Union Jack and the subsequent shift in their opinions to a closer resemblance to those of other parties. The other pertinent observation is that no matter what the form of the questions, Liberal supporters have always been more likely than others to favour the creation of a new national flag (see Table 41).

TABLE 40

CHOICE OF FLAG BY REGION, 1952–1963
(in percent)

Date	Question	Maritimes	Quebec	Ontario	Prairies	British Columbia
5/3/52	Of three alternatives, Canada should design a new national flag of its own [National: 46]	...	74	...	...	...
6/7/55	Approve of Canada having a national flag of its own rather than continuing to use the Union Jack	44	86	57	63	61
8/58[a]	Approve of Canada having entirely new flag, different from that of any other country	60	91	72	69	69
3/62[a]	Of three alternatives, Canada should de-sign a new national flag of its own	19	69	40	41	35
25/5/63	Of three alternatives, Canada should de-sign a new national flag of its own	23	74	35	35	35

[a] Month of interviewing rather than newspaper-release date.

TABLE 41

CHOICE OF NEW FLAG BY PARTY PREFERENCE, 1945–1962

(in percent)

Date	Question	Conservative	Liberal	CCF/NDP	Social Credit
3/11/45	Canada should have a national flag of its own rather than continue to use the Union Jack	49	74	71	...
8/58[a]	Approve of Canada having entirely new flag, different from that of any other country	76	80	69	100
3/62[a]	Of three alternatives, Canada should design a new national flag of its own	41	52	42	39

[a] Month of interviewing rather than newspaper-release date.

It is impossible to say when the shift in the views of CCF/NDP supporters took place; it appears that in 1945 they were almost as likely to favour a new flag as the Liberals. But in 1958 and 1962, the extent of their support for a new flag was more like that of the Conservatives.

Although based on only one survey, other tendencies which appeared were the lesser preference for a new flag from business and professional and farm households, those with an elementary or university education, and those in the older age groups. In 1962, the university-educated were most favourable to the Red Ensign but all other groups less desirous of a new flag supported the Union Jack.

The largest proportion, then, wanted a new flag during the times surveyed. Stable proportions continued to favour other alternatives. The differences in opinions of regional and ethnic groups also foretold the differences in opinions of regional and ethnic groups when a new flag was finally introduced in 1965.

THE ANTHEM

The Union Jack has retained a hard core of supporters, but the proportion of those wishing to continue with "God Save the Queen" as the national anthem has declined. "O Canada," which has never received the official sanction of the Red Ensign, has a larger body of supporters; by 1963, 72 percent were in favour of it, compared to 16 percent for the Ensign (see Table 42). Since Quebec respondents were highly favourable to "O Canada" in 1950 and again in 1963, we can assume that the over-all increase in approval for this anthem has come from other regions. Even so, regional differences are still noticeable, with the Maritimes considerably less in favour of "O Canada," followed by Ontario and then the West (see Table 43). Those who

TABLE 42

CHOICE OF NATIONAL ANTHEM, 1950–1963

Date	Question	Percent
9/8/50	Of four patriotic songs, the most suitable one for our national anthem is "O Canada"	61
28/2/59	Of four patriotic songs, the most suitable one for our national anthem is "O Canada"	67
29/5/63	Of four patriotic songs, the most suitable one for our national anthem is "O Canada"	72

TABLE 43

CHOICE OF NATIONAL ANTHEM BY REGION, 1950 AND 1963
(in percent preferring "O Canada")

Region	1950	1963
Canada	61	72
Maritimes	. . .	56
Quebec	89	90
Ontario	. . .	63
West	. . .	70

prefer "God Save the Queen" are most frequently found in the Maritimes and Ontario.

It is impossible to explain these differences in proportions between those supporting a Canadian national anthem and those supporting a Canadian flag, but several tentative suggestions are offered. It may be that for those residents of Canada to whom the expression "One Flag, One Throne, One Empire" [1] has emotional meaning, the Red Ensign contained an extraneous element in its inclusion of the Canadian Coat of Arms, perhaps even suggesting a conflict of loyalties. For the French-speaking Canadian the Union Jack contained in the Ensign is a constant reminder of the British conquerors, while even the Coat of Arms is characteristically British. For many of the remaining citizens, of no matter what origin, the Red Ensign lacked distinctiveness and uniqueness, taken over as it was from the British merchant navy. It has no romantic patriotism attached to it as do, for example, the flags of Republican France or the United States, flags created in the midst of revolutionary struggles and intimately bound up with the founding of these states.

In contrast, there is the comparatively widespread support for "O Canada" as the national anthem. Here is a national symbol acceptable to both French and English, even if more so to the French. It is, at the least, meaningful in both languages; it contains references to no country other than Canada; and the national sentiments it expresses are militantly patriotic. In speaking of Canada, it does not mention specific groups or regions of the country. Comparing "O Canada" to "The Maple Leaf Forever"—another contender for anthem but one which received only limited support—differences are readily apparent. Instead of the inclusive nationalism of the "O Canada," "The Maple

[1] The official slogan of the Imperial Order, Daughters of the Empire, a women's patriotic organization.

Leaf Forever" specifically calls attention to many historical situations which continue to divide Canadians. For example, it describes General Wolfe, the victor in the decisive battle of the Plains of Abraham, as "the dauntless hero . . . who planted firm Britannia's flag." In comparing the two symbols, then, we would suggest that the greater appeal of "O Canada" lies in its unifying, historically positive message. The findings also suggest that the move toward adopting Canadian symbols made by the Pearson government would have met with less disagreement if it had begun with the anthem rather than the flag.

THE GOVERNOR-GENERAL

Before 1952, the office of Governor-General had been filled by a person from Britain. The appointment of a Canadian came during a trend downward in favouring a British Governor-General from 32 percent in 1944 to 9 percent in 1957. In surveys containing a third alternative—that of abolishing the position of Governor-General—this served to keep down the proportion favourable to a Canadian. At the same time there has been a slight but steady decline in those favouring the abolition of this position from 27 percent in 1945 to 16 percent in 1957. Thus the trend has been increasingly favourable to a Canadian. In 1952, after Vincent Massey became the first Canadian Governor-General, 79 percent approved of this appointment (see Table 44). When Mr. Massey's first term of office drew to a close in 1956, Gallup Poll interviewers asked informants to choose the preferred next Governor-General from a list of five names. Listed were the Duke of Windsor; Lord Beaverbrook, a former Maritimer long resident in Britain; Major-General Vanier, a French-Canadian diplomat and career soldier; George Drew, a former leader of the national Conservative party and former premier of Ontario; and James Duncan, prominent businessman and, until 1961, chairman of the Ontario Hydro-Electric Commission. The Duke of Windsor received the largest number of choices of any individual, but the four Canadians combined were preferred by the large majority. In making these choices, respondents often seemed to be guided by considerations other than those of national unity. Thus, Beaverbrook was favoured by Maritimers, Vanier by those in Quebec and French-speaking respondents, Windsor by those in Ontario, and Drew by the Conservatives. These distinctions also appear in questions concerning the origin of the Governor-General. For example, there were major differences in opinions between residents of Quebec and Ontario in 1944. But these regional variations have declined considerably since. This has been also true

TABLE 44

DESIRED ORIGIN FOR GOVERNOR-GENERAL, 1944–1957

Date	Question	Percent
22/3/44	It has been the custom for the Governor-General to come from Britain. A Canadian should be appointed to this office	59
29/8/45	Of three alternatives, would like an appointment from Canada for Governor-General	42
19/3/50	Of three alternatives, would like an appointment from Canada	45
8/51[a]	Of three alternatives, would like an appointment from Canada	53
12/3/52	Approve of having a Canadian as Governor-General	79
10/56[a]	From this list of men, each of whom has been suggested as the next Governor-General, nominee would be:	
	Duke of Windsor	27
	Lord Beaverbrook	18
	Major General Vanier	16
	George Drew	14
	James Duncan	5
9/57[a]	Of three alternatives, would like an appointment from Canada	59

[a] Month of interviewing rather than newspaper-release date.

of differences between English- and French-speaking Canadians.[2] Liberal supporters have been characteristically more pro-Canadian, Conservatives have favoured a British Governor-General more than others. Conservatives, though, have become more like other party supporters since 1944. According to the 1957 survey, 32 percent of CCF supporters wanted to abolish the position of Governor-General. This is difficult to explain, particularly since in later surveys CCF/NDP supporters became less favourable to a new flag and more approving of the Union Jack and the Red Ensign. Perhaps they were objecting to the implicit inequalities that this particular symbol suggested to them. There may also be some differences with respect to social class, but this is not clear-cut. For example, in 1951, choice of a British Governor-General declined sharply from 30 percent for those in the highest socioeconomic level to 17 per cent for those in the lowest. But in 1956, it was those in the lowest socioeconomic level who most frequently

[2] French-speaking respondents in 1956 and 1957 were relatively high on no opinions.

chose the Duke of Windsor for the next Governor-General, and class differences were imperceptible in 1957.

THE ROYAL FAMILY

The suggestion that members of the royal family serve as Canadian Governors-General generally meets with disapproval. The one exception was the Duke of Windsor but opinion was closely divided concerning him, with 43 percent for him and 40 percent against. As noted he was distinctly less popular than a combination of four Canadians. There was less disapproval of the Queen Mother in 1957 than in 1952 when she was suggested as a possible Governor-General. During the later survey, Mr. Massey's term of office was drawing to a close, and she may not have seemed as unattractive at that time. But in the following year, a sizable majority again did not want Princess Margaret as Governor-General (see Table 45). The familiar regional differences

TABLE 45

OPINIONS ON MEMBERS OF ROYAL FAMILY AS GOVERNOR-GENERAL, 1952–1958

Date	Question	Percent
19/7/52	Would disapprove if Queen Mother invited to be next Governor-General	60
10/56[a]	Would approve of Duke of Windsor as Governor-General	43
10/57[a]	Would disapprove if Queen Mother invited to be next Governor-General	48
8/58[a]	Would disapprove if Princess Margaret appointed next Governor-General	59

[a] Month of interviewing rather than newspaper-release date.

appear again with Quebec most disapproving of members of royalty as Governors-General. In 1952 and in 1957 Maritimers were most approving of royalty; in 1956 it was Ontario residents and in 1958 those in the West, although this latter finding should probably be disregarded.[3] Accompanying these regional variations in opinions were those related to origin. Disapproval of the royal family in this position was greatest from French Canadians, Roman Catholics, and the Canadian-born (see Table 46). Usually, Liberal supporters were least ap-

[3] For some reason, this survey had an unusually small Western sample and all respondents in the West were supporters of the Conservative party.

TABLE 46

OPINIONS ON ROYAL FAMILY AS GOVERNOR-GENERAL BY ORIGIN, 1956–1958

Indicators of origin	Approve Windsor, 1956	Disapprove Queen Mother, 1957	Disapprove Margaret, 1958
English	48	46	55
French	35	52	65
Both	31	57	66
Religion			
Protestant	49	. . .	52
Catholic	35	. . .	66
Birthplace			
Canada	42	. . .	61
Elsewhere	50	. . .	54

proving of the royal family.[4] In 1957, the same year in which CCF supporters were most anxious to abolish the position of Governor-General, they were also most disapproving of having the Queen Mother become Governor-General. Otherwise, they were even more willing than Conservatives to have a member of the royal family serve in this capacity. Finally, some distinctions can be made by sex, but these are not consistent beyond the fact that women are generally less opposed to members of the royal family.

The conclusions to be drawn from these two sets of questions are that Englishmen, including members of the royal family, are becoming distinctly less popular as potential Governors-General. At the same time that appointments from Britain have declined in popularity, belief in the desirability of retaining this office has increased. Although group differences seem to have leveled off considerably, French Canadians, residents of Quebec, and Liberal party supporters are still most pro-Canadian in their choice for Governor-General.

Canadians appear to enjoy visits of the royal family, but the idea of having them as residents over a period of time does not meet with general approval (see Table 47). Before the 1959 royal visit, a former Canadian television star, Joyce Davidson, said on the Jack Paar Show that most Canadians were indifferent to the visit. In response to the furor that this aroused, the Gallup Poll took a telephone interview in several urban centres. The poll found a majority very interested

[4] The 1958 survey is again an exception but in this case the highly disapproving Social Crediters are based on a sample of six.

TABLE 47

OPINIONS ON ROYAL FAMILY, 1948–1959

Date	Question	Percent
25/9/48	Would be a good idea if the royal family came to live in Canada for part of each year	45
28/5/52	Would disapprove if Queen Elizabeth and her immediate family were to live in Canada for part of each year	51
27/6/59	Very interested in Queen's visit	48
27/6/59	Disagree with a Canadian commentator who claimed most Canadians are indifferent to the royal visit	54
4/7/59	This royal visit is a good thing for Canada	69
14/11/59	Might be a good idea if Queen Elizabeth's baby is a boy, he be given a Canadian title— perhaps the Duke of Ottawa	51

in the visit, in disagreement with Joyce Davidson's views, and of the belief that the visit was a good thing for Canada. Respondents in Montreal and Quebec City were considerably less interested than those in other centres, yet a majority of them as well felt that the royal visit was good for Canada.[5] In that year, in support of the symbolic ties which a majority feel with the royal family, 51 percent were in favour of having Prince Andrew given a Canadian title as compared to 22 percent who opposed this idea.

OTHER SYMBOLS

The appeal of "O Canada" suggested that Canadian symbols would be most often selected where they conveyed a unifying, historically positive message. This is particularly true when no invidious comparisons are made. Thus, approval for a new national flag is greatest when no other choices are available. This was also true of the desire for a Canadian Governor-General, although here the knowledge that a Canadian had already occupied this position probably contributed to respondents' preference. The conflicts inherent in questions of political symbols were further illustrated in a survey conducted in

[5] The Queen's 1964 visit to Quebec produced the most open controversy ever. A Gallup Poll, released June 27, 1964, found 63 percent approving her visit and 25 percent feeling the trip should be canceled. The latter views were mainly the result of fears for the Queen's safety in the face of threats from extremists in Quebec. During her visit to Quebec City she was greeted by some overt hostility, but this appeared to come from an exceedingly small minority.

TABLE 48

OPINIONS ON OTHER POLITICAL SYMBOLS, 1943–1959

Date	Question	Percent
24/12/43	Canada should be able to change her own constitution without going to the British parliament	64
1/6/46	Approve of Ottawa government changing the name of Dominion Day to Canada Day	46
13/2/52	This country has been known as "The Dominion of Canada." Would like to see this kept as it has been	45
9/54[a]	Agree that we should continue to use picture of the Queen on money and postage	50
9/9/59	When think "I am a Canadian," what first comes to mind is:	
	national pride	20
	sense of freedom	18
	count self fortunate	15

[a] Month of interviewing rather than newspaper-release date.

1954 (see Table 48). When respondents were asked if they would prefer continued usage of pictures of the Queen on postage and money, or pictures of great Canadians instead, 50 percent replied they wanted the Queen and 33 percent favoured great Canadians. In the face of the growing popularity of Canadian symbols, these results may suggest not so much strong feelings toward retention of the Queen's picture, as that respondents were troubled by the lack of Canadian heroes or the difficulty of choosing between French and English ones. Most frequent choice of the Queen's picture was made by Maritimers, residents in rural communities, English-speaking respondents, Protestants, Conservatives, and Social Credit supporters, women, those in older age group, the widowed or divorced, those living in business, professional, or farm households, and those with only elementary schooling. Aside from factors of region and origin, less tradition-oriented groups were inclined to select pictures of great Canadians. In this instance, this also included the better-educated.

Questions on other political symbols indicate that by 1943 a majority wanted Canada to be able to change her own constitution, even though parliament has yet to work out completely satisfactory arrangements for this. While the term "dominion" has a long and respectable history in Commonwealth terms, some Canadian politicians have felt that it smacks of colonial dependence and therefore have wanted to remove this stigma. Up until 1946, the first of July was know as Dominion Day, but since then it has been changed to Canada Day. Of respondents queried on this change in 1946, 46 percent approved, 29 percent disapproved, but 25 percent were indifferent to the whole matter. Removing the word "dominion" from the name of the country was disapproved of by 45 percent of a sample selected in 1952. Again, almost one-quarter had no opinion, leading us to assume that this is not an issue of great interest. On these questions, Quebec respondents were distinguished by their desire for greater autonomy. In addition, in the 1952 survey, 15 percent of those of French origin wanted to retain the word "dominion" as part of Canada's name as compared to 55 percent of those of all other origins. Finally, unstructured answers to the phrase "I am a Canadian" also produced differences related to origin. The most frequent response was that of national pride, given by 36 percent of the Canadian-born, 12 percent of those born in Britain or the Commonwealth, and 22 percent of those from Europe.

From the foregoing material it is apparent that approval for native Canadian symbols is high and has grown over the years. This is especially so when no comparisons are introduced between native institutions and those of Britain. Despite changes which have occurred over time, there remains a stable nucleus of support for British symbols, constituting about 20 percent of the population. Ethnic and regional differences are most apparent, but those relating to party, social class, age, and sex also have a bearing on the distribution of opinions.

VII   THE IMAGE OF CANADA

LIMITED THOUGH it is by the number and kinds of questions asked, a picture of Canada does emerge from these public-opinion polls. Between 1941 and 1963, consensus on the definition of national problems and their solutions was high only in limited areas, but both the extent of consensus and the number of issues producing greater agreement have grown over the years. As a result we can interpret that there is a growing yet cautious and diffident search for identity. In its relationships with other countries Canada's identity is still viewed within the confines of traditional ties and alliances. In meeting its internal problems the customary ways of doing things find most favour, and there is a new recognition attached to the importance of the French language.

The absence of an aggressive nationalism can be related to at least three sets of factors: regional-ethnic, regional-economic, and social class.

Ethnic heterogeneity, reinforced by geographic boundaries, has perpetuated two different world views. At the same time, even though the English culture dominates, the French has also been given legitimacy and this has usually served to restrain the nationalism of both groups. This has not, however, always been the case, as was demonstrated during three wars. But except during such national crises, Canadians are usually anxious to avoid internal conflict.[1] It is the cleavages between English-speaking and French-speaking Canadians which are emphasized by those French Canadian nationalists who expound the concept of "two nations," [2] and these are confirmed by public-opinion data. But it is noteworthy that at the same time that French Canadian nationalists are becoming more vocal, the opinions of the two language groups are also becoming more similar as English Canadians too become self-conscious about their national identity.

We have dealt here with the divisions between two cultural groups,

[1] For Latin American comparisons see C. C. Cumberland, "Political Implications of Cultural Heterogeneity in Latin America," in *Freedom and Reform in Latin America*, ed. by F. B. Pike, South Bend, Indiana: University of Notre Dame Press, 1959, pp. 59–80.

[2] A leading exponent of this view is Michel Brunet, *La Présence Anglaise et les Canadiens*, Montreal: Beauchemin, 1958, especially pp. 233–292.

but it is more accurate to speak of Canada as a multiethnic state. Although the Gallup Polls rarely report origin except in terms of official language, descent from an ancestry other than British or French, has important implications for political attitudes and behaviour,[3] particularly in the western provinces where about half of the population are of other origins. In Canada lack of a parallel concept to Americanization undoubtedly poses problems for the integration of these non-British, non-French groups into the nation, with consequences for the degree of consensus on the nature of Canada's identity.

Regional-economic factors also contribute to the slow unfolding of a unified national sentiment. There are those who argue, in fact, that the distinctiveness of Quebec is related as much to that province's economic inferiority and hostility to outside business interests as it is to ethnic factors.[4] But regional-economic factors are probably most important in accounting for responses of those resident in western Canada. Like other Western nations, Canada has become increasingly urbanized, but the prairie provinces, and Saskatchewan in particular, have remained largely rural. Experiencing similar social and economic conditions, rural residents are often readily led to accept a community of interest. In economically insecure one-crop agricultural areas, movements of agrarian radicalism have found ready support.[5] The attainment of office of the CCF in Saskatchewan and Social Credit in Alberta were both manifestations of this kind of radicalism. But in many respects both parties have become essentially conservative, and their supporters find no conflict in voting for the Conservatives in federal elections.[6] Social Credit in British Columbia has even been described as overtly reactionary. Despite the appeal of radical move-

[3] S. M. Lipset, *Agrarian Socialism*, Berkeley and Los Angeles: University of California Press, 1950, pp. 183–186, 190–192; Mildred A. Schwartz, "Political Behaviour and Ethnic Origin," in *Papers on the 1962 Election*, ed. by John Meisel, Toronto: University of Toronto Press, 1964, pp. 252–271.

[4] Brunet, *op. cit.*, pp. 221–232; Guillaume de Maillard, "Biculturalisme, bilinguisme, et émancipation économique," *Cité Libre*, 15, janvier, 1964, pp. 17–21; Ken Lefoli, "Quebec and Ontario Need an Honest Broker Before They Both Get Hurt," *Maclean's*, March 7, 1964, p. 4.

[5] S. M. Lipset, *Political Man*, Garden City: Doubleday, 1960, p. 233 for sources from a number of countries.

[6] According to one interpreter of the Social Credit movement, "It was not that the exigencies of government, as such, caused the leaders, on attaining office, to become orthodox both in their economic policies and in their practice of democracy. Rather, the exigencies of governing a society of independent producers, in revolt against outside domination but not against property, brought out the conservatism inherent in *petit-bourgeois* agrarian radicalism." C. B. Macpherson, *Democracy in Alberta*, Toronto: University of Toronto Press, 1953, p. 220.

ments under the special circumstances previously cited, rural residents in North America usually find political conservatism more attractive. The unique combination of radicalism and conservatism in the West appears to be related to the growing appeal of provincial rights, independence, and isolationism in that part of the country. This is the traditional response of a frontier society. The economic development of Canada thus remains sufficiently uneven that sectional interests can continue to command loyalties that would otherwise go to the state.

Support for the growth of a collective identity are also affected by the social-class position of those who most frequently give the dominant viewpoint. Generalizations here must be made with caution since only limited data are available from the polls. Yet, bearing this in mind, it is still most often those in higher-class positions, particularly the better-educated, who are in company with the majority. This is especially noteworthy since differences between classes are generally least apparent on questions with an obvious class-related content. In effect then, Canadian identity is a reflexion of the opinions of the middle class. But if the existing identity is mainly an outgrowth of middle-class views, it is also shaped by these class interests.[7] Because of the economic and political situation of Canada, it is understandable that a conciliatory approach to national problems would be more attractive to essentially conservative middle-class groups than one which might disrupt existing internal and external relations.

A fuller analysis of the effects of social class in shaping national identity would require another type of study, in particular one which permitted an examination of elite groups in Canada. In outlining the influences on formulating a national identity, the significance of elites was noted although the discussion, both generally and with reference to Canada, was confined to the intellectual elite. Intellectuals were discussed in their role as the vanguard of nationalism. But, because of the limitations in Canada on the mass media and the educational system as builders of national consensus, the intellectuals too are probably curtailed in effectiveness, which might be an additional factor in producing the present status of national identity. Further insight into the middle-class nature of Canada's identity probably would also emerge from a study of the economic elite. There

---

[7] In parallel terms, recent forms of nationalism in Quebec are seen as largely reflecting middle class concerns. Charles Taylor, "Nationalism and the Political Intelligentsia: A Case Study," Queen's Quarterly, 72, Spring, 1965, pp. 150–168.

is evidence that members of this group differ markedly in social characteristics and, presumably, in interests, from the majority of other Canadians. These differences are intensified by the fact that the economic elite is concentrated in central Canada, and its members are predominantly of British origin.[8] Assuming that the leadership role of the economic elite extends to issues of national identity, what is known about this body tends to support the preceding inferences that a middle-class base has shaped national identity into its present form. As the result of a host of conditions, some already described, some still to be dealt with, and some which this study cannot encompass, the innovative potential of the higher social classes is constantly restrained by the need for compromise. Those in positions of leadership are normally sensitive to the demands of their groups, and, in Canada, these demands can be basically incompatible, because of the cleavage structure of the society and the nature of the external ties. The solution, then, has been to fall back on tradition, including that which limits independence, in an effort to sustain the *modus vivendi* which has already been formulated.

The nature of Canada's identity and the way it has developed has been related to ethnic and economic factors, both with a regional base, and to the character of those representing the dominant viewpoint. Along with opinion differences associated with these characteristics differences were found which related to party preference. Among these were the greater preference of Liberal supporters for Canadian symbols, a decline since the mid-1950's in differences between Conservatives and supporters of other parties, the uniqueness of viewpoint of CCF/NDP supporters, the similarity between Social Credit and Conservative supporters until 1960, and the more independent viewpoints of Social Credit supporters since that time. The sources of these differences and their effects on national identity will be discussed in the next section. When the influences on the formation of national identity were outlined in Chapter II, the critical role assigned to political parties was related to the characteristics of their supporters, the nature of their appeal, and the type of organization. The interaction of these three dimensions served to determine the

---

[8] John Porter, "The Economic Elite and the Social Structure in Canada," *Canadian Journal of Economics and Political Science*, 23, August, 1957, pp. 376–394. See also John Porter, *The Vertical Mosaic*, Toronto: University of Toronto Press, 1965. The unrepresentative nature of the elite may in turn hinder their contribution toward national integration. See Juan J. Linz, "Regional Differences in the Social Structure of Spain and their Consequences for Political Integration," a paper submitted to the International Conference on Comparative Political Sociology, Tampere, August, 1963, p. 16.

kind of unity present both within a particular party and within the nation as a whole. The operation of the party system in Canada, as reflected in supporters' opinions on national problems, will again be given major importance and will provide the subject for analysis in Part III.

PART III

THE RELATION OF POLITICAL PARTIES TO A DEVELOPING IDENTITY

VIII   PARTY INFLUENCE ON OPINIONS

THE POLITICAL PROBLEM

The Gallup Poll surveys used in this study give evidence of slow-growing nationalism. Contributing to this are regional and ethnic cleavages, often of considerable magnitude, confirmed by every survey for which this information is available. The importance of such sub-group loyalties and the difficulties of transcending them constitute serious strains for the continuity of the polity. A federal structure permits some solution to the political problems posed. Federalism allows the day-to-day work of the country to be carried on, but does little toward creating a unified image of Canada. It is political parties in a heterogeneous society which may overcome the critical cleavages and help build a sense of national identity.

The typology introduced in Chapter II related eight possible party forms to the development of a national identity. The most effective types were broad-based parties of principle with either mass or cadre organization. Their effectiveness derived mainly from an ability to attract supporters from all significant strata in the society and to unite them through an appeal to some overriding principle. The one principle which appeared best able to mobilize support from all segments of the population was that based on militant nationalism. Yet, the very strength of such parties makes them potentially synonomous with the political state and thus with a denial of the legitimacy of opposition. When these parties are successful in suppressing opposition, national unity is achieved at the expense of equating political nonconformity with, at best, lack of patriotism, and, at the worst, treason. Our typology also suggested two other kinds of parties which could make a contribution to the achievement of national consensus, but without raising the same problems as do parties of principle. These are broad-based parties of electoral success, again with either mass or cadre organization. With such parties, principle is subordinated to getting elected, and, in achieving this, a more generally conciliatory approach is adopted to attain support from diverse groups.

The question is whether political parties influence the opinions of their adherents sufficiently to contribute to or suppress the development of national unity. Does party, for example, supply the same kind of meaningful frame of reference as do other social groups—in particular, those related to origin, region, and social class, to which individuals belong or with which they identify? The major assumption here is that membership or reference groups provide frameworks within which members or identifiers structure their opinions. Relatively distinct climates of opinion can result. The growing literature on climates of opinion generally focuses on a clearly defined institutional context of opinion, examining all members of a given group rather than samples. In the following analysis climates of opinion are examined through sample surveys, with the contexts here being political parties lacking in clear-cut membership boundaries.

METHODS OF DISCERNING OPINION CLIMATES

This study uses a large number of surveys obtained by admittedly questionable sampling techniques; it covers a variety of questions which must be treated in categories rather than individually; it deals with a large number of variables, most of which have no inherent order; and the issues cover a time span of more than a decade. What is needed, therefore, is an index for handling these data which meets the following requirements: it should be usable with ordinal data; it should make no assumptions about the normality of the population; it should not be affected by the shape of the tables; and it should have some statistical validity.

Raising the issue of validity brings along with it a number of *caveats* in the use of statistical tests of significance. Aside from the difficulties in selecting data and problems which warrant the application of tests of significance are those pertaining to the interpretation of the subsequent results. Critics of the indiscriminate use of statistical tests have been concerned with their being employed to prove or disprove single occurrences. But what is often important in sociology, and specifically in this study, is not the isolated instance but the behavioural or attitudinal pattern. With this in mind the task was to select a statistic which would help in discerning not so much significance levels but patterns of attitudes.

An index often used to show the relationship between contingency tables is the coefficient of contingency,

$$C = \sqrt{\frac{\chi^2}{N + \chi^2}}$$

But C is not useful where a comparison of degrees of relationship is to be made between tables of different size, since the maximum that C

can attain is a function of the size of the table. For example, in a 2×2 table $C_{max} = .707$, and in a 3×3 table, $C_{max} = .816$. In addition, the data to be used in this study are often found in asymmetrical tables. Further, in order to make comparisons between tables, we should have an index with a lower limit of zero and an upper limit of 1. The index developed for this purpose, to be known as the Index of Group Homogeneity (IGH), fulfills these qualifications.[1] The calculation necessary for it is:

$$\text{IGH} = \frac{C}{C_{max}} = \sqrt{\left(\frac{\chi^2}{N + \chi^2}\right)\left(\frac{r}{r - 1}\right)}$$

where r is the smaller number, r or c, in an $r \times c$ table, since C_{max} is a function of the smaller of the two numbers. For example, C_{max} for a 3×3, 3×8, or a $3 \times n$ table $= .816$.[2]

This index has limitations. The major shortcoming is that extremely low cell frequencies inflate the size of the IGH. This is not too serious here, however, because this study is not primarily concerned with levels of significance. Secondly, our concern is mainly with low IGH's rather than high ones.[3] That is, a low Index of Group Homogeneity will be used to indicate that within-group differences are slight and that the main variable is exerting an influence on opinion.

[1] My deep appreciation to Professor E. R. Oetting, now at Colorado State University, Fort Collins, who developed this index for me.

[2] The following corrective factors were then employed in the construction of the index.

Where r is:	C_{max} is:
2	.707
3	.816
4	.866
5	.894
6	.913

To give C a 0 to 1 range, a different corrective factor was used by Kelley, but his maximum is actually not quite 1, unlike ours. T. L. Kelley, *Statistical Method*, New York: Macmillan, 1924, pp. 266–268. Cramer uses a similar correction to ours, but his statistic is based on Phi rather than C. See Leo A. Goodman and William H. Kruskal, "Measures of Association for Cross Classifications," *Journal of the American Statistical Association*, 49, 1954, p. 740.

[3] Since our statistic follows a Chi-square distribution we will take as our cutting point a probability level of .10. Normally in testing the null hypothesis a compromise is sought between Type I and Type II errors by choosing a confidence level of .05 or .01. In this analysis our concern is with finding cases where intraparty differences are slight. But because of the nature of the data and our interest in patterns rather than single instances, it appeared advisable to select a probability level that allowed us to make a conservative estimate of the validity of our hypotheses. In this way, by using .10, while we are increasing slightly the likelihood of Type I errors, (i.e., of rejecting the hypothesis that intraparty differences are great when this is true), we do this to avoid undue occurrences of Type II errors, (i.e., of accepting the hypothesis that intraparty differences are great when this is false).

It is essential that we first clarify what is meant by "influence on opinions." Throughout our discussion it should be understood that "influence" is used very loosely. It means, most simply, that there is a statistical relationship between variable X and a particular distribution of opinions despite the presence of some second characteristic. When we find a relatively high proportion of such relationships out of the total possible number of opinion distributions, then we go on to infer that variable X has indeed caused at least some part of the relationships found, regardless of the pull from a second variable.

In this study respondents are classified according to the political party they would support in a coming national election, and by a number of other characteristics, one of which is whether some member of the household belongs to a trade union. For each question, IGH's are computed in two ways: across party lines, giving cross-party IGH's, and across union membership lines, giving intraparty IGH's. The purpose of these computations is to discover the existence of low IGH's, whether in union or in nonunion households regardless of the party supported by respondents, or in one or other of the parties, regardless of the union status of respondents. For Liberal supporters, for example, we find that in 84 percent of the 32 questions where both party and union affiliation are available, intraparty IGH's are below the previously designated probability level. From this we conclude that support for the Liberal party has exerted some measurable influence on opinions, regardless of the union status of the respondents' household. Again, of course, we must qualify with the statement that influence is our shorthand concept for describing the existence of a framework for opinions associated with a specific party.

Individual data on which patterns are based are not reported here, but throughout the following discussion we will give brief resumes of what these are.[4] In order to permit meaningful comparisons between groups, most data have been dichotomized according to whether or not groups expressed the dominant opinion. In a few instances, where responses could not be compressed into two categories, three were used.

EVIDENCE OF PARTY INFLUENCE

This analysis used 39 questions for which complete information was available. Because these covered a limited time period, the existence

[4] Data on which these tables are based are contained in Mildred A. Schwartz, "Canadian National Identity as Seen Through Public Opinion Polls: 1941–1963," Vol. II, unpublished doctoral dissertation, Faculty of Political Science, Columbia University, 1965.

of trends did not merit much attention. The relative influence of a party on opinions was considered in relation to the following attributes: region, community size, occupation of household head, trade-union status of household, education, interviewers' evaluation of socioeconomic level, official language, religion, origin or birthplace, sex, age, and marital status. While not all these attributes were given for each question, they represent the range of characteristics available.

In order to derive some general conception of the role of party support as a frame for opinions, the number of low intraparty IGH's across all available characteristics were added together for all parties and for all questions. As might be anticipated from our previous findings, within-party differences were greatest across regional and ethnic lines. Party homogeneity, as measured by the Index of Group Homogeneity was most evident with respect to union affiliation, type of community, and marital status. Party influence on opinion was of intermediate importance when compared with age, sex, and social class (See Table 49). Again adding together low intraparty IGH's for all parties, considering each kind of national problem separately, we

TABLE 49

OPINION CONSENSUS WITHIN TYPES OF SOCIAL GROUPINGS,
REGARDLESS OF PARTY SUPPORTED

Characteristics	Number of possible combinations with party	Percent low intraparty IGH's
Union household	123	85
Type of community	140	82
Marital status	111	76
Age	142	70
Sex	135	69
Evaluated socioeconomic status	147	67
Occupation	145	61
Education	101	61
Origin	36	61
Official language	115	49
Region	115	39
Religion	84	34

NOTE: The greater the proportion of low IGH's, the greater consensus in the parties. For example, in the 123 instances where intraparty IGH's were constructed in relation to residence in union households, parties displayed low IGH's in 85 percent of the cases. This means that party supporters in each party revealed similar distributions of opinion 85 percent of the time, whether or not they lived in a union household.

find greatest consensus within parties on questions pertaining to independence, internal cleavages, and symbols, and least on the role of government, while foreign commitments fall in between (see Table 50). Other kinds of variations emerge when we look at the number of low IGH's for each party and each issue type separately. According to the views of its supporters as these were measured by the Index of Group Homogeneity, the CCF/NDP was best able to control intergroup differences. The Social Credit party was somewhat similar in this respect, although generalizations about it were usually limited by the small number of supporters sampled. Of the two older parties, the Liberal party was least influential, as evidenced by the relatively large proportion of high intraparty IGH's (see Table 51). It remains now to examine these variations in detail and to account for their occurrence.

Before doing so, some comment is necessary about the order in which evidence of party influence is presented. Since our main concern was with the impact of political party preference on the views of supporters, we have begun with those variables which influence opinion less than party preference. These are trade-union membership and type of community. In the case of trade-union affiliation, this characteristic has been separated from other indicators of social class, since social class was relatively more influential on viewpoints

TABLE 50

RELATION BETWEEN PROBLEM AREA AND INTRAPARTY CONSENSUS
FOR ALL PARTIES

Problem area	Number of possible combinations between party and other characteristic ties	Percent low intraparty IGH's
Independence	478	78
Internal cleavages	276	74
Political symbols	264	74
Foreign commitments	82	65
Government activities	263	56

NOTE: The greater the proportion of low IGH's the greater consensus within the parties collectively. For example, in the 478 instances where intraparty IGH's were constructed in relation to all other available characteristics, low IGH's were found in 78 percent of the cases. This means that, in this proportion of the cases, party supporters in each party displayed similar distribution of opinion on issues of independence, regardless of other characteristics.

TABLE 51
RELATION BETWEEN PROBLEM AREA AND INTRAPARTY CONSENSUS FOR EACH PARTY

Problem area	Conservative		Liberal		CCF/NDP		Social Credit	
	Number of combinations between party and other characteristics	Percent low intraparty IGH's	Number of combinations between party and other characteristics	Percent low intraparty IGH's	Number of combinations between party and other characteristics	Percent low intraparty IGH's	Number of combinations between party and other characteristics	Percent low intraparty IGH's
Total	367	59	376	53	340	75	315	72
Independence	124	68	124	51	122	80	108	70
Foreign commitments	21	62	21	48	21	62	19	74
Internal cleavages	79	56	79	57	78	77	68	74
Government activities	66	52	66	44	66	60	65	69
Political symbols	77	56	77	62	53	81	55	75

NOTE: The greater proportion of low IGH's, the greater consensus in the party. For example, in 124 instances where it was possible to construct intraparty IGH's for Conservative supporters on questions of independence, low IGH's were found in 68 percent of the cases. This means that, in 68 percent of the cases, Conservative supporters displayed similar distributions of opinion on issues of independence, regardless of their other characteristics.

than party preference. Even though marital status tends to be like union and community, it will be discussed in conjunction with age and sex, since it also displays some similarity to these characteristics in relation to party affiliation, and fits in more naturally with them.

Trade-Union Affiliation

Political party appeared to have a strong influence on opinions expressed by trade-union householders. Although both union and non-union householders within a single party tended to hold similar views on national problems, in the few instances where intraparty differences did exist they resulted in greater homogeneity of outlook for those resident in union households (see Table 52). To determine whether

TABLE 52

RELATION BETWEEN PARTY PREFERENCE AND RESIDENCE IN TRADE-UNION HOUSEHOLD FOR CONSENSUS ON NATIONAL IDENTITY

| Households | Cross-party IGH's for union households | |
	Number of possible combinations with party	Percent low IGH's across party lines
Union households	32	56
Nonunion households	32	38

| Party | Intraparty IGH's related to union | |
	Number of possible combinations with union	Percent low intraparty IGH's
Conservative	32	84
Liberal	32	84
CCF/NDP	30	83
Social Credit	29	90

NOTE: The greater the proportion of low IGH's, the greater the consensus within the group.

these results were due to the great strength of political parties in imposing distinct climates of opinion on supporters or to some other reasons, some historical background on trade unionism in Canada is necessary.

Trade unionism in Canada.—In many countries trade unions have developed political arms or have become affiliated with political parties which can promote their interests in the legislature. As a result rank-and-file members have a distinct focus of identification. Labour parties of this scope have not developed in the United States, and some have argued that union members see the proper sphere of union activity confined to economic rather than political problems. Yet even when trade unions do not take an active role in politics, and even when their leaders are divided, union members in the United States display political characteristics different from nonmembers if occupation, education, and other relevant factors are constant.[5]

The experiences of Canadian trade unions differ markedly from those in the United States and contribute to the even lesser influence on members and their families.[6] The development of unionism in Canada was comparatively slow, and, even more than in the United States, internal dissension hampered the formation of a unified outlook. The nature of the Canadian economy with its recent and partial industrialization, reliance on foreign trade and capital, and specialized production also contribute to an economy

highly vulnerable to seasonal and cyclical fluctuations in price, income, and employment originating in foreign markets.

This fact in itself has tended to exert a modifying influence on labor-management relations in Canada, to temper union demands (other than in boom periods at least) and to stiffen employer resistance against recognizing or making concessions to unions.[7]

Economic factors have also aided the employer in achieving a stronger bargaining position toward his workers. The Canadian worker, too, has been comparatively more difficult to unionize because industrialization is relatively recent, with many workers from agricultural, more individualistic backgrounds, and others immigrated from foreign

[5] B. Berelson, P. F. Lazarsfeld, and W. McPhee, *Voting*, Chicago: University of Chicago Press, 1954, pp. 37–53; A. Campbell, G. Gurin, and W. E. Miller, *The Voter Decides*, Chicago: Row, Peterson, 1954, p. 154; Arthur Kornhauser, Albert J. Mayer, and Harold L. Sheppard, *When Labor Votes*, New York: University Books, 1956; Harold L. Sheppard and Nicholas A. Masters, "The Political Attitudes and Preferences of Union Members: The Case of the Detroit Auto Workers," *American Political Science Review*, 53, 1959, pp. 437–447.

[6] The following discussion on the characteristic attributes of Canadian trade unionism is based on Stuart Jamieson, *Industrial Relations in Canada*, Toronto: Macmillan, 1957, pp. 93–100. For an authoritative but early history of unionism in Canada, see H. A. Logan, *Trade Unions in Canada*, Toronto: Macmillan, 1948. Later sources are Eugene Forsey, "History of the Labour Movement in Canada," Canada, Dominion Bureau of Statistics, *Canada Yearbook*, Ottawa: Queen's Printer, 1958, pp. 795–802; Aranka E. Kovacs, *Readings in Canadian Labour Economics*, Toronto: McGraw-Hill, 1961.

[7] Jamieson, *op. cit.*, pp. 13–14.

countries. Large-scale immigration brought with it many ready recruits to the trade-union movement, but it also added to those with agricultural experiences. In addition these immigrants were often unable to speak one of the official languages, and thus found themselves at a disadvantage in competition for jobs, let alone in seeking to better their position through trade-union activity. Along with immigration there has been massive emigration to the United States, taking with it, according to some interpretations, those eager for opportunity which they saw as greater in the neighbouring country, who might otherwise have provided trade unions with their most militant supporters.

Mention has already been made of inter-union rivalries which derive in part from the regional and cultural cleavages in the country. One result has been the formation of Catholic trade unions in Quebec which, at least until recently, severely limited cooperation between unions. The development of a national labour movement with some internal coherence has been further hampered by the limited jurisdiction of the federal government on labour matters. As a consequence, regional differences in various worker benefits have been allowed to continue.

Like many other social institutions, trade unionism was brought to Canada and influenced first by the British, but more recently and more significantly by the Americans. Canadian unions affiliated with the AFL-CIO vary in the degree of their autonomy, but this is not the central issue here. Rather it is the contention that Canadian trade unions are affected by their "foreign" nature in such a way as to curtail the expression of Canadian nationalism in a manner that might have differed had trade unions originated and grown out of conditions completely indigenous to the country.

Special note must also be taken of the political activities of trade unions, and again these are different from American experiences. Legislation favourable to labour was slow in emerging in Canada, yet the dominant Trades and Labour Congress was reluctant to take direct political action. It confined itself to attempting to influence government by presenting briefs to the Prime Minister, the Minister of Labour, and other Cabinet members. Even when the CCF party was formed in the 1930's with a program somewhat similar to that of the Labour party in Great Britain, the Trades and Labour Congress declined to support it officially. Individual unions did, however, affiliate with the CCF. The Canadian Congress of Labour, a more militant industrial type of union organization, officially supported the CCF from its founding. When the two labour councils were negotiating their merger in 1956, the founding convention attempted to reconcile the opposing views toward political action by two resolutions. The first of these commended the CCF for its help in bringing about favourable labour legislation, and the second recommended that means of cooperating with the CCF be explored. These resolutions were obviously compromises and did not commit the new labour body to any concerted support of the CCF. But in the face of the failure of the CCF to win widespread support after World War II, particularly from organized labour, it was decided at a Canadian Labour Congress convention to set about founding a genuine labour party which would inherit the old support of the CCF and acquire a broader base. Yet in the first two federal elections (those of 1962 and 1963) when the New Democratic party, as the inheritor of the CCF is known, ran candidates, the results were hardly encouraging. Even with its own party, organized labour was far from acquiring a monolithic political outlook.

Because of the combination of conditions detailed above which have inhibited trade-union militancy, influence on the viewpoints of members and their families is probably minimized. The solutions which trade unions propose to national problems, as seen by the rank and file, do not appear different from those offered to other citizens. From another perspective, we can say that the cleavages implied by trade-union affiliation are not so great that they cannot ordinarily be restrained by political parties.

Within party differences related to union affiliation.—The history of trade unions in Canada may account for the lack of differentiation between union and nonunion households, but some differences did emerge from our data, and these seem worth examining in detail.

Opinions about responsibility for schools in 1954, and unemployment in 1957, differed among Conservative supporters, with those in union households more in favour of provincial responsibility. The questions pointed up the greater attraction of centralist solutions to Conservative nonunionists and the importance to union householders of the creation of a labour party and of immigration prospects.

It was in relation to the role of government that CCF supporters exhibited the greatest internal differences. Three questions from the same 1956 survey on a hospital plan, a medical plan, and competition with the CBC showed nonunion householders to be more favourable to government activity in these concerns. Yet before we can conclude that it was the nonunion CCF supporter who was most favourable to government intervention, we find that in 1955 union householders were relatively more favourable to government support

of cultural activities, and in 1957, although a majority of party supporters preferred government resource development, nonunionists
were more likely to favour private development while unionists were
comparatively reluctant to offer an opinion. But generally, union
householders in other parties were more consistent. Thus, those supporting the Liberal party in 1956 were less favourable to private development of a trans-Canada pipeline and more often opposed to the
size of the pension increase in 1957. Conservative supporters who were
also residents in union households were more likely to favour government resource development. Yet they too, like CCF supporters, were
more disapproving of government support of cultural activities than
were nonunionists. Where union affiliation does exert an influence in
this area, it appears to be in the direction of greater government participation in social and economic activities. There is some temptation
to suggest that it was nonunion CCF/NDP adherents who were more
ideologically oriented, but the data are inconclusive.

Questions dealing with national symbols showed a tendency for
nonunion householders to favour British symbols and for union
householders to disapprove. Thus, Liberal unionists were most likely
to disapprove of the Queen Mother as Governor-General. Nonunion
Social Crediters were largely in favour of the Queen's picture on
money and stamps. Some further support for this viewpoint comes
from other questions on symbols, but these did not produce important
differences.

Trends in party influence.—Some differences appeared with respect
to the long-range influence of party on the opinions of supporters.
These differences could be related to shifts in the character of supporters, the kinds of questions asked, and changes in the nature of
the parties. But because of the kind of data being used, little more
than suggestive evidence is available.

For example, there were more intraparty differences among Conservatives before 1958 than later but it is difficult to attach any meaning to this, since there was no consistency in the questions, nor has
the proportion of union supporters altered appreciably. For the
Liberals, intraparty differences have been more evenly distributed over
the years but again it is difficult to relate this to the nature of the
party or the questions asked.

On the basis of supporters' opinions, the CCF was least successful
in imposing a relative uniformity of viewpoint between 1955 and
1957. Since that time intraparty differences have been consistently
slight. It is not clear whether this change in influence is due to the
emergence of the NDP, or whether it is a result of the kinds of ques-

tions asked in the earlier period and not repeated later. These questions referred to the activities of government. It is possible, also, that the apparent increase in the effect of party is related to a shift in the character of supporters. Thus, as the NDP came into being with a promised commitment from organized labour, this could have been accompanied by a great increase in electoral support from union households, bringing with them a new perspective on national problems unlike that of earlier union supporters. An attempt to check this from our survey data unfortunately confirmed the limitations of the sampling techniques used. Yet while sampling variations did not permit clear determination of what proportion of CCF/NDP supporters were also affiliated with trade unions, it also appeared that there have been no major alterations in this support. It seems more fair to conclude, then, that the questions on the nature of governmental activities as much as the activities themselves contributed to variation in opinions.

It would be desirable to make a comparable examination of Social Credit supporters, but the smallness of their number makes it difficult to do so.

Lack of a trade union climate of opinion.—A detailed consideration of the problem areas, political parties, and time periods characterized by lack of intraparty consensus indicates that parties have been proficient in establishing a climate of opinion which restrains the expression of specific trade-union viewpoints. One reason for this finding could well be the way we have defined union affiliation. Following Gallup Poll usage, the concept of union encompasses all those resident in a household where at least one member belongs to a trade union. It could be argued that if we were to confine our category only to trade-union members themselves, we would get a clearer demarcation of opinion. This is possible, but present usage is favoured by those who see the results of trade-union activities such as work stoppages, increased wages, and welfare benefits as having a direct impact on all members of the household, and as a consequence, on their outlook.[8]

---

[8] The data did not allow us to separate union members from those merely living in households where someone did belong, but an attempt to ascertain the possible effects of combining these two kinds of respondents was made by controlling for sex. This attempt was based on the assumption that men would more likely be union members than women. A control for sex was introduced in eleven questions from three surveys. Since we are dealing with four parties, this procedure resulted in forty-four instances where sex and union affiliation were related to opinion. Of these, only seven instances showed appreciable differences within union households, within each party, according to sex. In all these instances women in union households resembled both men and women in nonunion households more than they did men in union households. However, this is not sufficient evidence from which

Another reason for lack of a distinctive union climate of opinion could be that the trade-union households were not interested in the questions put to them. If the proportion of "no opinions" is taken as an indicator of concern, there is little difference between union and nonunion householders.[9]

Thirdly, it could be inferred that there is a relative lack of differentiation between the two groups because unionists, while no less interested in the issues posed than other respondents, do not find them any *more* relevant. This interpretation would seem to be belied by such questions as the formation of a labour party, responsibility for unemployment, and opinions of immigration—all issues which affect labour households more than others.

The relative similarity which we found in the influence of parties on both union and nonunion householders seems to derive mainly from the circumstances of trade union development in Canada, rather than from the data examined. These circumstances have dampened the potential for trade-union militancy and, as a consequence, have permitted political parties to develop their own approaches to national problems, almost unhampered by specifically trade-union perspectives.

Type of Community

Similarly to residence in union households, residence in urban or rural areas influences opinions less than party affiliation. Rural respondents, however, manifest more of a common perspective than those who live in cities (see Table 53). A number of questions considered in Part II indicated that Canadian rural residents were historically more likely to respond in a conservative, traditional manner unless their interests appeared to be directly at stake. Nevertheless, in the great majority of cases, distinctions based on party were more important than those of community in shaping answers to national issues.

Sources of urban-rural similarities.—As in trade-union affiliation, the reasons why location of residence is so often overriden by party considerations are of greatest interest. From a variety of sources we have been led to believe that type of community will have an independent impact on opinions. Early students were impressed with the

---

to conclude that results quoted in the text would have been greatly different if sex had been controlled for all questions. It still, of course, does not answer the initial objection that union members may be different from other householders, but it does cast some doubt on such a conclusion.

[9] See Chapter XII.

TABLE 53

RELATION BETWEEN PARTY PREFERENCE AND TYPE OF COMMUNITY

Community type	Cross-party IGH's for community	
	Number of possible combinations with party	Percent low IGH's across party lines
Rural	36	61
Urban	36	39

Party	Intraparty IGH's related to community	
	Number of possible combinations with community	Percent low intraparty IGH's
Conservative	36	83
Liberal	36	81
CCF/NDP	34	79
Social Credit	34	85

NOTE: The greater proportion of IGH's, the greater consensus within the group.

psychological concomitants of city life; more recent views have stressed the manifold structural effects of urbanization.

An excellent clue to the economic and social development of an area is the growth of cities. For this there are two reasons. First, the city *reflects* the changes in every sphere of social life. Its growth stems from all the factors that change illiterate agriculturalism to literate industrialism; it is correlated with increased industry and commerce, enhanced education, more efficient birth and death control—in short, with the whole process of modernization. Second, the city is a *source* of change in its own right. It is a diffusion center for modern civilization, providing a milieu in which social ferment and innovation can take place. City expansion therefore helps to determine as well as reflect the trend toward more modern conditions.[10]

The trend toward urbanization has had some implications for political life, even if the character of these influences has not always been uniform. Kornhauser, for example, in his survey of fifteen Western nations, found considerable difference between urban and rural centres in the support for various kinds of mass movements.[11] In the United

[10] Kingsley Davis and Ana Casis, "Urbanization in Latin America," in *Cities and Society, The Revised Reader in Urban Sociology*, ed. by Paul K. Hatt and Albert J. Reiss, Jr., New York: Free Press, 1961, p. 141.

[11] William Kornhauser, *The Politics of Mass Society*, New York: Free Press, 1959, pp. 143–150.

States, the large urban centres have been the stronghold of the Democratic party. The influence on political opinions of residence in a rural setting would appear to be even greater than that of urban residence because of the greater homogeneity of the rural population. Situations of economic distress have often been followed by support for protest movements of a radical bent, but usually in stable societies rural residents hold to politically conservative views. Although urban-rural differences have been treated as though they were dichotomous, they more often shade off into each other and are affected, in urban communities, by relative size. These distinctions have been further complicated by the growth of suburban communities. The suburbs have inspired both studies and speculations about new political alignments although the outcome of these alignments appears still to be uncertain.

With evidence from a number of countries on political differences related to type of community, the expectation of similar cleavages in Canada seemed appropriate. Even though numbers sampled usually prevented the treatment of urban respondents according to city size, while suburbs could not be distinguished at all despite growing suburbanization in Canada, the experiences of other countries led us to believe that gross distinctions between rural and urban would be politically significant. But, although there were some differences in communities, particularly rural ones, they were not significant. Again we must inquire into the circumstances in Canada inhibiting the differential perception of national problems. Studies of Western farmers have produced well-documented accounts of agrarian radicalism,[12] which, however, often proved to be a response to local conditions, even when these had national ramifications. Furthermore, as conditions have changed, farmers have become more conservative, the only apparent exception being the more favourable attitude of rural CCF adherents in 1956 to government welfare policies. One explanation, then, for the lack of rural-urban differences in Canada is the decline of radicalism among Western farmers.

It might be argued that the lack of differentiation is related to the relative recency of urbanization in Canada. More than 70 percent of Canadians were resident in locales with a population of at least one thousand by 1961, but in 1941 it was only approximately 50 percent. Many of our respondents therefore could be immigrants from, or have family connections with, rural areas. As such, the urban community

---

[12] S. M. Lipset, *Agrarian Socialism*, Berkeley and Los Angeles: University of California Press, 1950; C. B. Macpherson, *Democracy in Alberta*, Toronto: University of Toronto Press, 1953.

may not yet have had sufficient time to make its mark on the outlook of all its residents. It is possible that the opinions of party supporters were internally consistent because a majority were responding with a rural outlook despite residence in an urban community.

Without denying the possible validity of the foregoing argument, it could also be said that there is little difference between town and country because of the pervasiveness of urbanism as a way of life. This has been achieved in the modern world by the extension of communication networks which allow all people, no matter where they live, to share in information, aspirations, and a sense of community. To partake of an urban way of life, rural residents must have ready access to such communication media as telephones, radio, television, newspapers, and magazines. Data indicate that ownership of radios is as widespread in rural as in urban communities, although there is still a sizable gap in ownership of telephones and television. With respect to radio and television, the Canadian Broadcasting Corporation and, more recently, the Board of Broadcast Governors, attempted to provide special rural services plus a conception of broadcasting that is more national in scope.[13] The reading public of newspapers and magazines is different for rural and urban communities, but there are many common links, and exposure to national advertising in these media helps create some uniformity in wants and their satisfaction. Rural isolation has also been broken down by the increase in travel, and widespread ownership of cars provides an indicator of ability to do so. A pattern which is becoming more common, at least on prairie farms which are characteristically large in size and mechanized, is for farmers to spend part of each year in town, thus taking part directly in urban life. These indicators all point to greater urbanism for Canadians, but their growth has been relatively recent, having gained momentum in the postwar years, which still leaves open the question whether urbanism has had sufficient time to take effect.

The lack of pronounced urban-rural differences within parties, then, is likely to be a reflection of three factors: rural problems are often perceived as local rather than national issues; urbanization has been a relatively recent phenomenon; and an urban way of life is spreading through the entire society. All these factors in combination permit political parties to develop their own opinion climates without regard to the urban or rural character of their supporters.

The nature of urban-rural differences.—We affirmed the overriding significance of party in relation to urban and rural residence. It is also

[13] For a general statement on the purposes of broadcasting in Canada, see *Report, Royal Commission on Broadcasting*, Ottawa: Queen's Printer, 1957, pp. 74–76.

worth paying attention to those instances in which parties were not successful in establishing a climate of opinion. Consideration of each question in which intraparty differences occurred is not warranted since the direction of these differences has already been indicated. An exception is made, however, where the interaction between party and community produces unique patterns of response. Differences were slight for NDP adherents, but the tendency was for them to be more disapproving of a labour party if they lived in an urban community. Yet a survey conducted in 1956 disclosed the opposite situation. Since these are only tendencies rather than distinct differences it could be that in the earlier survey CCF supporters in cities were opposed to the creation of new political alignments, but in 1962, once the NDP had come into being, it was rural supporters who felt themselves most threatened by the intrusion of organized labour into their formerly agrarian-base party. In keeping with their more conservative attitudes, rural respondents in 1961 were more in favour of immigration restrictions within all parties. The question asked the preceding year on the admission of nonwhite immigrants did not produce much intraparty difference, but there was some tendency for urban residents to be less discriminatory. However, in 1954, when feelings against immigration were not as widespread, and there were no pronounced differences within three of the parties, CCF supporters in urban areas were most disapproving of the effects of immigration. Here we may have a manifestation, not of the rural residents' distrust of strangers, but of the urban workers' fear of job displacement. Presumably if such feelings existed in other parties, they were more readily submerged by the more diversified ethnic and class character of urban supporters.

Questions on the role which government should play in the life of the country produced the most distinctive rural-urban variations for each party, even though intraparty differences were almost always low. Thus, in 1956 government financing of a trans-Canada pipeline was most favoured by farm respondents; and they were less disapproving of lack of competition with the Canadian Broadcasting Corporation than were urban residents, with some variation by party. We can account for some of this variation by suggesting that city dwellers would be most likely to see themselves as benefiting from a diversity of cultural activities, and from social-welfare plans, whereas those in rural areas would feel more dependent on the noncommercial orientation of the government-operated CBC. Where the latter is not true of rural respondents, we can only infer that they live in more populous areas such as Ontario and Quebec where they could expect to be serviced by commercial radio and television stations. The finding that rural CCF adherents in 1956 were the greatest supporters of a medical and hospital plan run by the government fits in with our previous observation that the greatest approval for these measures come from nonunion households where agrarian socialism exerted the strongest influence.

Where differences occurred on questions of symbols, they generally were such that urban respondents were more disapproving of British symbols and more in favour of characteristically Canadian ones.

There was no evidence of distinct shifts in the influence of party as compared to type of community, nor were there real differences between parties beyond the fact that type of community was slightly more troublesome to the CCF/NDP.

We have discussed here situations in which the political party supported by respondents assumes greater significance in affecting viewpoints than does the type of community in which they live. The differences which do appear are most often related to the development of rural perspectives on national issues. From a consideration of Canadian circumstances, we have related the relative lack of urban-rural differentiation within parties to the local nature of rural issues, the recent origin of urbanization, and the diffusion of urban ways. In whatever manner these operate in Canada, their effect is to permit a high degree of intraparty consensus. All four parties then are to a large extent able to control the cleavages that might otherwise be associated with types of community. In so doing, the solutions which parties offer to problems underlying the definition of national identity need not take into account rural-urban divisions except for some concessions to the greater traditionalism of rural areas.

IX   BARRIERS TO CONSENSUS

REGIONALISM

It has been well documented from a number of countries other than Canada that the region where people live has a bearing on their political outlook. The bases of regionalism may be related to the settlement of distinct social or ethnic groups, the development of regional subcultures through isolation, or the economic conditions peculiar to an area. These factors all have some relevance to the Canadian experience and contribute to the difficulty faced by parties in counteracting the effects of region. This generalization needs to be qualified by the observation that not all regions in Canada are equally

TABLE 54

RELATION BETWEEN PARTY PREFERENCE AND REGION IN CANADA

	Cross-party IGH's for region	
Region	Number of possible combinations with party	Percent low IGH's across party lines
Maritimes	30	80
Quebec	30	60
Ontario	30	57
Prairies	29	62
British Columbia	29	59

	Intraparty IGH's related to region	
Party	Number of possible combinations with party	Percent low intraparty IGH's
Conservative	30	23
Liberal	30	20
CCF/NDP	28	61
Social Credit	27	56

NOTE: The greater the proportion of low IGH's the greater the consensus within groups.

146

homogeneous in opinions. Looking at regional (or cross-party) rather than intraparty Indices of Group Homogeneity, we find the Maritime provinces most homogeneous, followed by the prairie provinces, Quebec, British Columbia, and Ontario (see Table 54).

Maritimes

Among the factors promoting Maritimers' unanimity of outlook are the economically shaped conditions of life. Compared to other Canadians, those in the Maritimes are most likely to be engaged in primary industry, they have had the highest unemployment rate, a below-average annual growth rate, and they are least likely to be urbanized. Economic depression is not of recent origin in the Maritimes but goes back to the years of Confederation. The existence of sizable settlements of French, particularly in New Brunswick, constitutes the only major variation from the predominantly British character of the region. The chief religious denominations are Anglican, United Church, Roman Catholic, and Baptist without the proliferation of fundamentalist sects found in other parts of the country. More important is the fact that more than 96 percent of the population were native born in 1961, compared with 84 percent for the whole of Canada. Long settlement under similar conditions of life has thus contributed to an identity of interest which cuts across party lines. This has been further reinforced by the absence of third parties which mobilize discontent in other parts of the country. That is, one of the ways in which a common outlook is achieved is by submerging differences within the two major parties.

On three of the questions large interparty differences were a result of the opinions of supporters of minor parties.[1] In other instances where considerations of party overrode those of region, the pattern of opinions was similar to the national distribution. However, there were two exceptions to this, both from a 1957 survey, where Liberal supporters were less favourable than Conservatives to foreign resource development and United States investment, a reversal of usual Liberal views. Local conditions influenced party supporters in a direction different from that of the national party. At that period Liberals, who were out of office both provincially and federally, were urging

---

[1] These were from the 1957 survey concerning the level of government which should run schools, where CCF supporters were most pro-federal; the 1951 survey concerning a Governor-General, where minor party supporters were totally in favour of an appointment from Canada; and the 1958 survey, when CCF supporters were less approving of Canada having an entirely new flag.

greater economic expansion for the Maritimes through federal government intervention.

Prairie Provinces

No region duplicates the Maritimes in homogeneity but the prairie provinces come closest. Peopled to a larger extent than any other region in Canada by those of non-British, non-French origin, some identity of interest has no doubt emerged from the relative isolation of a largely rural population and one which has been comparatively bypassed by the large numbers of postwar immigrants. Out of their own peculiar economic conditions, strongly affected by periodic crop failures and by the depression of the 1930's, they responded with political parties of agrarian protest.[2] Particularly in recent years, the appeal of these parties has been confined to provincial politics, and federally the major parties, especially the Conservatives, have won their support. It should be remembered then, that in considering opinions about issues with a bearing on identity formation, we have divided respondents according to the expected vote in a federal election, and this plays down the significance of local issues. It is noteworthy that prairie respondents showed a similar distribution of opinions on questions on symbols regardless of party affiliation, but that those pertaining to independence and cleavages were most often affected by party. Party differences emerged in the 1957 questions on responsibility for education and unemployment, in disapproval of increased immigration in 1960, and disapproval of a labour party in 1962. Questions pertaining to independence included the 1954 question on continuing in the Commonwealth, the 1956 questions on the United States and Britain losing friends as a result of their foreign policy, and the 1957 questions on foreign resource development and United States investment. These party differences usually follow the national pattern, but some parties tended to take independent perspectives. Not only did the prairie climate of opinion exert a leveling influence on opinions but also, when differences did emerge, these were, for supporters of major parties, sometimes unusual. For example, in 1954, Conservative supporters, along with those of the Social Credit,

[2] It can be argued that the homogeneity of the three prairie provinces only emerges in contrast to the remaining provinces. Particularly in recent years, the three have become increasingly differentiated from each other, as Manitoba becomes industrialized and Alberta benefits from its rich resources of oil and gas. The political contrasts between Alberta and Saskatchewan are especially interesting. Still there is much precedent for treating these provinces collectively, and this policy will be followed here.

most opposed participation in Indochina. In 1956 and 1957, Conservatives were, like the CCF, most often convinced that the United States was losing friends as a result of her foreign policy and most disapproving of United States investment in Canada. It was the Liberals in 1960 who were least disapproving of increased immigration, while the Conservatives were most so. Finally, supporters of the Social Credit party in the prairie provinces differed from those in the rest of Canada by being more favourable to the pension rise in 1956 and highly disapproving of a labour party in 1962. We can conclude from these instances that even though party differences emerged, they were strongly shaped by regional conditions. This will be elaborated when we conclude our discussion of regionalism.

Quebec

Quebec is ethnically the most homogeneous province in Canada, with about 80 percent of its population of French origin. From the time of the British conquest, the retention of ethnic and religious identity has always been of serious concern to French-speaking Canadians.[3] Since that time, domestic issues and involvement in foreign wars have kept open the deep cleavages between the two dominant ethnic groups. As a result, the political responses of French Quebec have often been unique. For example, in the general election of 1945, when feeling against conscription was still close to the surface, two members of Bloc Populaire, a new party strongly oriented to French-Canadian nationalism, were elected to the federal House. In that year's election, one-third of the popular vote in Quebec went to solely provincial parties. At the provincial level, the Union Nationale party provided the focus for French-Canadian nationalist feelings from its first election in 1934 until its defeat by the provincial Liberal party in 1960. Victory in the 1966 provincial election probably derived, though, from other sources than Union Nationale's nationalist appeal. Sentiments favouring a militant French-Canadian nationalism had some connection with the new strength of the Social Credit party in the 1962 federal election, and the multiplicity of separatist movements in that province. The nationalism of French Canadians also has an important economic component as they become increasingly concerned about the economic dominance of English Canada and the inadequacies of a classical college education as preparation for

[3] Though not without its detractors, the best single source on French Canada is Mason Wade, *The French Canadians*, Toronto: Macmillan, 1956. Another useful source is Marcel Rioux and Yves Martin, *French-Canadian Society*, Vol. I, Toronto: McClelland and Stewart, 1964.

a modern competitive technical society. We would expect that these forces would curtail the expression of party differences and lead opinions in the highly pro-Canadian direction noted in Part II. It is perhaps surprising then, that consensus across party lines is not greater. Yet considerable region-based pressure does exist and, in particular, serves to level distinctions between Conservatives and Liberals. The consequence of residence in Quebec was to make Conservative party supporters less differentiated from the more pro-Canadian Liberals. To the 1958 question on a new flag, Conservative supporters were even more frequently approving than either Liberal or minor party supporters.

There is some evidence that the Liberal party has been able to override the influence of regionalism. Responses to the 1954 questions on immigration and education followed the national pattern, but on the 1957 question on responsibility for unemployment, it was Liberal supporters who were most in favour of federal responsibility. Although the Liberal party generally is not considered highly centralist in its policies, this is an instance where a party climate of opinion was able to restrain the expression of sectionalism and bring opinions more in line with those of the nation as a whole.

The apparent opinion differences which are characteristic of Quebec in contrast to other regions are generally related to minor-party support. Thus in 1954, CCF supporters were most in favour of foreign development of resources. In that same year Social Credit supporters were most anti-Commonwealth and had a high rate of no response. In 1962 again, Social Crediters were most frequently in favour of independence, while the few CCF supporters in the sample were pro-Commonwealth. Neutrality was most favoured by the CCF in 1960, while the few Social Crediters interviewed were most often against it. On questions pertaining to the role of government the national pattern was followed on government assistance for cultural activities and opinions of the raise in pensions in 1956. But in the latter question, it was Social Credit supporters who were most disappointed with the size of the pension raise rather than the few CCF supporters. On symbols, the questions concerning the Governor-General in 1951, the Duke of Windsor in 1956, and a new flag in 1962, Social Credit supporters were distinguished by their rate of no opinion. The intense French Canadian nationalism evidenced in the pronouncements of the Quebec leadership of the Social Credit party, did not show up in the responses of party supporters because of the latters' reluctance to express opinions.[4]

[4] The significance of this will be elaborated in Chapter XII.

British Columbia

British Columbia follows Quebec in the extent of its homogeneity of outlook. Characterized by a socially diverse population and increased industrialization and urbanization, British Columbia's geographic isolation from central Canada has served to accentuate the separateness of that province. Politically, British Columbia has shared the experience of other western provinces in the lessening appeal of the two major parties, both federally and provincially. At the provincial level, the Provincial party won 24 percent of the popular vote in 1924, while in both federal and provincial elections, the CCF/NDP have had considerable voter appeal since the 1930's and the Social Credit since the 1950's. Social Credit has formed the provincial government since 1952. Isolation from the remainder of Canada and a history of support for radical parties hence contribute to a regional climate of opinion influencing views on the issues which we have interpreted as contributing to a definition of national identity.

It is mainly on questions concerning internal cleavages that party considerations are more important than residence in British Columbia. Differences between parties appeared in the 1954 survey on effects of immigration, the 1954 survey on responsibility for education, the 1957 survey on responsibility for unemployment, and the 1962 survey on the participation of organized labour in politics. In the area of independence, party differences were also prominent in the 1954 and 1957 questions on foreign development of resources and United States investment.

In those cases where cross-party differences were low for questions asked of British Columbia residents, region was pushing the supporters of all parties in a similar direction. Responses of Conservative and Liberal supporters were markedly different from their counterparts elsewhere even in several instances where cross-party differences were great. Thus, while Conservatives nationally were more approving of the Duke of Windsor as Governor-General in 1956 and, in 1957, more in favour of federal responsibility for unemployment, and only moderately more approving of foreign development of resources than Liberals and CCF supporters, the opposite was true in British Columbia. On the question of resource development through foreign capital they were most highly approving and, in 1962, much more strongly opposed to labour participation in politics than were Conservatives in general. Liberals in British Columbia were also distinguished by their high preference for foreign development of resources in 1954, their even more frequent opposition to participation in Indochina than Social Credit supporters, and their greater preference for the Duke of Windsor as Governor-General. These examples of variations in outlook of supporters of the major parties deserve further comment, which will be reserved until the conclusion of the discussion of regional influences.

Ontario

Socially diverse, Ontario is also the most populous, consistently prosperous, industrialized, and urbanized province in Canada. Despite large settlements of continental Europeans, particularly since World War II, those of British origin remain the dominant ethnic group, if not numerically, at least in terms of influence. Political experimentation is not foreign to Ontario, and in the 1920's, the United Farmers of Ontario played a prominent role in provincial politics. In the 1940's, the CCF had its greatest appeal, but since that time the Conservatives have been in the ascendency, both federally and provincially. The Social Credit party has yet to make significant inroads into the province. Given these social, economic, and political characteristics, we find the greatest amount of party differentiation in this region of the country. In addition, unlike responses elsewhere, there were no responses expressing party viewpoints peculiar to Ontario. This means that in general party differences followed the national pattern. But it might be more accurate to say that it is Ontario which sets the pattern for the nation. Exposed to, or experiencing directly, all the stresses inherent in Canadian life and succeeding nonetheless, residents of Ontario thus help contribute to the essentially conservative, "don't rock the boat" status of the nation's identity.

Party Influences

This examination of the interplay between party and region suggests several explanations for variations in the influence of party on the formation of Canada's identity; these stem from the distribution of party supporters, the stability of party loyalties, and the existence of regional climates of opinion.

Distribution of party supporters.—Parties which appeal to limited groups in the population rather than to a broad spectrum of voters are more likely to influence the opinions of their supporters in a uniform fashion. Thus the relatively strong influence of the CCF/NDP on supporters' opinions can be related to the small number of supporters it has been able to attract in the Maritimes and Quebec.

It has not had to accommodate to the special interests of residents of these regions. Homogeneity of viewpoint is reinforced as well by that party's attraction of support with a limited occupational base, drawn particularly from workers and farmers. From its founding, the CCF has made a deliberate attempt to educate its followers in its policies and to allow them a role in formulating programs. It is noteworthy that CCF/NDP supporters showed greatest homogeneity across regional lines on questions of independence and political symbols, two areas where other parties failed to achieve this unanimity (see Table 51). But success in achieving a climate of opinion in this manner means also the CCF/NDP's continuity as a minor party, particularly when, as seen in Part II, the views of its supporters are so often at variance with those of other Canadians.

The Social Credit party, although less able to cut across regional lines than the CCF/NDP still appeared more effective than either the Liberal or Conservative parties. Again this was partly achieved by a minimal appeal in some regions, in this case Ontario and the Maritimes. Unlike the CCF/NDP, however, in western Canada, where it has received its greatest share of the popular vote in general elections, it has attracted support from a broad occupational base. But in Quebec its support comes mainly from farmers and small shopkeepers in the smaller towns. It is perhaps surprising that under these circumstances Social Credit has been as influential as it has. Other factors affecting that party's impact on the opinions of supporters may be more important than the lack of appeal to all regions, especially since it has been making electoral inroads in Quebec. These will be discussed in relation to our other explanations.

An uneven distribution of party supporters appeared to contribute to the homogeneity of viewpoint found among those of the CCF/NDP, and perhaps to some extent of the Social Credit. The Conservatives and Liberals, as parties which historically have appealed to all regions of Canada, have thus been hindered in acquiring the united outlooks which might result from attracting supporters only from particular regions.

Stability of party loyalties.—We can also hypothesize that party influence will be weaker during a period of electoral shift when a party is expanding its social base and attracting new types of voters. This is well exemplified by the Conservatives. Until they took office in 1957 the Conservatives had been in opposition for twenty-two years. Having last served as the governing party during the depression of the early 1930's, and being associated with the dominant British Protestant group in central Canada, it was important, if the Conservatives were to attain office, that they create a new image for themselves. In doing so, they were fortunate to have as their leader a small-town western lawyer with none of the stereotyped characteristics of a Tory. But as the election of 1957 approached, it was also evident that the Conservatives would be able to benefit from the general feeling of dissatisfaction with the Liberals and the notion that it was time for a change. As a result, the Conservatives were able to capitalize on these new circumstances by appealing to more voters from all regions in Canada. This was not accompanied, however, by the creation of a party climate of opinion. Thus, between 1951 and 1956, intraparty differences across regional lines were high in 67 percent of the questions, but between 1957 and 1959, the years of greatest popularity, they had risen to 91 percent. The dropoff in voter appeal indicated in the elections of 1962 and 1963 was anticipated by a drop in high intraparty IGH's between 1960 and 1962 to 71 percent of the questions asked.[5] Even if not too much is read into this last finding, it does still suggest that the Conservatives were best able to achieve cross-regional homogeneity when their appeal was restricted primarily to those to whom voting Conservative had become a customary practice. This tends to be further substantiated by inspection of IGH's constructed according to whether respondents were supporting the Conservatives for two elections. There was an accumulation of high IGH's between 1956 and 1957, during a time when the electoral trend was in favour of the Conservatives. That is, the attraction of new voters is often *not* accompanied by their incorporation into a party point of view (see Table 55). The Liberals exhibit similar tendencies. At the time of their greatest electoral strength, they also showed the highest proportion of intraparty differences: 91 percent between 1951 and 1956. While they were in opposition between 1957 and 1959, intraparty differences were lowest, 64 percent of the questions. In 1960 to 1962, 71 percent of the IGH's were high, a proportion identical to that of the Conservatives. While the Liberals increased their share of seats in the House of Commons in the elections of 1962 and 1963, their share of the popular vote remained similar to that of the Conservatives, indicating that they had not appreciably broadened their electoral base. For Liberals, examining IGH's on party stability gives us no further insight, since these are dispersed without any apparent pattern through the years for which we have information.

Considering responses over the time span available, no trend toward greater or lesser influence could be discerned for the CCF/NDP.

---

[5] Number of questions used was: twelve for the 1951–1956 period, eleven for 1957–1959, and seven for 1960–1962.

Table 55

TRENDS IN DISTRIBUTION OF HIGH INTRAPARTY IGH's ACCORDING
TO STABILITY OF PARTY PREFERENCE, 1951–1962

Year of survey	Number of combinations of party preference and stability of preference	Number of high intraparty IGH's			
		Conservative	Liberal	CCF	Social credit
1951	2	0	0	1	0
1954	5	2	1	1	2
1955	1	0	1	0	0
1956	7	4	2	1	2
1957	11	3	2	3	2
1958	2	0	1	a	a
1959	1	0	1	0	a
1960	4	2	0	1	2
1961	2	0	1	0	1
1962	3	0	0	1	1

a Not calculated.
NOTE: The greater the number of high intraparty IGH's, the greater the lack of consensus within parties.

There was, however, some slight suggestion of greater party influence since 1956.

Generalizations must be made with caution because similar questions were not asked every year, yet the influence of Social Credit on opinions seems to have operated in a curve. It was low up to 1956, greatest between 1957 and 1960, and low again in 1962. Between the general elections of 1953 and 1957 Social Credit gained strength in Manitoba and Saskatchewan and lost slightly in Alberta and British Columbia. These changes in supporters in the West may have then contributed to a greater homogeneity of outlook. But it was in 1962 that the impact of new voters from Quebec was felt. Intraparty differences were great on all three questions asked that year: on the Commonwealth, a new flag, and a labour party. For example, prairie respondents were highly opposed to the formation of a labour party, those in British Columbia were slightly less opposed, but the majority in Quebec thought that such a new party would be good for Canada.

A further indication of the impact of new kinds of supporters comes from examining intraparty IGH's for respondents who favoured Social Credit in two elections, those who switched parties, and those who do not remember how they voted; a large share of the latter are likely to have not voted (see Table 55). Generally such IGH's on voting stability are low for all parties, but the difference between new and more stable supporters was great for Social Crediters in 1960, 1961, and 1962 on questions on independence. No control was introduced here for region, but it is most likely that new voters in Quebec were reducing party unanimity.

Regional climates of opinion.—From evidence supplied by Gallup Polls, and from scholarly observations on the course of Canada's development, it is reasonable to conclude that, up until now at least, sectionalism has inhibited the development of a concept of nationhood for which a political party could find wide support in all regions. If anything, traditions of the British parliamentary system have helped control much of the sectionalism inherent in Canadian life.[6] It is a frequent and now commonplace observation that sectional interests have led to the emergence of minor parties in Canada; but these same interests have also shaped the two older parties. As a result, the older parties have favoured compromise and the avoidance of ideological consistency in an attempt to appeal to as many disparate groups as possible. When the opinions of supporters of the same party in different localities are compared, we can more truly appreciate the difficulty of achieving this wide appeal. The difficulty may be partly explained, in the modern era of rapid communication, in terms of a conflict between policies and pronouncements made on national issues and the response of provincial parties with the same name, as well as federal candidates, to local conditions. Among these local conditions are the existing political climates of opinion and the natures of the parties contending for power. For example, Ross Thatcher, leader of the provincial Liberal party in Saskatchewan and a former member of the CCF, has often publicly declared himself opposed to the mildly left-of-centre policies of the national Liberal party. In Manitoba, the provincial Liberals are considered more conservative than the Conservatives, while in Alberta the provincial Liberals are essentially a third conservative party. In the 1963 provincial election in that

[6] Lipset has interpreted the problem of parties in Canada as lying specifically in an incompatibility between the social structure and the political institutions. "Canada's political party problem is a result of the fact that its social structure and bases for political division are essentially comparable to the American and French pattern, but it retains a form of government which requires disciplined parliamentary parties, and which does not permit cross-party alignments in the House of Commons, sharp divergences among the federal programs of the parties from province to province, or democratic methods of solving internal party cleavages. Whenever a section, class, ethnic group, or province finds itself in basic conflict with its basic party allegiance, its only alternative is to go over to the other party, with which it may be in even greater disagreement on other issues." S. M. Lipset, "Democracy in Alberta," Part II, *Canadian Forum*, 34, December, 1954, p. 197.

province, the Liberals attempted to campaign on the issue of provincial takeover of electric power in an area where some utilities are already publicly owned. This program was played down, however, in the face of opposition from those within the party—a stance which Liberals in central Canada found hard to accept.[7] Such differences in approach by parties bearing the same label have undoubted consequences for the outcome of federal elections and the shaping of opinions. For example, in the 1957 survey on government versus private resource development, the order of preference for private enterprise by Liberal supporters was, beginning with the most favourable, British Columbia, the prairie provinces, Ontario, the Maritimes, and Quebec.

Regional differences also have implications for the minor parties. Social Credit did not begin growing as an important electoral force in Quebec until 1960 but even before that time differences in outlook were apparent between the eastern and western wings of the party. But the West itself is not homogeneous, and in most surveys where regional differences emerged, although these were largely due to the distribution of opinions in Quebec, variations also existed between British Columbia and the prairie provinces. For example, in the 1954 questions on foreign development of resources, most opposition was in Quebec, but it was also high in British Columbia. In that year's question on the Commonwealth, most respondents in favour were in British Columbia, fewer in the prairies, and fewest in Quebec. Those in favour of the Queen's picture on money and stamps were most often found on the prairies, less often in British Columbia, and least often in Quebec. British Columbia was more disapproving of the Duke of Windsor as Governor-General in 1956 than the prairies, while Quebec respondents were high on "no opinions." The 1962 survey on the flag found a majority favouring the Red Ensign in British Columbia, the Union Jack in the prairies, and a new flag in Quebec. While the data used here have indicated that Social Credit has been fairly successful in controlling regional differences, this is partly related to the unevenness in sampling of Social Credit supporters. Differences

---

[7] These generalizations are derived from newspaper reports, information about party conventions, and interviews with party supporters and officials. A systematic examination of regional differences within parties of the same name has been neglected by Canadian political scientists, although there has been some published comment concerning the controversy between the Ontario Liberals under Mitchell Hepburn and the federal Liberal government. See, for example, H. M. Clokie, *Canadian Government and Parties*, Toronto: Longmans Green, 1946, p. 200. Regional differences within parties make up part of the subject of study in Frederick C. Engelmann and Mildred A. Schwartz, *Political Parties and the Canadian Social Structure*, Toronto: Prentice-Hall of Canada, 1967.

which do appear suggest that there are distinct climates of opinion in each region.

If regional factors have more significance for the major parties, this is because these parties are forced, by their very nature, to cope with the problem of supplying national leadership in a diversified society. Sectionalism has restrained the growth of national parties, and with them, the development of an unambiguous public conception of the nation.

ORIGIN AND PARTY

We will consider "origin" here to refer to religion, official language (whether English, French, or both), and birthplace (usually of respondents but, in a few instances, of their parents). In Part II, information on these characteristics indicated that on questions of independence Protestants, foreign-born, and English-speaking respondents were relatively favourable to British and Commonwealth ties, whereas Catholic and French-speaking respondents were more likely to approve of independence and ties with the United States. On questions of foreign commitments, Protestants and English-speaking respondents were more inclined to take an interventionist stand. Although sufficient data were not available on questions of internal cleavages it did appear that English-speaking Canadians were becoming more receptive to bilingualism. They differed from the French in being more favourable to federal responsibility for unemployment problems, but there was little difference between the language groups with respect to attitudes toward education. The advocacy of Canadian symbols was a source of difference between origin groups, the French-speaking and Catholics being most in favour. The position of origin groups was less clear with respect to the role which government should play. Thus, the French-speaking vacillated in their approval of private enterprise, but the French-speaking, Catholic, and Canadian-born tended to be less in favour of social-welfare measures than their opposites, while at the same time being more receptive to government cultural activities. This brief summary, then, may serve as a reminder of the ways in which origin relates to opinion.

Religion

Our concern in this section is not with these over-all effects but with the interaction between party and origin in helping shape a national identity. In examining first those surveys for which a religion and party were available, we found that religion was the one factor affecting opinion over which party had least effect. Religion here was even more critical than region. Cross-party Indices of Group Homogeneity for Catholics and Protestants showed, not surprisingly, greater unanimity for Catholics across party lines. This is understandable in the light of denominational differences within Protestantism and the correlation of Catholicism with French origin and residence in Quebec. And, according to the 1961 census, approximately 90 percent of those of French origin were also Catholic, and 30 percent of the remaining Catholics in Canada were of other origins. The relation between religion and politics, as manifested in voting behaviour, was also present, albeit not as strongly, outside Quebec.[8] Catholics are a much more homogeneous group than Protestants, but they lack a complete coincidence of origin characteristics. As a result, low interparty IGH's occurred for Catholics in only about half the questions, so that we cannot consider the opinions of these respondents to be highly uniform[9] (see Table 56).

TABLE 56

RELATION BETWEEN PARTY PREFERENCE AND RELIGION

Religion	Cross-party IGH's for religious groups	
	Number of possible combinations with party	Percent low interparty IGH's
Protestant	23	39
Catholic	23	52

Party	Intraparty IGH's related to religion	
	Number of possible combinations with religion	Percent low intraparty IGH's
Conservative	23	13
Liberal	23	26
CCF/NDP	21	62
Social Credit	17	35

NOTE: The greater the proportion of low IGH's the greater the consensus within the group.

[8] Robert R. Alford, "The Social Bases of Political Cleavage in the 1962 Canadian General Election," in *Papers on the 1962 Election,* ed. by John Meisel, Toronto: University of Toronto Press, 1964, pp. 203–234.

[9] An attempt to differentiate within the Protestant and Catholic groups between those who were frequent churchgoers compared with those who were not did not produce any consistent findings.

Religion and party support.—Yet although neither religious group can be considered highly homogeneous in its opinions, religion is important in hindering a united outlook by party supporters. With few exceptions, the two major religions directed their adherents into the positions we have already indicated, regardless of their party affiliation. At times, this resulted in cross-party consensus within a religion. This was true, for example, of the Catholics with respect to the 1961 question on Britain joining the European Common Market, the 1960 question on neutrality for Canada, and the 1954 question with respect to pictures of the Queen. This was also true for Protestants in the 1960 question on continued immigration, the 1956 question on choice of the Duke of Windsor as Governor-General, and the 1955 question on government activities in cultural areas.

But even more interesting are many of the remaining questions where each party had its own climate which affected the expression of religious points of view. These appear to be neither strictly religious nor party positions, but combinations of the two. For example, there were three questions available on Canada's continuation in the Commonwealth. On each of these Protestant, Conservative party supporters were most in favour of continuing Commonwealth relations. This view was slightly less pronounced among Protestant Liberals and dropped off considerably for Protestant CCF/NDP and Social Credit supporters. Generally, a similar direction of opinion followed for Catholic party supporters, although in the 1954 survey it was Catholic Liberals who were most in favour of the Commonwealth. Yet, among Catholics, Conservative and Liberal differences were much less pronounced than among Protestants, although for all parties internal religious differences were great.

Religious differences, both inhibited and exaggerated within parties, serve mainly as the basis for significant political cleavages. Their continued impact in what otherwise can be seen as a modern industrialized country bespeaks the importance of traditional values in Canada despite some evidences of growing secularization.[10] Up until the present at least, according to Alford's analysis of Gallup Polls taken before federal elections, religion, and in particular Catholicism, has been critical in hindering the development of class-based voting

---

[10] This is represented by the growth of a laical movement in Quebec, the proposal to subordinate religious authority over the school system to the state in that province and the increase in interfaith marriages. See David M. Heer, "The Trend of Interfaith Marriages in Canada: 1922–1957," *American Sociological Review*, 27, April, 1962, pp. 245–250; Charles Taylor, "L'État et la laïcité," *Cité Libre*, 14, février, 1963, pp. 3–6.

such as is found in other Anglo-American democracies.[11] In addition
to the relatively low level of secularization of the country as a whole,
the importance of religion as a political influence is reinforced for
the majority of Catholics by the possession of a common language and
territory.

Sources of religious influence.—Our analysis of political problems
has not included specifically religious questions since these do not
often become political concerns at the federal level. Religion plays
a prominent role in education, but this comes under the jurisdiction
of provincial governments. At the time of Manitoba's admission into
Confederation the provision of separate schools to its Roman Catholic
residents did become a national issue, but the responsibility has since
been transferred, although the problem remains current in that
province and in others. The present emphasis on education and
the concern of religious bodies, Protestant as well as Catholic, with
socializing the young through the school system contribute to the
saliency of religious divisions. Although education is a provincial
matter, its importance and its tie-in with religion contribute to the
primacy of religion at the national level.

Divorce, though not as pressing an issue as education, is another
example of the way religious concerns affect legislative processes. Because of the general reluctance of politicians to disturb significant
interest groups, religion plays a part in restricting changes in either
the grounds for divorce or the procedures for obtaining it in Quebec
and Newfoundland.[12] Thus religious affiliation is regarded as both a
critical social characteristic and one with implications for the political
process.

The primary emphasis of this study is on the way political parties
and other social groups structure political opinions rather than on
the social bases of party support. But affinities of social groups for
different political parties, particularly over periods of time, have implications for the responses of those groups to a party climate of
opinion. Our own data suggest two ways this may operate; either by
the attraction of a religious group to a party, or its opposition to a
party.

The effects of attraction.—We contend that when a party attracts

[11] Robert R. Alford, *Party and Society,* Chicago: Rand-McNally, 1963, especially
pages 272–278.

[12] Neither province provides legal means for divorce and residents wishing to
dissolve their marriages must appeal to the Parliament of Canada. New procedures
were introduced in the 1964 session as a result of the tactics of two NDP members
of Parliament.

large numbers of supporters from religious groups which have, in at least some respects, opposing views on politically significant issues, this will result in a strain on party consensus. Catholic supporters are most often found in the Liberal party, yet religious cleavages are held in check in only about one-quarter of the instances examined here. It might be argued that this indicates an unstable attachment of Catholics to the Liberal party and that, as they become aware of the incompatibility of their viewpoints with those of Protestant supporters, presumably through education and the mass media, they will leave this party for another. For example, Meisel found in his study of one Ontario community that those closest to the Church were more likely to vote Conservative, while rank and file Catholics favoured the Liberals. He argued from this that the former were responding to the Church's position on political issues and, unlike the latter, were not carried along by traditional loyalties.[13] One possibility is that if the laity were to become informed of this position, it also would change its party preference, at least in some cases.

The ability of a party to appeal to both Catholics and Protestants and at the same time impose a party viewpoint on supporters is more likely to come about when circumstances call for strong partisanship. This could happen when the issues at stake are seen as more significant than religious loyalties or when the party is engaged in a struggle that requires a high level of commitment from its supporters. For example, the distribution of high intraparty Indices of Group Homogeneity over time suggests that the Liberal party was slightly more effective in overcoming religious cleavages during a time when the party was out of favour with the electorate generally. At that period, the need for party loyalty was sufficiently strong to subdue internal differences. This might suggest that, for the Liberals, party consideration can be of paramount significance only when less committed supporters are excluded. Yet, because of the position which the Liberal party takes on most issues, this does not necessitate the wholesale exclusion of large segments of the Catholic population, as is the case with the CCF/NDP, where some religious loyalties may also be at stake.

Attraction of support from various religions may play a positive role in the development of a united party outlook where the major religious bodies have the opportunity to contribute to the dominant climate of opinion. This has been true at times for the Liberals. Al-

[13] John Meisel, "Religious Affiliation and Electoral Behaviour: A Case Study," *Canadian Journal of Economics and Political Science,* 22, November, 1956, pp. 481–496. The affinity of the Catholic Church for the Conservative party, especially in Quebec, has a long history. See, for example, Mason Wade, *The French-Canadian Outlook,* Toronto: McClelland and Stewart, 1964, p. 63.

though Protestants and Catholics agree, partly, only on questions of internal cleavages, here it is the Catholic position which appears to have affected the viewpoints of Protestants in their evaluation of immigration and their preference for provincial powers. Party homogeneity is attained, then, through the influence of the majority Catholics in affecting the dominant climate of opinion. This is unlike the case of the CCF/NDP where *party* policies and ideology are the major determinants of the opinions of supporters.

The effect of having large proportions of Catholic and Protestant supporters is further complicated by the nature of the identification that members of a religion have with the church. For example, although those directly connected with the Catholic Church hierarchy may find a particular party attractive, this may have little influence on rank and file Catholics because the latter identify with their religion more as a subcommunity than as an association.[14] The most notable example of identification with a subcommunity going contrary to that with an association is that of Wilfrid Laurier and his leadership of the Liberal party. The party at that time was still, in the eyes of the Catholic Church, suspected of the anticlerical radicalism of continental liberal parties, but the assumption of leadership by Laurier, himself a Catholic, was sufficient to attract Catholic support to the party despite the Church's animosity. In other instances as well, the candidacy of coreligionists provides a further impetus for supporting a particular party. Visibility of the success of Catholics in the Liberal party is another factor serving to tie Catholics to it. In itself, however, it does little to insure the unanimity of views between Catholics and Protestants within the party, although it does provide some basis for establishing a minimal consensus.

The interrelation between religion and political party is best illustrated by a comparison of Liberals and Conservatives. The latter are a major political party which is almost totally unable to restrain divergent viewpoints among its Protestant and Catholic supporters. The Conservatives, like the CCF/NDP, count Catholics as only a minority among their supporters. Even so, unlike the newer party, they do not offer sufficiently strong partisan solutions to national problems which might overcome religious cleavages, nor as in the case of the Liberals, do they permit at least some instances where Catholics may help create the dominant party climate of opinion. It was noted at the conclusion of Chapter VII that Conservative party supporters were becoming more

[14] See Gerhard Lenski, *The Religious Factor*, rev. ed.; Garden City: Doubleday Anchor, 1963, for discussion on the differences between these two concepts and their implications for political behaviour.

like those of other parties. Yet this movement toward a national consensus is not yet reflected within the party with respect to religion.
We have no evidence to indicate whether this means that the Conservative attraction for Catholics is a tenuous one, but the evidence
of continuing religious differences at least means that the Conservative
party's contribution to a definition of national identity is hampered
by its lack of internal consensus.

From the surveys it appears that, of the minor parties, the Social
Credit party has always attracted more Catholic support than has the
CCF; this support increased with its popularity in Quebec. Opposite
to expectations, this change in the character of supporters was no
strain on party consensus and did not lead to pronounced intraparty
differences. If anything, increased support from Catholics for the
Social Credit party was accompanied by a trend toward greater consensus. In addition, a number of questions indicated unusual response
patterns for both religious groups. This atypicality may be related to
the smallness of the Social Credit samples which might produce an
unrepresentative picture. If this is so, then we must regrettably conclude that we do not know the effects of religion on Social Crediters.

The effects of opposition.—The case of the Liberal party demonstrated some of the possible effects of large-scale support from the
two major religious groupings. Of special interest was the ability of
the Liberal party to obtain support from Catholics, even though, at
some points in the party's history, the Church actively opposed it.
When Church opposition is effective, a low level of support from
members of the religious body should result. When, however, group
members do favour the opposed party, their opinions are likely to be
strongly in keeping with the party position. For example, the CCF/
NDP is, of the four parties, best able to control religious cleavages. At
the same time, compared with the others, it receives least support from
Catholics. Faced with the historic opposition of the Catholic Church
to socialism, and the identification of the CCF with centralist policies,
presumably inimicable to many Catholics who are also provincial
rightist French Canadians, those Catholics who support the CCF/NDP
must make some significant break with tradition. Presumably this
break is more likely to occur in the highly industrialized provinces
of Ontario and British Columbia, where socioeconomic factors assume
greater relevance.

Language

Religions presumably have been able to establish a communality of
outlook extending to political issues, but this aspect of their influ-

ence has undoubtedly lessened as societies become more secular. Yet religious bodies in countries such as Austria, Italy, and Germany continue to play an overt role in politics through their connection with specific parties. But even in countries where religious parties do not exist, religion has a bearing on political behaviour. In these countries, largely the Anglo-American ones, which are a prototype of what Almond has called "homogeneous, secular political cultures," [15] religious identity probably owes a good deal of its political significance to the strength of communal rather than associational ties.

Unlike religion, language is not affected by moves toward secularization and provides an important medium for communicating a common outlook. One of the first tasks in developing a national consciousness is the creation of a literature which inspires and reinforces national pride. In Canada, a writer in English is constantly faced with comparison with other English-speaking writers who proceed from a richer cultural heritage. The result has been said to inhibit Canadian artistic development. The French writer is not faced with quite the same problems, but he too is affected by the circumstances of Canadian existence. In Canada, however, the French language more than any other single factor provides the most important ethnic cleavage and focus of loyalty. This tends to be confirmed by our own data. Despite the fact that religion, when compared with party, has a stronger effect on opinion than membership in a language group, specific linguistic groups—the French and bilingual—are both considerably more homogeneous than any religious group (see Table 57).

French-speaking Canadians are more often like each other than like others supporting the same political parties. The French language through the school system, the mass media, and normal discourse has provided the essential means for the continuation of French existence. Provision for the strengthening of such communication and education are regarded as essential by many French-speaking Canadians. In particular, the Canadian Broadcasting Corporation is seen as an important agency for the dissemination of French language and culture, and pressure for the extension of French language teaching outside Quebec is greater than at any other time in Canadian history. The opinions of those who give their official language as both French and English are similar although not identical to those of French-speaking respondents. We can expect that much the same factors which promote an identity of interest among the French-speaking operate for the bilingual as well. We can also expect that facility in the two languages

[15] Gabriel A. Almond, "Comparative Political Systems," in *Political Behavior*, ed. by Heinz Eulau, S. J. Eldersveld, and M. Janowitz, Glencoe: Free Press, 1956, p. 36.

TABLE 57

RELATION BETWEEN PARTY PREFERENCE AND OFFICIAL LANGUAGE

Language	Cross-party IGH's for language groups	
	Number of possible combinations with party	Percent low IGH's across parties
English	30	37
French	30	67
Both	29	76

Party	Intraparty IGH's related to language	
	Number of possible combinations with language	Percent low intraparty IGH's
Conservative	30	37
Liberal	30	33
CCF/NDP	24	79
Social Credit	28	57

NOTE: The greater the proportion of low IGH's the greater the consensus within the group.

and thus exposure to more than one culture would make the bilingual person even more self-conscious than the unilingual.[16] Consensus is not a feature of the English-speaking group. Unlike the French, those who answer that English is their official language represent a variety of ethnic backgrounds and social interests. In this instance, party preference is much more significant as a factor influencing opinions.

The major parties and low consensus.—At the outset of this discussion on origin the general effects of language on opinion were stated. Examined in more detail, it appeared that no trends existed in the relative strength of language versus party. The most prominent finding was that parties which draw on greater numbers of French supporters are also characterized by less internal consensus.

The Conservative and Liberal parties were similar in their inability to establish intraparty consensus, yet there were some notable features distinguishing their supporters. For example, bilingual respondents in 1954 expressed themselves as most in favour of the development of resources through foreign capital, while the French-speaking were least

[16] This last point tends to be substantiated from our analysis of "no opinions." See Chapter XII. There is also evidence from our surveys that the bilingual are better educated than the unilingual, especially the French.

in favour. This difference was sharpest among Liberal supporters. Although in most cases the bilingual respondents tended to be more like the French, in this case their views approving of foreign development were even more pronounced than those of the English. This may have indicated less fear on the part of those who share in the two cultures of increasing their contacts with outsiders when it is to their economic advantage. On issues of social welfare also, the Liberals were most troubled by differences in outlook. Thus, in 1957, French-speaking respondents were much more satisfied with the raise in old-age pensions than were either English-speaking or bilingual respondents. In 1956, the English in particular were most approving of a government-operated hospital or medical plan. These last questions were not troublesome to Conservatives, since the French-speaking and bilingual were as much in favour as their English-speaking counterparts, making them in fact more approving of these welfare measures than their fellows among Liberal supporters. These responses could be considered as indications that the French, historically more secure in the Liberal party, were, at least at that time, responding with a traditional distrust of the federal government's activities in social welfare, even though the party had been moving in this direction for many years.

French Conservatives, who are more likely to be party switchers, have fewer of these traditional loyalties and might then be expected to react like their English compatriots. Yet examination of questions about internal cleavages and political symbols showed that even though the percentage of high intraparty IGH's was similar for the Liberals and Conservatives, the former were much less polarized along language lines. The one exception concerned opinions of the Duke of Windsor as a possible Governor-General, a question asked in 1956. In this instance, the French-speaking and bilingual respondents were about as approving of the Duke of Windsor as the English-speaking. But the principal concern here is with patterns of responses, and these suggest the existence, although highly tenuous, of a Liberal party viewpoint at least with respect to questions on cleavages and symbols. This is a finding which tended to emerge, although again in this indistinct manner, in connection with the interaction of religion and party support.

The minor parties and high consensus.—Of the four parties, the CCF/NDP was best able to control language differences. When language did take precedence over party in the CCF/NDP, differences in opinion followed the national pattern. The exceptions were based on such small numbers that they were hardly worth considering.

Social Credit followed the CCF/NDP in internal similarity. Yet again the small size of the French-speaking sample prevented an adequate examination of differences between the language groups.

In considering why the CCF/NDP, and to a lesser extent the Social Credit party, can control internal differences much more effectively than either of the two major parties, there arises the problem of interpreting results from a small sample. There were many instances, especially after 1954, when French-speaking and bilingual respondents supporting these parties were so few that differences, even if they did exist, did not have the opportunity to emerge. This may have been partly a result of sampling, since the two parties did not attract a large share of supporters and thus included few French-speaking and bilingual persons. But it is also true, as in regional differences, that these parties have avoided the problem of reconciling opposing viewpoints among the language groups by not attracting them into the party fold. Even when they did become supporters of the minor parties, the French and bilingual represented such a small minority of their groups that they were likely as well to be atypical members. Aside from the problems posed by sampling errors and small numbers, there was the further disadvantage of having only one survey conducted after 1958 in which information about language was available. Yet it was in this later period that Social Credit increased its strength in Quebec and consequently among the French-speaking. Further evidence would have likely lent support to our contention that a larger proportion of French-speaking supporters, particularly if they were recruited suddenly without the opportunity to become socialized into a partisan point of view, would result in a lessening of party consensus. The one question asked in 1962 on organized labour supporting its own party did in fact show a sharp difference between French and English within the Social Credit party, but this is not evidence for any firm generalizations. In the light of the available information it was only possible to suggest the mentioned reasons for the greater homogeneity in viewpoints of CCF/NDP and Social Credit supporters.

Birthplace

The continued settlement of Canada by large numbers of immigrants and the increase in those of non-British and non-French origin, requires a careful examination of the ways in which these groups establish ties with the political community. Yet aside from impressionistic writings, little systematic information on the political behaviour of immigrant groups is available. Data from the Gallup Polls in this area were also limited, although we can presume that country of birth would have important implications for views on Canada's identity. Information was available on respondent's birthplace for only seven questions and these were from two surveys. Another two questions gave parents' birthplace, and a final one provided information on national origin. The nature of the responses made one doubt even the representative nature of the foreign-born. Compared with those born in Canada, the foreign-born appeared more favourable to Britain and to British symbols, and more often opposed to American policies. This suggested that most of the foreign-born interviewed, or their parents, were immigrants from the British Isles. Considering the usual problems of interviewing, it was hardly likely that in a national survey interviewers would seek out the foreign-born, particularly if this meant that they were not fluent in either English or French.

The one instance where a notable difference which also related to party affiliation appeared between native and foreign-born respondents concerned questions on government activities. The foreign-born among the Liberals were more consistently in favour of government participation. Although this tendency appeared in most instances in other parties, it was most distinct for the Liberals. Beyond conjecturing that the sharp contrast within the Liberal party may have stemmed from the fact that the foreign-born were more likely to have been exposed to government economic planning and welfare activities in their homelands, while Liberal supporters would include a larger proportion of French Canadians opposed to government involvement in these areas, the data were insufficient to press analysis further. As usual, the CCF/NDP had the fewest intraparty differences, the Liberals had the most (see table 58).

Influences of Origin

This examination of the interaction between party and origin points up the great influence of religion on political opinions. At the same time, however, both Protestants and Catholics are also influenced by the political parties they support. This differs to some extent from the influence of membership in an official language group; French origin, as indicated by language, leads to a greater homogeneity of outlook, transcending influence of party, than membership in any religious group. Country of birth is probably another important dimension of origin, but data were not sufficient to permit adequate generalizations.

TABLE 58
RELATION BETWEEN PARTY PREFERENCE AND BIRTHPLACE

Birthplace of respondent or parent	Cross-party IGH's for birthplace	
	Number of possible combinations with party	Percent low IGH's across parties
Canada	9	33
Elsewhere	9	78

Party	Cross-party IGH's related to birthplace	
	Number of possible combinations with birthplace	Percent low intraparty IGH's
Conservative	10	60
Liberal	10	40
CCF/NDP	8	87
Social Credit	8	62

NOTE: The greater the proportion of low IGH's the greater the consensus within the group.

The two major parties are somewhat alike with respect to internal homogeneity, but the Liberal party is more effective than the Conservative in managing religious differences among its supporters. Of the four parties, the Liberal has the broadest social base. The evidence is, at least on internal national issues, that origin tends to be subordinated to party. This suggests that the party may make an appeal based on principle in respect to these issues. If this could be extended without at the same time losing the support of diverse origin groups, the Liberal party would have the opportunity of adding considerably to the definition of Canada's identity.

Although the Conservative party has a relatively broad social base, its dominant climate of opinion has not had a strong influence on those origin groups which constitute a minority within the party. They are willing to offer their votes, but they have not yet been encouraged to make the commitment which would allow widespread consensus on the Conservative view of Canada's nature.

Of the four parties, the CCF/NDP appeared best able to control opinion differences associated with origin. This is, as we have noted, partly the result of its narrow social base; Catholics and French Canadians are not attracted to the party in great numbers. Usually when they are, the explicitness of the party's position on social issues presupposes some commitment to the party's stand in order for them to become supporters. As a consequence, intraparty consensus tends to be high, yet the contributions which the party may make to the development of a national identity are for the same reasons relatively low.

The Social Credit party is perhaps similar to the CCF/NDP in its degree of intraparty consensus, but it has been difficult to examine this adequately because of sampling limitations. However, the tensions following from the sudden influx of Catholic and French Canadian supporters to the party in 1960 illustrate the difficulties of such parties in extending their social bases and adapting their principles to encompass these new groups. The breakup of the national party into two wings, one of which is centred in Quebec, indicates how inadequately the cause of national unity is served by the activities of this party.

THE CONSEQUENCES OF DIVERSITY ✗

Detailed analysis of responses grouped according to region and origin has confirmed the continuing significance of these factors in shaping the outlook of Canadians. Compared with them, political parties have a more difficult task in establishing climates of opinion. The relative success of the minor parties in this respect is related to their narrow social base, their appeal to principle, and, at least for the CCF/NDP, more widespread membership participation.[17] A shifting social base has been considered to be one source of difficulty in creating a united outlook. This seems to have occurred most noticeably in the Conservative and Social Credit parties, with the result that, during periods of change, voters may have been attracted without at the same time a marked impression being made on their opinions. Of the two older parties, the Liberal has appeared better able to handle potential differences associated with origin. On the basis of available information, we have related this to a broader social base, a longer history of appeal to diverse groups, and the possibility that the party has arrived at a more consistent position, at least with regard to internal problems.

[17] Although the Social Credit party originally used the study groups which had provided the nuclei for the United Farmers of Alberta, no information is available about the role which rank and file play in the party at present, but it is not believed to be great.

X THE PULL BETWEEN PARTY
AND OTHER CHARACTERISTICS

SOCIAL CLASS AND PARTY

SOCIAL CLASS is important because it determines life style. Social classes, by structuring opportunity, can lead to the development of relatively distinctive systems of values which permeate various aspects of their members' lives. Sharing opportunities and values, members of social classes may unite either to protect their advantages or to overcome their disabilities. This union need not be formally organized for it to become politically significant. It is sufficient that class members recognize some communality of interest and see these interests best served by one or more political parties. Political parties, on the other hand, recognize and reinforce this through class-based appeals. Lipset says, for example, that

in every modern democracy conflict among different groups is expressed through political parties which basically represent a "democratic translation of the class struggle." Even though many parties renounce the principle of class conflict or loyalty, an analysis of their appeals and their support suggests that they do represent the interests of different classes. On a world scale, the principal generalization which can be made is that parties are primarily based on either the lower classes or the middle and upper classes. This generalization even holds true for the American parties, which have traditionally been considered an exception to the class-cleavage pattern of Europe.[1]

Yet a detailed study of class-based voting in Britain, Australia, the United States, and Canada indicates that there is least evidence of this in Canada.[2] Canada, then, appears to be an exception in modern industrialized societies.

The low incidence of class voting is further confirmed by our own findings on the extent of class factors affecting opinions, and comparisons of cross-party and intraparty Indices of Group Homogeneity. In

[1] S. M. Lipset, *Political Man*, Garden City: Doubleday, 1960, p. 220.
[2] Robert R. Alford, *Party and Society*, Chicago: Rand-McNally, 1963; Robert R. Alford, "The Social Bases of Political Cleavage in the 1962 Canadian General Election," in *Papers on the 1962 Election*, ed. by John Meisel, Toronto: University of Toronto Press, 1965, pp. 203–234.

general, region and origin were more important factors than social class. At the same time, the findings also indicated at least a moderate degree of importance for class which merits closer scrutiny, especially if Alford is correct in predicting that social class may become a more important basis of political behaviour in the future.[3] In any case, our concern, unlike that of Alford, is with the relation between social class, party preference, and *opinions*. Again, unlike Alford's study, despite the difficulties posed by sample size, the present study has attempted to evaluate the effects of minor parties as well as the two major ones.[4]

Part II discussed the general effects of social class on the development of Canada's identity. High social class position tended to be associated with greater preference for traditional external ties. Internally, population expansion and diversity was favoured, but no clear-cut point of view emerged about federal-provincial cleavages. As would be expected, high social class position also accompanied preference for private enterprise. But, surprisingly, there was little differentiation between classes with respect to government social-welfare measures. Political symbols did not produce distinctive viewpoints according to social class, but there was some suggestion that the desire for Canadian symbols was greatest in the middle class. Lower-class opinions tended to be less favourable to traditional external ties, to immigration, and to private enterprise. Finally, farm households, which are ordinarily difficult to classify in social-class terms, tended to resemble the upper and middle classes except in their opinions on issues of immigration and government activities in the cultural field, when they were more like the working class.

With this, then, as our background, we may look more closely at the way social class affects definitions of the nation's identity.

Occupation

Most researchers have found that the best single indicator of social class is occupation. In the subsequent discussion, the categories employed were derived from the occupation of the respondent's household head. This classification may account in part for the apparently moderate effects of social class on party opinion, but a primary contention of most theories of social class is that the main unit is the

[3] Alford, *Party and Society*, p. 285.
[4] In arriving at his estimations of class-based voting in Canada, Alford omits Social Credit supporters and combines CCF and Liberal supporters. In his 1965 paper, however, he treats the four parties separately.

family, and all members of that family resident in the same household normally share the same social-class position.

Some variation appeared in the degree of internal consistency of viewpoint among the occupational categories in this analyses. Greatest consensus across party lines was revealed by persons in farm and blue-collar households, while the business and professional groups had the smallest percentage of low cross-party Indices of Group Homogeneity. Yet it must also be noted that these variations were not great (see Table 59). All categories of course included a range of occupations; although farmers represent a single occupation, that category too included many types, facing different problems, and receiving different rewards. Even so, both blue-collar and farm households share sufficiently common conditions of life to make them more uniform than other groups in their opinions. These two groups in Canada, as well as in other countries, have often provided the basis for special-interest parties.

There was also some variation in the problem areas for which the

TABLE 59

RELATION BETWEEN PARTY PREFERENCE AND OCCUPATION OF HOUSEHOLD HEAD

| | Cross-party IGH's for occupational groups | |
Occupation	Number of possible combinations with party	Percent low IGH's across parties
Owners, managers, professionals	38	47
White collar	38	55
Blue collar	38	58
Farmers	38	63

| | Intraparty IGH's related to occupation | |
Party	Number of possible combinations with occupation	Percent low intraparty IGH's
Conservative	38	58
Liberal	38	53
CCF/NDP	36	67
Social Credit	33	70

NOTE: The greater the proportion of low IGH's the greater the consensus with the group.

various occupational categories showed relative agreement. For example, in white-collar households the greatest degree of cross-party consensus prevailed on issues of independence, whereas in blue-collar households consensus about symbols was greatest, and in farm households most agreement was about the role of government. Beyond the likelihood that farm households face similar social and economic conditions which make them more responsive to government activities, the data suggest no further reasons for this particular distribution of IGH's.

The major parties.—Among Conservatives and Liberals, questions about internal problems pertaining to cleavages and the role of government produced the largest proportion of intraparty differences. To a lesser extent, this was also true for the Liberals with respect to questions of independence. An examination of questions on internal cleavages did not indicate any unusual response patterns for either party or for any of the occupational categories. But it did show that opinions on internal cleavages were an important indicator of class differences within the two parties. Questions on government activities resulted in two unusual response patterns. Respondents in farm households, who also supported the Conservatives in 1956 and 1957, tended to favour government development of resources and pipelines, thus resembling blue-collar workers. Otherwise, the opinions of occupational groups within the Conservative and Liberal parties were along expected social-class lines. Opinions on independence showed class differences of the sort noted in Part II and at the outset of this section to be greatest in the Liberal party.

No distinctive trends in the distribution of high intraparty IGH's appeared for the Conservatives. The Liberals, however, manifested the familiar pattern of greater internal consensus across occupational lines during a time when electoral opposition toward the Liberal party was most pronounced. Social-class differences, like differences of origin, were less apparent in the viewpoints of Liberal supporters when the base of support was restricted to those more likely to have a relatively strong commitment to the party, despite its opposition role (see Table 60).

The minor parties.—The CCF/NDP showed greater internal homogeneity than either of the two older parties. Of all the parties, however, it had the fewest low intraparty IGH's on questions relating to the role of government. This is particularly noteworthy since this party has had the most explicitly class-based appeal. Many questions asked in this area previously proved troublesome to the party in establishing internal consensus, with trade-union affiliation and type

TABLE 60

TRENDS IN DISTRIBUTION OF HIGH INTRAPARTY IGH's
ACCORDING TO OCCUPATION OF HOUSEHOLD HEAD

Year	Number of possible combinations with occupation	Percent high intraparty IGH's			
		Conservative	Liberal	CCF/NDP	Social Credit
1951–1956	16	44	50	50	37
1957–1958[a]	13[b]	31	31	27	18
1960–1962	9[c]	33	67	11	33

[a] Information on occupation was not available for the 1959 survey.
[b] Results for the CCF and Social Credit are based on eleven questions.
[c] Results for Social Credit are based on six questions.
NOTE: The greater the proportion of high IGH's, the greater the lack of consensus within parties.

of community having greater influence on opinion. In 1956, residents in nonunion households and rural community residents were more likely than union and urban respondents to favour government action on social and economic policies. On these same questions, respondents in farm households were again more likely to take a progovernment stand than those in blue-collar households. But this was not true of questions asked in other years. Thus, in 1951, blue-collar householders favored an old-age pension without a means test as much as the farmers did, while those in business and professional households disapproved of this measure. But a question asked in 1955 on government support for cultural activities found business and professional householders most in favour, and farmers least so. Finally, a 1957 question about the raise in old-age pensions showed that white-collar householders were most dissatisfied with the raise while farmers were more likely to approve. It is difficult, then, to evaluate these results. We are again forced to ask whether the survey taken in 1956 was an unusual one or whether, if these questions had been repeated in later years, similar patterns would have emerged. Other problem areas showed both greater intraparty consensus and fewer unexpected responses. When differences did occur, even as tendencies rather than clear-cut differences, they suggested that it was the middle-class supporters of the CCF/NDP who helped to establish the dominant climate of opinion, even when by so doing they acted as "class traitors." Thus, in 1956, business and professional householders supporting the CCF tended to be less favourable than other groups to the United States and to the Commonwealth; in 1957, to be most opposed to the Queen Mother as a prospective Governor-General; and in 1962, to be most in favour of the formation of a labour party. In 1960, those in white-collar households were most clearly agreeable to Canada pursuing a policy of neutrality.[5]

The CCF/NDP has shown some trend to greater consensus since 1960. This may be related to a number of factors. While the NDP had not yet been officially so designated by 1960, the formation of a new party was clearly in the offing, and, in a federal by-election during the same year, a candidate running in a traditionally Conservative constituency in Peterborough, Ontario, as a representative of this New Party, was elected. The excitement generated by this victory suggested to some observers that indeed a new party with a new appeal was coming into being.[6] One possibility, then, is that the formation of the NDP brought with it the means for bringing about greater internal consensus. This could be achieved through the alteration of the party's social base. Thus, if the differing viewpoints of blue-collar workers and farmers were a major source of tension it could be reduced if, since 1960, only those farmers who were in relative agreement with blue-collar workers continued to support the party. The theory is difficult to support but election results indicate that it might be valid. When NDP candidates ran for the first time, in 1962 and 1963, the results, anticipated to some degree in 1958, showed how the party's federal strength had shifted from rural to urban centres. Almost every seat won in those years was, if not in an urban industrialized constituency, at least in one in which agriculture did not predominate. Farm organizations had been important nuclei of support for the old CCF, but the more active partnership with organized labour which was to result in the NDP was apparently not attractive to many farm bodies, and few were represented at the 1961 founding convention of the party. A further indication of the shift in the character of supporters for the NDP appeared in the Gallup Poll surveys. From the surveys it is clear

[5] The greater concern of middle-class voters with what we have termed external problems (see for example Table 74), undoubtedly means that in whatever political party they find themselves, they will influence the dominant views on such issues. But in class-oriented parties, this is much less likely to be true for internal, particularly economic, problems, where class interests may be more often expressed by those of the working class. For example, the Greenwich study found that middle-class supporters of the Labour party were most in favour of self-government for parts of the Empire (one of the Labour party's election pledges), but on economic issues, there were sharp class differences within the party. Mark Benney and Phyllis Geiss, "Social Class and Politics in Greenwich," *British Journal of Sociology*, 1, 1950, p. 322.

[6] Pauline Jewett, "Voting in the 1960 Federal By-Elections at Peterborough and Niagara Falls: Who Voted New Party and Why?" *Canadian Journal of Economics and Political Science*, 28, February, 1962, pp. 35–49.

that, at least since 1960 and possibly even since 1958, support from farmers had dropped off, and that from blue-collar workers had increased.

If in fact a trend toward greater internal consistency is emerging in the NDP, it may be due in part also to the more deliberate attempts of the party to indoctrinate supporters in party viewpoints on issues and to involve them in party activities. Insofar as these attempts aid in overcoming occupational distinctions, party policies could be designed either to encourage class consciousness, even though it would mean that upper- and middle-class supporters must deliberately adopt working-class stands, or to provide a similar focus for all supporters regardless of their social class. Such policies would also help to account for the trend in the CCF/NDP toward lessened distinctions between trade-union and nonunion households. However, whether such increased indoctrination and membership participation has in fact occurred within the NDP is a matter of conjecture.

The kinds of issues which were suggested to respondents may also explain the apparent trend toward greater intraparty homogeneity in the CCF/NDP. As we have emphasized, the most divisive area has been the role of government. Yet questions about this have not been repeated in recent years. It is, therefore, impossible to know whether this area continues to be a source of division among occupational groups, or whether shifts in supporters (which we are fairly sure have occurred), or changes in the communication of policy (which we can at this point only suggest as a possibility), have either singly or in combination helped produce greater homogeneity of viewpoint.

Like the CCF/NDP, the Social Credit party was more homogeneous with respect to occupational differences than the major parties. The central problem in analyzing data on the Social Credit has been the inadequate sample with which we must work. As usual, this hindered us in generalizing. However, it does appear that usually when high intraparty IGH's occurred, opinions manifested occupational differences similar to those in the sample as a whole. The most distinctive difference was associated with the 1962 question on a new flag. On this issue business and professional and white-collar householders were most highly favourable to a new flag, while remaining occupational categories tended to favour the Red Ensign and the Union Jack. In the other parties business and professional householders were considerably less likely to respond in this manner. Little more can be added to this discussion of the Social Credit beyond repeating that it apparently shares with the CCF/NDP the ability to establish internal consensus which cuts across occupational groups.

A fuller analysis of these findings will be left until other indicators of social class have been examined. At the moment, however, a number of noteworthy points need to be emphasized. It is known from other sources that class-voting in Canada is relatively infrequent. Yet taking into account the opinions of occupational groups, it appears that class conflict, if such a strong term can be used here, takes place *within* the major parties. In the CCF/NDP, those in higher-class positions, attracted presumably on ideological rather than pragmatic grounds, presented the working-class point of view even more strongly than did those actually in such occupations. When the relations between region and origin and party were examined, it was found that the two older parties, and in particular the Liberal party, were best able to achieve internal consensus on questions concerning internal problems and not on those pertaining to external and symbolic ones. When the relations between occupation group and party were examined, however, the results were the contrary, with internal problems a major source of cleavage within the Liberal and Conservative parties.

Education

Education is also an important component of social class. The strong correlation between the social class of parents and the likelihood that children will be given an advanced education is due not only to the expense but also to the values which different social classes attach to education. When a particular educational level has been attained, it is also highly correlated with the kind of occupation that can be achieved. Most studies, then, find the same kind of behavioural and attitudinal distributions for various educational groups as for related occupational levels. If there were a perfect correlation between education and occupation as indicators of social class, there would be no need to treat education separately, but education appears to have distinctive features. Higher education in particular exposes individuals to a variety of experiences, deliberately attempts to broaden their horizons, and often results in changing their attitudes from those which they acquired from earlier agents of socialization. Advanced education may not always result in high social class. Individuals in this anomalous position often display political attitudes opposed to the *status quo*. The alienated intellectual then may become a ready recruit for radical political movements. For these reasons, the effect of education on opinion merits special attention. In addition, in this study classification of respondents was according to their own educational attainment unlike the classification of occupation, which was that of the head of the household. This allowed the direct effects of education to be manifested as they relate to the impact of parties on the opinions of their supporters. These supporters are conceived not as individuals with distinct occupations, years of schooling, origins, and so on, but rather as separate strata, in this case divided according to educational level.

In support of the contention that higher education will have the greatest impact on opinions we found that those with some university education displayed the greatest degree of opinion consensus across party lines (see Table 61). Differences between problem areas were not great, but the high-school educated were least homogeneous on issues of internal cleavages, and those with elementary schooling showed most variation on symbolic issues. Only two questions were available on the role of government, and it was difficult to predict what the results would have been if there had been a greater number and variety of such questions.

An examination of the impact of level of respondents' education on

TABLE 61

RELATION BETWEEN PARTY PREFERENCE AND EDUCATION

| | Cross-party IGH's for educational groups | |
Education	Number of possible combinations with party	Percent low IGH's across parties
Elementary	29	59
High school	29	55
University	29	66

| | Intraparty IGH's related to education | |
Party	Number of possible combinations with education	Percent low intraparty IGH's
Conservative	29	62
Liberal	29	38
CCF/NDP	27	70
Social Credit	16	81

NOTE: The greater the proportion of low IGH's, the greater the consensus within the group.

opinions shows the CCF/NDP and Social Credit to be internally the most homogeneous parties. They were followed in this respect by the Conservative party; the Liberal party was noticeably lacking in consensus across educational lines.

The major parties.—The most interesting question centres on the reasons for the different ways in which educational levels affect homogeneity of opinion in the Conservative and Liberal parties. The two parties also differed in their capacity to control occupational viewpoints, but this was not as pronounced as it was in the case of education. Comparing distinctive response patterns for the two parties on questions of independence, it was the less educated Conservatives in 1957 who favoured Canadian television and the more educated among the Liberals. In 1960, Liberals with some high-school education were most likely to favour an independent course for Canada.

On cleavages in 1960, the better educated among the Conservatives tended to be anti-Quebec, and among the Liberals to be anti-Ontario. This presumably reflects differences in the ethnic bases of the two parties, especially since the bilingual, unlike those speaking only French, also tend to have a large proportion with at least secondary schooling. These better-educated bilingual respondents are more often found among Liberal supporters. This difference in outlook is also probably related to the greater awareness of the better educated generally. They would thus be more cognizant of the more centralist viewpoint of Conservatives and have greater sympathy for provincial rights among Liberals.

The 1957 question on resource development found preference toward private enterprise increasing with more education in the case of Conservative supporters. But Liberals with some university education were most often in favour of government development.

In that same year support for a Canadian rather than an English Governor-General was inversely related to increased education for Conservatives. Here again it was university-educated Liberals who were most in favour of a Canadian Governor-General. From these responses it appears that increased education tends to make Liberal supporters more nationalistic. Yet at the same time, it does not necessarily make them similar in outlook to others in their own party.

The minor parties.—In the CCF/NDP, the usual differences in opinion were found when respondents with elementary and secondary-school education were compared. The university educated, however, often took unique stands, appearing, for example, the most anti-American, pro-neutralist, most in favour of the formation of a labour party, and most in favour of the exercise of federal authority. Yet they did act more like their educational and social-class counterparts in other parties when, in 1954, they favoured the Queen's picture on stamps and money, and, in 1957, were most often satisfied with the old-age pension increase. More often however, the uniqueness of the university educated in terms of responses served to make them the most consistent representatives of their party's position. Yet insofar as the low level of ideological orientation found among most North American voters is also characteristic of the CCF/NDP to some extent, the attitudinal consistency of the better educated must produce a strain on the party which the relatively large proportion of low intraparty IGH's tends to belie. The achievement of this apparent degree of consensus, at least for the samples here, may therefore have been partly due to the relatively small number of university-educated respondents.

Social Credit supporters showed some unusual response patterns relative to educational level. But for the most part, the differences were generally too small to be distinguished by the Index of Group Homogeneity. It may be a good guess that consensus is fairly widespread across educational levels—partly due to the low level of support from university educated—but sampling problems forbid a more intensive analysis of the sources and direction of variation.

The impact of higher education.—If the better educated are also more likely to assume leadership roles within their party, either as decision makers or as opinion leaders, then wherever they represent a specific point of view they will aid in giving their party its dominant orientation. In effect, this helps account partly for the anti-Americanism and centralism of the CCF/NDP and the pro-Canadian outlook and preference for provincial rights and government activity of the Liberals. At the same time, the more a party focuses its appeal on principle, the more potential strain is engendered, hindering the achievement of consensus. (Although if principles are instrumental in attracting supporters, they should also contribute to consensus.) It was noted, however, that consensus was greater for the CCF/NDP than for the Liberal party. We suggested that for the CCF/NDP this was at least partly due to the ideological bridge reaching from the better educated to the pragmatic interests of the less-well educated. For the Liberals such a bridge between educational levels did not appear to exist. By contrast, responses of Conservative supporters at the different educational levels tended to be similar to those for their related occupational groups. But these internal class differences were held relatively well in check, possibly because, in the absence of any explicit formulation of party principles, class differences are allowed to remain implicit. Although class differences do exist, they may not be considered by voters to be an important factor affecting their partisan choice.[7]

Some of these intraparty differences may also be affected by the character of party supporters. Trends in intraparty consensus are most noticeable for the Liberals. Between 1957 and 1959, when popular support was at its lowest, the party showed fewest internal differences. The opposite was true when the Liberals were in office in 1954, and again when popular favour picked up beginning in 1960. To a much lesser extent, an opposition role was also associated with greater internal consensus for the Conservatives. However, there are no discernible trends for either the CCF/NDP or the Social Credit. This might suggest that the opposition role, especially for the Liberals, led to a consolidation in the ranks of supporters. But in keeping with our previous discussion, the consolidation might also be associated with a disproportionate loss of supporters in one educational level. Because of their special position, changes in support from the university educated should presumably have the greatest impact. We repeat our former caution about using these survey data for determining with any degree of accuracy the social bases of party support, yet in this instance we note some fairly consistent patterns. Most significantly, those periods when internal consensus for the Liberals was at its lowest were accompanied by an increase in the proportion of university-educated supporters. When general support was on the increase, the university educated were presumably attracted to the Liberal party as a focus for their nationalist sentiments, which were in contrast to the views of less-well-educated supporters. The Conservatives, who were not so much affected either by high intraparty IGH's or by trends in these, seemed to have a more even pattern of support from the university educated (see Table 62). The proportion of university-educated supporters of the CCF/NDP appeared to fluctuate without any relation to the distribution of high intraparty IGH's.

In attempting to account for the relative lack of consensus in the Liberal party between different educational groups we have drawn attention, although often in conjectural terms, to the role which the better educated play in all political parties. For the Conservatives this has not been so overt as to seriously affect party unity. The better-educated CCF/NDP supporters have played a more critical role in that party. Yet there has often been sufficient community of interest

---

[7] Robert T. McKenzie and Allan Silver, "Conservatism, Industrialism and the Working-Class Tory in England," *Transactions of the Fifth World Congress of Sociology,* Vol. III, 1964, pp. 191–202, where the authors give some of the reasons leading working class voters to support the British Conservative party.

TABLE 62

TRENDS IN SUPPORT FROM THE UNIVERSITY-EDUCATED FOR
CONSERVATIVES AND LIBERALS, 1954–1962

Year	Number of surveys used	Percent university-educated	
		Conservatives	Liberals
1954	3	11	12
1957	4	10	8
1958	1	9	5
1959	1	11	8
1960	1	8	8
1961	1	8	10
1962	2	9	13

NOTE: Figures given are percentages of total number of supporters with some known level of education.

to moderate differences between educational groups. The Liberals, however, have been most strongly affected by the divergent viewpoints of the better educated, preventing a coincidence of the party's orientation (which is presumably adopted by them), with that of the dominant climate of opinion.

We did have one additional means of classification, the interviewers' assessment of the respondents' socioeconomic status, based on a social and economic ranking of residential area, the exterior of the respondents' house and style of life, if this was visible. Intensive analysis shows, however, that this classification, used in our over-all assessment of relative opinion consensus, is an unreliable indicator of social class. For this reason we are not presenting further details on socioeconomic status.

The Effects of Social Class

The effects of social class are not as pronounced as those of origin or region, yet social class nevertheless is important for the unfolding of a national identity. For one thing, the popular assessment of national problems does not obviate class differences even though social class itself is not a major determinant of party preference, as Alford has described. Class differences, instead of being accentuated between political parties, exist within parties. This was particularly true for the Conservatives and Liberals. To some extent it was also true of the CCF/NDP, but in that party class differences were often not manifested, as middle class, better-educated supporters most clearly adopted the party's leftist, centralist, and isolationist orientation. Noteworthy as well was the fact that for all parties, class differences were centred on internal issues.

The implications for national identity are several. Since class conflict as such does not pose a difficult problem for any party, there is no polarization of parties along class lines to hinder the development of a national consensus. Yet it has been argued that this very lack of class polarization limits the emergence of a clear-cut *national* identity since such a lack is often associated with loosely organized political parties which cannot have a strong influence on their adherents, and with political issues and activities stressing localism and particularism.[8] This may be the long-range result of the absence of class-based parties, but class differences within parties still have some effect. In particular, intraparty consensus is limited by class differences on internal problems. The definitions and solutions offered by any party to internal problems are therefore affected by the extent to which the party is deliberately concerned with reconciling class differences in order to achieve electoral success, its success in attracting a varied class base, and its possession of recognizable programs and policies with a class content. Class differences have a greater effect on opinions on internal issues than on opinions on symbolic and external issues. Parties, then, have a much greater potential for flexibility in defining external and symbolic problems. At the same time we recall that this flexibility is seriously limited by factors of origin and region.

The better educated establish each party's dominant philosophy, yet in so doing they produce a strain on intraparty consensus. That is, insofar as there is an appeal based on principle, or a party line, this immediately points to the need for consensus. But to the extent that this principle has been formulated by the better educated, it also may sharply indicate the extent of social cleavages within a party.[9] From our data it appeared that the difference between educational levels was most apparent for the Liberals and the CCF/NDP, although, in the latter, this did not emerge from the Index of Group Homogeneity. In these parties the better educated were most often associated with the dominant policies and programs characteristic of each party. Where these policies and programs partake of a radical approach, as they do in the nationalism of the Liberals and most of the CCF/NDP

8 Alford, *Party and Society*, pp. 292–302.

9 See, for example the complaints of working-class supporters of European Socialist parties about the beliefs and activities of intellectuals in their parties. Robert Michels, *Political Parties*, Glencoe: Free Press, 1958, pp. 332–346.

approaches to national problems, then this may mean that the restraint on these parties' definitions of Canadian identity comes not from those in upper-class positions but from those in lower positions.

PARTY AND AGE, SEX, AND MARITAL STATUS

Age

Age and sex have somewhat less influence on the opinions of party supporters than social class. Marital status, though frequently discussed along with age and sex, will not be discussed here in detail. It resembles the characteristics which are of less importance than party in influencing opinions. Regarding age separately and independently of party affiliation, dominant trends reported in Part II indicated that older age was associated with more traditional responses. This finding is consistent with those derived from studies conducted in other political settings. The sociological significance of biological age derives from two sources. The first of these has been described by Eisenstadt as allocative. Age, he writes, "becomes a basis for defining human beings, for the formation of mutual relationships and activities, and for the differential allocation of social roles." [10] In addition to giving rise to different social roles with their attendant relationships and obligations as a result of being at different age levels, each stage in development may also be shaped in its outlook by the historical context. Yet given these reasons for attaching significance to age differences, it is still clear that in our data age differences were secondary in influencing opinions.

Ages of respondents were divided into four categories, beginning with age twenty-one, and grouping all those of age fifty and older together. Cross-party IGH's for each of these age groups show that low cross-party IGH's became proportionately fewer with increasing age. There is considerable evidence from other sources that political party loyalties become more stable with age, and that, therefore, partisan viewpoints are likely to develop.[11] Some substantiation of the greater tendency of the young to be attracted by political experimentation comes from a study conducted in Canada. In a mailed survey conducted after federal by-elections in two Ontario constituencies in 1960, it was found that greatest support for the New Party, the name

[10] S. N. Eisenstadt, *From Generation to Generation*, Glencoe: Free Press, 1956, p. 21.

[11] Robert E. Lane, *Political Life*, New York: Free Press, 1961, p. 300.

informally adopted before the official creation of the New Democratic party, came disproportionately from those in the youngest age groups.[12] With the political loyalties of younger voters less fixed, presumably the influence of party on their opinions should also be less distinct. This was indeed our own finding (see Table 63).

TABLE 63

RELATION BETWEEN PARTY PREFERENCE AND AGE

| Age | Cross-party IGH's for age groups | |
	Number of possible combinations with party	Percent low IGH's across parties
21–29	37	70
30–39	37	68
40–49	37	62
50 and older	37	54

| Party | Intraparty IGH's related to age | |
	Number of possible combinations with age	Percent low intraparty IGH's
Conservative	37	70
Liberal	37	76
CCF/NDP	35	63
Social Credit	33	73

NOTE: The greater proportion of low IGH's, the greater the consensus within the group.

Within party differences.—Generational differences were not acute for any of the parties. They were somewhat more apparent in the CCF/NDP than in the older parties. Conservatives showed an inclination toward greater anti-American feelings among the youngest, although at times these feelings also appeared among the oldest respondents. Younger supporters were also more inclined to favour a pluralistic conception of the nation, for example, with respect to the formation of a labour party and the exercise of provincial responsibilities, but this did not extend to favouring immigration. Like the young in other parties they were most desirous of Canadian political

[12] Pauline Jewett, "Voting in the 1960 Federal By-Elections at Peterborough and Niagara Falls: Who Voted New Party and Why?" *Canadian Journal of Economics and Political Science,* 28, February, 1962, p. 39.

symbols. Younger Liberals were somewhat similar to Conservatives in their anti-American responses. However, the former differed in being more favourable toward immigration. Yet the young of both parties were significant exponents of what has become the dominant expression of Canadian nationhood.

Among the noteworthy responses of CCF/NDP supporters were a decrease in restrictive attitudes toward immigration with age in 1961 and in 1962. In general, however, older respondents were somewhat more likely to be unfavourable to all aspects of immigration about which they were questioned. In respect to the role of government, questions on hospital and medical plans in 1956 found those in both the oldest and youngest age groups most opposed to these plans. In the previous year, however, the issue of government support for cultural activities served to differentiate the eldest and youngest, with the former opposed and the latter in favour. On other questions, older respondents, like those in other parties, were inclined to give traditional responses.

Some comment is in order concerning the greater extent of generational differences in the CCF/NDP. As a result of the shorter history of the CCF compared with either the Liberal or Conservative party, and the recency of the New Democratic party, these parties do not have the advantages of a common outlook across age lines accruing to the parties with long-established loyalties and traditions. Another relevant factor is the appeal of radical political movements to the young. Since the CCF/NDP is one of the apparently radical political parties in Canada, youthful supporters may be attracted for this reason, which is then reflected in their opinions. Older supporters may, with increasing age, either have lost this radicalism or have been drawn to the party for other reasons. Consequently, we could expect and do perceive greater evidence of strain among age groups in a party like the CCF/NDP where ideological appeals of a radical nature play a prominent role. In those instances where the youngest supporters were like the oldest, the results were probably affected by the indifference of the young as compared with the conservatism of the old.

Comment about the Social Credit party is omitted here because generational differences were not great, and small sample sizes prevented an adequate analysis.

The assessment of generational differences.—The existence of some generational differences, particularly as evidenced by the nationalistic responses of the young in all parties, raises an important question. Does this portend the direction of opinions for an even greater proportion of the population, or will increasing age reshape the opinions of the young? To distinguish in terms of long-range consequences between the effects of age *per se* and the historical circumstances in which different age groups happen to find themselves, William Evan has suggested a method of cohort analysis for survey data.[13] To carry out such an analysis the surveys must cover discernibly different time periods. Unfortunately, the data available were not always clearly associated with significant historical events. All that can be done is to examine the questions separated by at least eight years (in order for twenty-one-year olds to at least approach the next age group).

In the area of independence two relatively comparable questions were asked on the Commonwealth: in 1954, whether it was good to continue in the Commonwealth; in 1962, the Commonwealth was one of several alternatives which respondents might choose for Canada's future. In 1954 the youngest respondents were reaching their political majority during the transition from a "hot" to a "cold" war and during serious crises over Berlin and Korea. In 1962 major trouble spots had shifted to such places as the Congo and Cuba. The Commonwealth itself was coming in for new scrutiny. With increasing membership from coloured nations, it appeared anomalous to have as a member a country that was highly discriminatory against its own coloured residents. As a result, the Union of South Africa was expelled from the Commonwealth, and Prime Minister Diefenbaker played a leading role in this action. Given these differing sets of circumstances to which young people were exposed, we still find that the young were less favourable than the old to the Commonwealth to a similar extent at both times. This was true of all parties except the CCF in 1954, when the young were more favourable to the Commonwealth than the older respondents. Comparing the responses of similar age groups at the two times, that is, focusing on the historical situation, events appear to have had little impact. There is only a slight suggestion that older respondents were more affected by events in the case of the over-all total and of Liberal supporters. The CCF, again, did not conform to this pattern, but indicated a movement to greater preference on the part of the old and less for the young (see Table 64).

With respect to foreign commitments, party breakdowns were not available for the earlier questions, so that only over-all trends can be considered. The majority response to the 1952 question was that sending troops to Korea was not a mistake; to the 1960 question, that neutrality for Canada was undesirable. The circumstances at

---

[13] William M. Evan, "Cohort Analysis of Survey Data: A Procedure for Studying Long-Term Opinion Change," *Public Opinion Quarterly*, 23, Spring, 1959, pp. 63–72.

TABLE 64

RELATIVE EFFECT OF AGE AND HISTORICAL SITUATION ON
OPINIONS OF COMMONWEALTH

	Ratios of percentages favourable to Commonwealth			
Effect of age	Total	Conservative	Liberal	CCF/NDP
$\dfrac{21–29 \text{ in } 1954}{50+ \text{ in } 1954}$	.81	.92	.86	1.14
$\dfrac{21–29 \text{ in } 1962}{50+ \text{ in } 1962}$	.86	.92	.92	.53
Effect of historical situation				
$\dfrac{21–29 \text{ in } 1954}{21–29 \text{ in } 1962}$	1.21	1.31	1.35	1.43
$\dfrac{50+ \text{ in } 1954}{50+ \text{ in } 1962}$	1.30	1.31	1.45	.67

SOURCE: Information on which this table is based can be found in Mildred A. Schwartz, *Canadian National Identity as Seen Through Public Opinion Polls: 1941–1963*, Vol. II unpublished doctoral dissertation, Faculty of Political Science, Columbia University, 1964.

these times were similar to those which have been described for the questions asked regarding independence. The difference would be that the events were much more immediate, both in 1952 and 1960. The older age group in 1952 probably did not contain many veterans of World War II. It was much more likely to have members from the war generation, however, in 1960. As we have seen in our earlier discussion, the young were not consistent in their opinions about foreign intervention. They were most often favourable to the Korean venture and less likely to oppose neutrality. Hence, there is little to be gained from an examination of these questions beyond the fact that age differences were greater in 1952 than in 1960. It might be that in 1952 the young were more optimistic about the operations of the United Nations and prospects for world peace than their more cynical elders who had already lived through two world wars and wished to avoid being involved in another one.

The area of government activities is represented by a 1942 question on a contributory medical plan and a 1956 question on a government-operated medical plan. Since the former question does not give party breakdowns, this comparison cannot be made. Those coming of age in 1942 were children of the depression, many of whom had experienced war at first hand. At this time, however, government welfare measures were limited. In contrast, the young in 1956 had grown up during World War II, but had not served in it. Their childhood had taken place during a time of domestic prosperity, and at the same time government welfare measures were becoming more customary. The aged in 1942—in this particular survey categorized as those sixty and older—were probably already well-established in their occupations by the time the worst years of the depression occurred, so they may have had sufficient resources to carry them through this financial crisis. On the other hand, there is evidence that older persons, especially when they are living on fixed incomes, are most seriously affected by major economic upheaval. In 1956, the older age group was made up of those aged fifty and over, and thus not completely comparable to the older age group in 1942. Its members were far removed from the depression years, which may, nevertheless, have left their impact on them at a time when they were beginning families and careers. Presumably because of changed economic and social conditions, age differences in opinions were greater in 1942 than in 1956. Also the younger age group changed more between the two points of time than did the older. In this case this represents a shift in a conservative direction for the young, since they became less favourable to a medical plan. It may be that the generally less traditional youth are more responsive to immediate conditions, both of depression and of prosperity (see Table 65).

Comparable questions on symbols asked about preferred pictures on money and postage in 1954, and about a preferred flag in 1962. To compare the two questions, respondents who preferred Canadian pictures in 1954 and a new flag in 1962 were selected. Although the first Canadian Governor-General had been appointed only two years earlier, in 1954 there was relatively little publicity on Canadian symbols. By 1962, however, not only had symbols become a popular issue in the mass media, but a flag and anthem were election issues for the Conservative, Liberal, and Social Credit parties in the 1962 federal election. At both times the young, collectively and in each party, except for the NDP in 1962, were much more favourable to Canadian symbols than were their elders. In the NDP, however, older supporters in 1962 were much more approving than younger supporters of a new flag. In the other parties, however, by 1962 the older age group began catching up with the more pro-Canadian youth. As a result the older age groups were more unlike each other at the two intervals in time than were the younger. Except for the CCF/NDP,

TABLE 65

RELATIVE EFFECT OF AGE AND HISTORICAL SITUATION ON OPINIONS
OF GOVERNMENT ACTIVITIES

Effect of age	Ratios of percentages favourable to a medical plan
$\dfrac{\text{21–29 in 1942}}{\text{60+ in 1942}}$	1.16
$\dfrac{\text{21–29 in 1956}}{\text{50+ in 1956}}$	.96
Effect of historical situation	
$\dfrac{\text{21–29 in 1942}}{\text{21–29 in 1956}}$	1.52
$\dfrac{\text{60+ in 1942}}{\text{50+ in 1956}}$	1.26

SOURCE: For details on the 1956 survey, see source note, Table 64. Information on the 1942 survey comes from a newspaper release and sample size was not given.

where the sample size was so small that it is probably not meaningful, the responses to these questions indicate the greater nationalism of youth, and, along with the conservatism of the older age group, a greater responsiveness on the part of the latter to events. This may seem paradoxical, but as the mass media and the political parties make public their views on political symbols, older people are made more conscious of the uniqueness of their outlook. The pressure for change, then, may be perceived as relatively great. The young, meanwhile, who are in the forefront of those with nationalistic viewpoints on political symbols, have much less ground to cover in responding to circumstances (see Table 66).

Youth and increasing nationalism.—The foregoing analysis attempted to find some clues to the sources of differences between age groups with a view to evaluating the significance of these differences. Among the most consistent differences found, particularly for the major parties, although also to some extent for the CCF/NDP, was the greater frequency of young people taking a nationalistic stand, that is, one opposed to traditional ties, on issues of independence and political symbols. From our analysis we have some indication, although not too conclusive, that these opinions of young people affect the dominant climate of opinion and thus have implications in the long

TABLE 66

RELATIVE EFFECT OF AGE AND HISTORICAL SITUATION ON OPINIONS
OF POLITICAL SYMBOLS

| | Ratios of percentages favourable to Canadian symbols | | | |
Effect of age	Total	Conservative	Liberal	CCF/NDP
21–29 in 1954 / 50+ in 1954	1.64	1.39	1.63	1.37
21–29 in 1962 / 50+ in 1962	1.18	1.21	1.24	.36
Effect of historical situation				
21–29 in 1954 / 21–29 in 1962	.89	.95	.85	1.65
50+ in 1954 / 50+ in 1962	.64	.82	.64	.43

SOURCE: See Table 64.

run for the views of their elders. In each party, then, the impact of youthful ideas is likely to have repercussions for the continuing formulation of Canada's identity.

Sex

Like older respondents, women tend to be more traditional in their approach to national problems. Female supporters of the Conservatives and Liberals, in particular, when compared with men, appeared more parochial in their outlook. They were more likely to be opposed to involvements with the United States and other foreign countries, positions which we could consider nationalistic, except that they were also less favourable to Canadian symbols. In attempting to account for these differences manifested in another political situation, that of a British general election, the authors of *How People Vote* write:

Part of the explanation may be found by extending the reasons suggested for an age difference in voting. If a Labour vote is a social novelty which the old, whose habits were fixed in an earlier period, adopt more reluctantly than the young, it may be that women lag behind because, in a changing world, their social contacts are more limited than those of men. . . . It is possible then that women's political conservatism results partly from a greater social isolation which makes them slower than men to change their opinions and attitudes.[14]

Probably related to these tendencies of women, their proportion of low cross-party Indices of Group Homogeneity was higher than for men. In other words, the influence of party on opinions was less for women than for men. There were some variations among parties, with the Liberals having relatively fewest low intraparty Indices of Group Homogeneity. (see Table 67). With some exceptions (most notably,

TABLE 67

RELATION OF PARTY PREFERENCE AND SEX

| | Cross-party IGH'S for sex | |
Sex	Number of possible combinations with party	Percent low IGH's across parties
Men	35	49
Women	35	60

| | Intraparty IGH's related to sex | |
Party	Number of possible combinations with sex	Percent low intraparty IGH's
Conservative	35	69
Liberal	35	46
CCF/NDP	33	85
Social Credit	32	78

NOTE: The greater proportion of low IGH's, the greater consensus within the group.

the 1954 question on which men were more favourable to the Commonwealth and the 1957 question on which women were more approving of government resource development—a position, we might add, true for women of all parties), Liberal women adhered to traditional approaches to national problems. Several reasons can be suggested for these sex differences. Men may vote Liberal, at least some of the time, because they are attracted by that party's principles, but this is much less likely to be true of women. With the lesser interest of women in politics, women will often vote in a particular fashion because their husbands do so, and they are more likely to be concerned with the

[14] M. Benney, A. P. Gray, R. H. Pear, *How People Vote*, London: Routledge and Kegan Paul, 1956, pp. 108–109.

personalities of candidates than with issues. The effects of these factors on normally conservative women are more likely to show up in the relatively more radical Liberal party than in the Conservative party. That sex differences do not play a prominent part in the CCF/NDP speaks for a greater political commitment on the part of women in that party.

Marital Status

When respondents were classified according to marital status political parties were seen to have great influence. Even though traditional solutions were most attractive to the widowed and least so to the single, neither group makes up a sufficiently large percentage within the body of voters to make its influence strongly felt. The married group, numerically most important, while faced with common family responsibilities, usually differed along party lines in their views on national problems. For the parties this permitted minimizing internal differences in respect to the marital status of supporters. Further discussion on marital status are omitted since there were insufficient single, widowed, or divorced persons to permit an intensive analysis.

The Relative Influence of Age, Sex, and Marital Status

In conclusion, it appears that different experiences and attitudes associated with age, sex, and especially marital status, are not, at least in terms of the issues we have considered, of paramount importance in preventing a high measure of intraparty consensus. Different perspectives on national problems do exist, but in the case of marital status, they are related to the numerically insignificant single and widowed, separated, and divorced. In sex differences, however, it is possible that the traditionalism of women may be at least a potential brake on the approach which each political party takes to national problems. This traditionalism could conceivably serve as the basis for the development of a national consensus on critical issues cutting across party lines. Over the time span considered, however, opinions highly favourable to traditional ties and ways of managing the affairs of the country have been consistently eroded, and have been replaced, although slowly and in a limited fashion, by ones which presume a more self-conscious nationalism. Since the latter is the position most often taken by the young in all parties, their views will probably have greatest implication for the future definition of Canadian identity.

XI   THE SIGNIFICANCE OF PARTIES

CANADIAN PARTY TYPES

The Conservatives and the Liberals; Broad-based Cadre Parties of Electoral Success

USING THE information supplied by the polls and analyzed in this and the preceding section, and using whatever other material is available on the nature of party organization, we are able to begin the placement of Canadian parties into the eight-fold typology introduced in Chapter II. The Conservative and Liberal parties, like the Republican and Democratic parties in the United States, are essentially broadbased cadre parties of electoral success. Yet there are a number of critical differences between the two Canadian parties. Compared with the Conservatives, the Liberals have a broader ethnic base; they have also been more successful in establishing a united outlook regardless of the origin of supporters. Regionally, however, in recent years the Conservatives have attracted a broader base of supporters than the Liberals, particularly from the western provinces. At this level, as well as some others discussed in the foregoing chapters, the Conservatives have been more successful in holding in check divergent viewpoints. On the basis of trends in the distribution of responses, it appeared that the success of the Conservatives was at least partly due to their lengthy period of opposition. During that time, support was more likely to come from those strongly committed to the Conservative party and influenced by the party climate of opinion. Although the accession to power of the Conservatives in 1957 and 1958 went along with a new concern with membership participation, it was not accompanied by increased internal consensus. Presumably, increased responsiveness to the wishes of the rank and file would need to continue for a longer period before it would be manifested in a greater degree of intraparty consensus. For parties of this type, however, an opposition role often provides greatest opportunity for consolidation of differing viewpoints. This appeared to be true as well for the Liberals when they lost favour with the voters.

How ironic it would be if parties could present a united front only when they were out of office! Fortunately both our data and our typology suggest other alternatives. The available data provide some examples of instances in which the ability of the Liberals to attract and hold the loyalty of large proportions of significant groups in the society, specifically those of French origin, meant that the latter could participate in creating the dominant climate of opinion. The party's resultant definition of national problems and solutions was then able to provide some basis for national integration. But, although bridging the hiatus between French and English-speaking Canadians is undoubtedly of paramount significance today as it has been throughout Canada's history, the information used in our analysis does not suggest that even the Liberals have been highly successful in this respect. And certainly at times they have been even less effective than the Conservatives in controlling other important cleavages in Canadian society. For other possible solutions we therefore need to consider the contributions to Canadian problems made by other party types in our typology.

The Broad-Based Party of Principle; Its Place in Canadian History

We postulated that the party inducing most consensus would be a broad-based one of principle. Ideally it should have a mass organization in order to ensure the widest participation and support. But cadre organizations would probably also be effective as long as the other conditions were satisfied. The most notable examples of such parties have been nationalistic and concerned with breaking colonial ties. While such "national liberation fronts" have been lacking in Canada, there have been times when the existing parties have approached the broad-based party of principle. For example, before Confederation, French and English-speaking Reformers united under LaFontaine and Baldwin to oppose the policies of the Governor of Canada, Lord Sydenham. Although the coalition did not emerge into a genuine party but broke up after the leaders' retirement, "the LaFontaine-Baldwin coalition was . . . the first example of what has become the most striking and distinctive feature of our Canadian politics—the bi-racial party which for the moment overcomes differences between French and English and brings them together inside one party to conduct a government on principles on which they can agree." [1]

The principles in this case pertained to responsible government.

[1] Frank H. Underhill, *Canadian Political Parties*, historical booklet number 8; Ottawa: Canadian Historical Association, 1960, p. 13.

Later parties followed this example of partnership between the two language groups under a leader of the one language and a lieutenant of the other. Such a partnership was maintained by permitting local autonomy while emphasizing some unifying program or policies at the national level.

Whatever sentiments, ideals or interests may divide the two main communal groups in Canada, they have in common an interest in material economic expansion. . . . Macdonald and Laurier always tried to keep economic expansion before the minds of the voters as the best way of keeping their minds off the racial and religious differences which were apt to divide them so bitterly.[2]

Presumably this form of solution is still available to Canadian parties, but it has become much more difficult to carry out. Up to and after Confederation, the main centres of population were in central Canada. The economy of the country was much less diversified and French and English could agree that prosperity lay in westward expansion. But especially since the outbreak of World War II, in effect the time period covered by our Gallup Polls, the fragmented nature of the society, regionally, economically, and ethnically, has been accentuated. As a result, Canadian parties have a more difficult task at present, both in attracting a wide base of support and in formulating an approach to national problems which can unify the people. In the future, unless some principles can be adopted which transcend subgroup loyalties, the major political parties will be restricted in their integrative roles, and the task of "nurturing consensus" will remain with those parties which at least are able to attract and hold supporters from all major segments of the population.

The Narrow-Based, Mass Party of Principle: The CCF/NDP

Of the remaining parties, the CCF and its successor most closely resemble the narrow-based mass party of principle. According to our model and the empirical data, such parties are characterized by a high degree of internal consensus. This consensus is promoted by considerable membership participation, an ideological orientation, and the consequent preclusion of support from important groups. Hence, the solutions to national problems offered do little to advance a national consensus.

It is possible that the definition of national identity which a narrow-based party of principle proposes is one which is the forerunner of

[2] *Ibid.*, p. 14.

popular opinion, and which, after some time lapse, becomes adopted by a wider spectrum of the population. For example, while CCF proposals in the 1930's and early 1940's to equalize opportunity through social-welfare measures did not make that party dominant on the national scene, they were still highly influential. They stimulated the Liberals to enact legislation in these areas, and, as our polls indicated, the legislation in turn resulted in widespread approval. But as far as other aspects of national problems are concerned, the survey results do not suggest that the CCF/NDP had a broader leadership potential. We were led to this conclusion by evidence that the opinions of CCF/NDP supporters had been at variance with those by supporters of other parties. Moreover, this was as much the case when we looked at the views of the better educated and the young in the major parties, who form the base from which present and future leaders are drawn; they too hold opinions divergent from those of the CCF/NDP. For the period covered by the polls, then, we must regard the CCF/NDP as internally united, but standing for causes unattractive to the majority of Canadians.

The Social Credit Party; Its Changing Nature

Throughout our analysis we have been limited in the generalizations made about the Social Credit party by the meagreness of our data. This limitation also extends to our difficulty in categorizing the party. At its formation, Social Credit was perceived as a movement (the leadership still persist in terming it such) which demanded the whole-hearted commitment and active support of its members. But, from the comments of present members, it appears that the party has become increasingly less of a mass organization and more like a cadre organization. Originally, also, its appeal was based explicitly on a unique approach to monetary problems. But over the years this too has been played down to ensure electoral success, particularly in Alberta. Yet the character of supporters has continued to be regionally, ethnically, and economically unrepresentative. The upsurge of support for the Social Credit party in Quebec in recent years would appear, in the light of the breaking away of part of the Quebec faction in 1963 to form Le Ralliement des Créditistes, to be a short-lived attempt to become a national party. As such it is difficult to treat this party seriously as a promoter of national integration. However, it remains as an important indicator of the fragmented nature of Canadian society.

DIFFERENCES BETWEEN PARTIES

Sources of Difference

The discussion in the preceding three chapters has centred on reasons for the presence or absence of a relationship between party support and opinions. Considering all questions for which this information is available, it appears that, with the exception of the CCF/NDP, cross-party differences are less great than those within the parties. In addition, however, differences between parties have altered over time and vary with the problem area. This raises two noteworthy questions: what are the sources of cross-party differences, and what are the factors making for a lack of party differentiation?

Party differences may be examined by pairing parties and classifying parties as "different" if there is a spread of 10 percent or more in the opinions of the two parties' supporters on dominant views. When the parties were so treated, we found that on questions pertaining to external problems, only the Liberals and Social Crediters, and Conservatives and Liberals were relatively similar in their views (see Table 68). The difference between CCF/NDP and Social Credit supporters was greater than 10 percent on questions relating to independence, but when these were combined with the one question on foreign commitments, the difference declined to slightly less than 10 percent. Conservative and CCF/NDP supporters were most distinctive in their answers and were divided most strongly on questions regarding the Commonwealth and, to a lesser extent, on those relating to trade. The Commonwealth was also the source of dissension for Conservative and Social Credit supporters, while trade questions were most divisive for Liberal and CCF/NDP supporters.

On internal problems, parties were most similar to each other. Here the major difference was between CCF/NDP supporters and those of the Liberal and Conservative parties. Although the greatest differences in outlook between parties occurred before 1950 in response to questions of an ideological nature, the parties continued to differ even on social-welfare issues.

At first glance problems of symbols appeared to be most closely identified with a partisan outlook. However, on closer examination, it was apparent that this was partly caused by the inclusion of two questions from a 1958 survey when only six Social Crediters were interviewed. When these are omitted, party differences were much less great and exceeded 10 percent only in the case of the Liberal and CCF/NDP supporters and supporters of the Conservative party. For

TABLE 68

SIMILARITIES IN VIEWPOINTS BETWEEN PARTY SUPPORTERS, BY PROBLEM AREA

	External	Internal	Symbolic[a]
Least different[b]	Liberal and Social Credit Conservative and Liberal CCF and Social Credit	Conservative and Liberal Conservative and Social Credit CCF and Social Credit Liberal and Social Credit	Conservative and Social Credit Liberal and CCF Liberal and Social Credit CCF and Social Credit
Most different	Liberal and CCF Conservative and Social Credit Conservative and CCF	Liberal and CCF Conservative and CCF	Conservative and Liberal Conservative and CCF

[a] Two questions asked in a probably unrepresentative 1958 survey have been omitted.
[b] Line divides differences of greater or less than 10 percent.

the Conservatives and Liberals, this was the one problem area of the three where the supporters of both parties were not highly similar. We recall that this was due to the fact that Liberals have favoured Canadian symbols while Conservatives have been more responsive to British ones. But as noted in the conclusion to Chapter VII, these differences are declining as Conservatives become more approving of Canadian symbols. Divergence between Conservatives and CCF/NDP'ers followed a more uneven pattern, but there has been some decline in this since about 1950. This has come about not so much through the greater desire for Canadian symbols from Conservatives as from a number of instances where CCF/NDP supporters strongly favoured British symbols.

The Historical Background of Cross-party Differences

External problems.—Election promises and party actions throughout Canada's development are important sources of party differentiation. It is easier to discern historical trends for the two older parties, but we will also attempt to take account of the policies of the newer ones. To begin with, let us consider party responses to external problems.

The Conservatives have long revealed their nationalism in economics, especially in devising and defending the protective tariff, in building and upholding railways during the first trying decades of federal union, and in attacking and defeating the reciprocity proposals of 1911 as a menace to a national economy erected on east-west trade. But in the more purely political sphere the Liberals have led in pressing for those measures that would assert the national status and independent action of the Dominion. They have been more status-conscious than the Conservatives, more zealous for the symbolism of an independent nationality.[3]

For recent years these differences are still apparent; in the campaigns of 1957 and 1958, and to a lesser extent 1962 and 1963, the Conservatives were relatively anti-American and showed themselves anxious to increase ties with Britain and the Commonwealth. The position of the CCF/NDP on issues of independence has appeared at times to be equivocal. Party intellectuals have often been outspokenly anti-American—and this outlook may be attractive to rural supporters of the CCF—but the labour element in the party has been much more restrained. This derives in part at least from the close ties between organized labour in the United States and Canada. Because the locus

[3] Alexander Brady, *Democracy in the Dominions*, 3d ed.; Toronto: University of Toronto Press, 1958, pp. 105–106.

of Social Credit strength has been in the more isolated provinces of Alberta and British Columbia, and to a lesser extent recently in Quebec, pronouncements on external problems have not occupied a prominent place. The opinions of supporters of that party are thus strongly determined by other characteristics, such as ethnic origin.

The nature of Canada's foreign commitments constitutes another part of external problems. After World War II, Canadian foreign affairs were conducted in such a way as to assure tripartisan consensus. This extended to Canada's participation in international organizations at the end of the war.

All parties concurred in the establishment of the United Nations and the Canadian delegation which went to the first session of the United Nations had included delegates from each of the major parties. Similarly the idea of NATO met with enthusiasm at the political conventions of the three major parties in 1948 and the treaty was ratified unanimously in 1949.[4]

In more recent years, however, the degree of cross-party consensus has changed considerably. The CCF and later the New Democratic party, for example, have been concerned with withdrawing from NORAD and, under certain circumstances, from NATO. The Liberals and Conservatives have also differed with respect to policy on NATO commitments. The Liberals, in addition, have complained that when the Conservatives took office in 1957, Canada's role in the United Nations became much less significant. A recent difference related to the acquisition of nuclear weapons, with the Liberals in favour, and the Conservatives and CCF/NDP opposed. Again it is difficult to determine Social Credit policy on these issues. In our data, information on opinions about specific foreign commitments according to party preference was limited to one question, and consequently party policies did not warrant much attention. The most distinctive difference was between Conservative and all other party supporters with respect to traditional ties. This can be related, then, to the greater pro-British, pro-Commonwealth policies of the Conservative party.

Internal problems.—Party differences on internal problems were not as pronounced as those on external problems, even though the Conservatives have a popular image of being mainly English, Protestant, and in favour of centralized government, while the Liberals are seen as French, Catholics, and the upholders of provincial autonomy. The lack of differentiation is due, according to Underhill, to the need for compromise.

[4] Derek R. F. Fraser, "Conservative Foreign Policy," *Conservative Concepts*, 2, Spring, 1960, p. 21.

All these Canadian parties now profess to be progressive, all present advanced social security programmes, all propose some degree of state regulation of the economy for the masses. . . . Whatever their moral indignation at the potential iniquities of totalitarian socialism, the parties on the right will continue to move in a socialistic direction. . . . And whatever its moral indignation at the actual iniquities of monopoly capitalism, a socialist party which, in the process of becoming a national party capable of government, has made adjustments to the points of view of French Catholics, individualist eastern farmers, and a perplexing variety of middle class groups may not be so clear-cut in its doctrines as the CCF seems . . . to be at present.[5]

But this is an oversimplification. Over the years, the Liberals have been at least moderately in favour of economic planning, particularly as it pertains to the equalization of regional opportunities and the expansion of social-welfare services. They have also been favourable toward the expansion of trade, with some leanings toward low tariff policy. It is true that the Conservatives differ mainly in degree. Their approach to planning is more piecemeal and their trade policies somewhat more protectionist. Compared with previous policy statements, those made during the 1962 and 1963 elections were much less specific than when the Conservatives were in opposition. But, looked at in this light, Underhill is indeed correct in stating that similarities between the Liberals and Conservatives are great, and this is reflected in Gallup Poll surveys.

Yet while the surveys also indicate little difference between the responses of the two major parties and those of the Social Credit, party policies of the latter are distinctive. In particular, the Social Credit party has expressed strong opposition to the participation of government in the economic life of the country, although the application of its monetary theories would in effect mean the opposite. Especially in French Canada, the Créditistes' campaign and the responses it brought forth from the electorate are analogous to Poujadism. Interestingly enough, the party's official approach to national problems had little effect on the views of supporters in terms of creating a unique party climate of opinion, separate from that of the Liberals and Conservatives. This of course may have been partly the result of the questions asked which do not represent significant indicators of Social Credit feeling. We hasten to add also that our statement about the apparent lack of an *official* party climate of opinion does not contradict our earlier finding that there was an appreciable

[5] Frank H. Underhill, "Political Parties and Ideas," in *Canada*, ed. by George W. Brown, Berkeley and Los Angeles: University of California Press, 1950, pp. 351–352.

measure of unanimity among Social Credit supporters. Although that unanimity bears some relation to party policy, it has also been shaped and modified by the character of supporters.

Underhill's generalization, however, has least relevance to the CCF/NDP. That party's dedication to the extension of public owner-ship and social-welfare measures and to control by the central govern-ment, contributes to the variant definition of internal problems shared by its supporters.[6]

Symbolic problems.—The Liberal party has been most concerned with symbolic problems. This has been manifested in a search for specifically Canadian symbols, even though the party's major achieve-ment in this direction was confined, until 1964, to the appointment of the first Canadian Governor-General. The Conservatives have officially been the most jealous defenders of the retention of British symbols. Yet in recent years they too, probably in response to the pressure of public opinion, have come to acknowledge the need for Canadian symbols. In the 1962 election, for example, the Conservative party pledged the adoption of a new flag by 1967. While party policies have changed more slowly than the opinions of supporters, there has been a trend toward favouring Canadian symbols reflected in the lessening differences between Conservative and Liberal supporters. The two minor parties have been both less outspoken and more vacillating on their position toward symbolic problems. This unevenness is reflected in a comparative analysis of the views of supporters.

The Party System

Party roles in a parliamentary system of government.—The impact of party policies on opinions should be reinforced, theoretically at least, by a parliamentary system of government. Under such a system, unless there is a coalition, one party serves as government and the other as official opposition. Where there is more than one party in opposition, differences between them may detract from their com-bined effectiveness in opposing the government. In all cases however, the government party is required to formulate policy, while parties in opposition must not only criticize the government, but present alternatives. As a result parties have a strong connection with issues,

[6] No attempt is made here to present detailed examinations of party policies over the years. These may be obtained from party literature and newspaper re-ports. Published sources include John Meisel, *The Canadian General Election of 1957*, Toronto: University of Toronto Press, 1963. Policies in 1962 have been summarized in an unpublished paper by Martin Westmacott, University of Alberta, Calgary.

a connection which may or may not be perceived by voters. Given the parties' concern with issues which arise during their parliamentary experiences, it is also likely that these issues will form the basis of election campaigns. Campaign organizers, especially in recent years, have been concerned with creating leader and party images, but the policy content of campaigns plays the necessary role of aiding voters in seeing meaningful differences among parties. In practice parties may of course gloss over policy stands, especially where these are seen as hindering their electoral success.

Party discipline.—The parliamentary system increases the likelihood that parties will influence the views of their supporters because of its demand for party discipline. On all major issues party members in the House of Commons are expected to a vote according to party lines. While divergent views may be presented in caucus, at least a semblance of consensus is displayed for the public. Theoretically at least, there should be little doubt where a party stands, particularly in relation to an issue that has been brought to vote. In Canada, where regional and ethnic cleavages have often assumed major proportions, disciplined parties have not always been able to control conflicts of interest. Whenever the divergence of interests has appeared irreconcilable, support for splinter parties has emerged. Party discipline in itself then tends to reinforce similarities within parties and differences between them, with the effect again of aiding the voter in discerning distinctive party positions.

Internal organization.—Another source of party influence derives from internal organization, as discussed in relation to mass and cadre parties. Our thesis has been that when party organizations permit a wide representation of the membership to participate in the formulation and critical examination of policies, the party can expect a high commitment to its program. The CCF/NDP is the only Canadian party we are considering which approaches a mass-type organization, and, as we have seen, also displays a high degree of internal consensus.

Parties as frameworks for issues.—The party system, by its very existence, also provides a ready made framework for new and changing issues.

Every party system constitutes a frame imposed upon opinion, forming it as well as deforming it. The party system existing in a country is generally considered to be the result of the structure of its public opinion. But the converse is equally true: the structure of public opinion is to a large extent a consequence of the party system.[7]

[7] Maurice Duverger, *Political Parties*, London: Methuen, 1954, p. 372.

By their persistence over time, parties form the basis for political attitudes, giving even new issues and campaign concerns an added colour because of their association with a particular party. The association between specific questions and party may survive as part of that party's image even after the original issues have disappeared. At any one point in time, disputes over political questions could assume unwieldy complexity if all shades of opinion and involvement were given free reign. Particularly through election campaigns, these disputes are made less complicated and fewer in number, so that broad divisions of opinion can result. In this view, the political process is seen as "a system for organizing disagreements." [8] In the same manner, parties may act to organize antagonisms by dividing them according to already existing groupings.

Party images.—The operation of parties as frameworks for opinion is reflected in the images associated with the four Canadian parties. Since responses to specific questions on party images were not a central concern of this study, no systematic attempt was made to collect questions on this subject. But, from the ten questions which we did have, some tentative generalizations can be made. Party supporters were naturally inclined to evaluate their own party most favourably. Support for a party then aided in the discernment of that party's image. But controlling for this tendency to associate one's own party with more admirable characteristics, there still appeared the impression that, of the two major parties, the Liberal party was more closely associated with prosperity than the Conservative. The former also emerged as the party which was conceived of as doing a better job if hard times should come to the country and for one's own family. Among other noteworthy tendencies was that of Liberal supporters to see their party as being for the common man. The workingman's party was even more frequently associated with the CCF by that party's supporters. Of all parties, the Social Credit was most likely to evaluate the CCF in ideological terms. Finally, there was some tendency for CCF/NDP supporters to be more favourable to the Liberals, and the Social Credit to respond this way to the Conservatives. The existence of such party images, then, contributes to the likelihood that party will influence opinion.

CROSS-PARTY CONSENSUS

A closer scrutiny of the questions used as indicators of party images revealed that while general policies were associated with parties,

[8] B. Berelson, P. F. Lazarsfeld, and W. McPhee, *Voting*, Chicago: University of Chicago Press, 1954, p. 183.

a considerable proportion of voters also saw no distinction between them. Although about 80 percent of party supporters were able to select a party which would be best for such situations as prosperity or hard times, when respondents were asked to distinguish between party programs and policies, from one-half to three-quarters were incapable of doing so (see Table 69). In this instance general questions were much more likely to produce an opinion than specific ones. Respondents' evaluation of parties was such as to produce an indistinct, undetailed image. This kind of image may be effective in guiding judgements about issues into a partisan context. Yet the lack of detailed information about party stands may suggest that voters are but weakly directed into opinions on issues by their perception of party positions. The Canadian Gallup organization has on three occasions asked respondents whether they thought it made much difference which political party ran the country. In 1953, 63 percent answered in the affirmative; in 1958, 57 percent; in 1961, 44 percent. (In the latter year 46 percent said that it did not make much difference.) In 1961, 43 percent of Conservative supporters, 51 percent of Liberals, and 56 percent of those favouring other parties expressed concern with the outcome.[9] The declining concern about which party wins may be related to the closeness of the 1962 and 1963 general election. That is, desire to be on the winning side did not produce any appreciable bandwagon effect. The responses to these questions can also be used to substantiate further the premise that cross-party differentiation, particularly between the two major parties, is of lessening significance in Canada.

Finally, the differences between pairs of parties, which we noted earlier in our discussion of cross-party differences, were generally not of great magnitude. This was especially true of Liberal and Conservative supporters on issues relating to external and internal problems and, more recently, to problems of national symbols. That differences among the major parties, at least, are not greater bespeaks a political characteristic which Canada shares with other Western democracies: the institutionalization of patterns of both consensus and cleavage. This means that government policies are usually received with some minimum degree of approval even by those supporting the opposition. While parties may draw supporters in disproportionate numbers from certain groups in the population, democracy could be endangered if important social and political affiliations completely coincided. Thus, although political parties derive from significant cleavages

[9] The total percentage distribution varies from the results for each party because undecided voters are included in the total.

TABLE 69

PARTY SUPPORTERS WITH NO OPINIONS ON PARTY DIFFERENCES
(in percent)

Date	Question	Conservative	Liberal	CCF/NDP	Social Credit
12/57	Party best for hard times	21	16	19	14
7/60	Party best for keeping country prosperous (of Conservative, Liberal, CCF)	26	18	12	52
7/60	What Conservative party stands for	53	74	53	56
7/60	What Liberal party stands for	65	59	50	52
7/60	What CCF stands for	64	76	24	52
7/61	Party best for keeping country prosperous	16	15	27	9
7/61	Party under which self and family would be better off	16	13	9	6
7/61	Differences between Liberals and Conservatives: —little, none, don't know	62	49	87	74
3/62	Party under which self and family would be better off—all the same, undecided	17	14	14	14
3/62	Of Conservatives and Liberals, party best for keeping country prosperous—both, same, undecided	19	14	34	14

within the population, and, by their existence, encourage and rein-force these cleavages, they must also, in order to achieve office, be willing to conciliate opposing interest groups and appeal to as broad a base of the electorate as possible. When a party becomes the gov-ernment, it must consider that it governs its opponents as well as its supporters. On the other hand, consensus must not be so great that leaders lose their partisan identity, or issue stands become so similar that meaningful political alternatives are obviated. Specific areas of disagreement, by being placed in a content of agreement on some basic essentials, primarily the legitimacy of the political system, can exist without destroying the over-all unity.

A high degree of cross-party consensus is also encouraged by con-ditions peculiar to Canada. Among these is the need for parties which expect to form a majority government to appeal to a highly diversified electorate. In doing so, the likelihood is increased that they will seek compromise solutions and avoid those liable to alienate important segments of the population. This has resulted in many instances in a low level of differentiation between Conservatives and Liberals.

POLITICAL CONSEQUENCES

On the basis of data surveyed and the available documentary evidence, it seems fair to conclude that the Conservative and Liberal parties represent Canadian examples of broad-based cadre parties of electoral success. Each, however, displays internal tension as a result of trying to attract a broad representation of the electorate, and, at the same time, impose on it a partisan outlook.

We have described the CCF/NDP as a narrow-based mass party of principle. As evidenced by responses of its supporters to survey ques-tions, the contribution of this party to a national consensus has been low. We have related this to the unrepresentative nature of its sup-porters and the character of its appeal. In the case of the latter, during the time period covered, its definition of national problems and their solutions has not been well-articulated with the conditions of Cana-dian existence.

Throughout our discussion it has been difficult to make more than tentative statements about the Social Credit party because of paucity of survey data and because existing literature does not reflect present conditions. Using the terminology of our party typology, Social Credit probably resembles a narrow-based cadre party of both electoral suc-cess and principle. With these present characteristics, we could antic-ipate the instability reflected by the breakup of the Quebec wing of the party. Since making inroads into Quebec, Social Credit has re-inforced its image as a focus for cleavages rather than consensus. Yet up until this time, at least as far as we were able to determine from our survey data, intraparty consensus was relatively high, as was the resemblance of supporters' opinions to those of other Canadians.

PART IV

CONFRONTATION WITH NATIONAL PROBLEMS

XII THE IMPACT OF NATIONAL PROBLEMS

THE MEANINGFULNESS OF ISSUE

DESPITE the concern of this study with national problems contributing to the definition of identity, we have thus far avoided the question of how meaningful these issues are for the public generally. From other sources we know that some disagreement exists on the importance of issues for understanding political behaviour, particularly voting. As Berelson, Lazarsfeld, and McPhee point out, there are those who argue that issues have no real importance for election campaigns, but are merely presented by parties as window-dressing to disguise self-interested actions. The other extreme is stated by those who say that elections are won or lost on the basis of issues in the forefront.[1] Although the concern of this study is not with the part that issues play in a specific election campaign, but rather with their impact on the electorate through time, it is still worthwhile to consider the evidence offered on the importance of issues, even when this centres on campaign questions.

Studies which find issues relatively unimportant in their effect on voting decisions emphasize the overriding importance of social relations.

The "issues" are in general too numerous and specific to provide a focus, the individual can directly "care" about only a minority of them, and the chances are good he will disapprove of his candidate's stand on some. . . . In this situation the individual seems to vote, other things being equal, with the people whom he most directly feels to be "his own kind." . . . It may be said that the question is not so much . . . *for what* he is voting as it is *with whom* he is associating himself in voting.[2]

For example, Coleman felt, in reviewing the Trow study of support for McCarthy, that this support was related more to integration into the

<hr />

[1] B. Berelson, P. F. Lazarsfeld, and W. McPhee, *Voting*, Chicago: University of Chicago Press, 1954, p. 182.

[2] Talcott Parsons, " 'Voting' and the Equilibrium of the American Political System," in *American Voting Behavior*, ed. by Eugene Burdick and Arthur J. Brodbeck, Glencoe: Free Press, 1959, p. 96.

local and national community than to attitudes toward the substantive issue of Communist subversion.[3]

Other writers take an opposing view by emphasizing the importance of issues, maintaining that there is some underlying conception of rational decision-making, and a relationship between concrete events and subsequent attitudes. A study designed to support this view was based on two Survey Research Center surveys; the first consisted of interviews before and after a sharp slump in the grain market, and the second of interviews with respondents before and after Malik's speech offering to negotiate an end to the Korean war. With some qualifications on the impact of these events on different segments of the population, the author could still conclude that people react in a rational manner to generally significant economic and political events.[4]

Another view of the importance of issues stresses their variation according to context. In the 1952 United States presidential election, issues as well as candidates were more important than they had been in 1948. Foreign policies had emerged as crucial concerns to voters, and, for many of Eisenhower's supporters, the source of his appeal was his perceived ability to deal with these problems.[5] During some elections, such as the one in 1952, events have greater importance for the electorate; in others, partisan loyalty or the personal attractiveness of candidates is paramount.

Finally, the significance of issues is affected by their nature and subject matter. Those who take a deprecating view of Western society as made up of uninformed and unconcerned masses could find reinforcement from public-opinion surveys which reveal that often only minorities of the population have even heard of important pieces of legislation. Yet if we turn from specific legislative acts or policies to more general ones we are more likely to find that most people hold some opinion. Another approach to issues which was fruitfully employed in *Voting* distinguished between position issues and style issues. Position issues are those which may be described in response to the query, "In whose *interest* should the government be run?" Position issues are less likely to be created by party propaganda; they are more likely to emerge from socioeconomic conditions. For this reason they tend to have long-range implications with relatively direct consequences for the group that is able to achieve its objectives. Style issues

---

[3] James Coleman, *Community Conflict*, Glencoe: The Free Press, 1957, p. 19.

[4] James C. Davies, "Some Relations Between Events and Attitudes," *American Political Science Review*, 46, September, 1952, pp. 777–789.

[5] A. Campbell, G. Gurin, and W. E. Miller, *The Voter Decides*, Evanston: Row, Peterson, 1954, pp. 175–177.

lend themselves more readily to manipulation by political parties, dealing with more subjective aspects of a "way of life." According to the authors, they have relatively short durability, and the result is "indirect subjective symbolic gratification for the successful group." [6] But these gratifications may give them an enduring quality, especially in those countries where stable economic interests have not emerged to supplant other group loyalties.[7]

The significance of political issues cannot be grasped if they are dismissed as trivial because large segments of the population often hold no opinion about them. Instead they should be seen as highly variable, dependent on such things as group loyalties, situational context, and subject matter.[8] The relative salience of issues is derived from people's awareness of them, involvement in their outcome, and intensity of feelings about them. Awareness seems to be related to the complexity, specificity, and currency of issues. The less complex and more general issues are more likely to produce a high degree of awareness. Along with this, the more current issues, the ones subject to most debate through the mass media, are those also more likely to produce some opinion. National circumstances probably determine the appeal of position issues and style issues, as well as the extent to which people become involved in them. It is difficult to predict the kind of issue which will arouse the greatest feeling, but one undoubtedly important factor is the threatening content of the issue. That is, insofar as an issue concerns a problem area which poses a threat to the existence or integrity of a group, the intensity of response will be particularly high, especially from the threatened group.

INDICATORS OF SALIENCE

Ideally an adequate measure of salience should involve a series of questions beginning with whether respondents had heard anything about the issue. In the case of the informed we should also know how strongly they hold their opinions and how involved they personally

[6] Berelson, et al., op. cit., pp. 184–185.

[7] This may have, in the case of Canada, some relation to its low level of class-based voting behaviour. R. R. Alford, Party and Society, Chicago: Rand McNally, 1963, pp. 311–318.

[8] Although it has not been possible in this study to evaluate effectively the consequences of having different groups of individuals hold opinions, individuals and groups do vary in their strategic placement in the social system. For example, not all opinion holders will manifest their viewpoints through political action, nor are the political activities of all citizens of equal significance. For relevant discussion of these subjects see V. O. Key, Jr., Public Opinion and American Democracy, New York: Knopf, 1961, especially pp. 85–152, 228–233.

feel in the outcome. The Gallup Poll data used here either did not yield this sort of information or, when they did, their utilization would have made analysis unduly cumbersome. Instead we employed two rough indicators of salience. The first was the proportion of respondents who were not able to give a reply to a question either because of unfamiliarity, indifference, or confusion, an indicator obviously available for all questions. A second indicator was whether the subject under discussion was seen as a critical issue or a major problem facing Canada. This was not as readily available, and only a few of the surveys used asked for such unstructured responses. None of the questions were asked in such a way as to yield a measure of intensity, but one of the surveys used included a question on the degree of interest of respondents in the forthcoming election. This question may provide some useful insights into the relative salience of other questions asked in the same survey.

Awareness

Distribution of "no opinions."—The questions which produced the highest proportion of responses referred to political symbols (see Table 70). Questions tapping awareness of problems of national symbols elicited especially few "no opinion" responses when references to royalty were eliminated (see Table 71). Internal problems ranked next in salience. For Canada, internal problems were subdivided into questions on internal cleavages and on the role of government. Collectively there was little difference in the proportion of "no opinions" for either category of questions, but among the responses to

TABLE 70

EXTENT OF AWARENESS OF PROBLEM AREAS

	Number of questions		Percent no opinions	
Symbolic problems	30		10	
Internal problems	119		15	
Cleavages		49		16
Role of government		70		15
External problems	78		19	
Independence		55		18
Foreign commitments		23		21

questions about internal divisions, those on population and French-English relations stood out for their high level of awareness. This was also true of responses to questions on social-welfare measures (see Table 72). Questions on external problems yielded the highest proportion of no responses. This problem area, too, was subdivided, and

TABLE 71

AWARENESS OF SYMBOLIC PROBLEMS

	Number of questions	Percent no opinions
Total symbols	30	10
Anthem	3	4
Flag	9	9
Governor-General	7	10
Royalty as Governor-General	4	15
Royalty	3	16
Other	4	12

TABLE 72

AWARENESS OF INTERNAL PROBLEMS

	Number of questions		Percent no opinions	
Total internal	119		15	
Total cleavages	49		16	
French-English relations		4		8
Population		14		8
Preferred influences on government		4		17
Specific federal-provincial responsibilities		9		17
General federal-provincial relations		5		20
Organized interest groups in politics		8		23
Confederation		5		25
Total government	70		15	
Social welfare		16		10
Price control		10		12
Ideology		12		14
Public ownership		26		19
Culture		6		19

in this case it was issues of independence which appeared more salient than those of foreign commitments. Independence covered a number of topics, and, of these, the Commonwealth was highly salient, the United States less so, Britain least. For the latter, "no opinions" were especially high on questions relating to trade and other economic measures. Variations were also present with respect to foreign commitments; questions on Canadian troops serving abroad resulted in respondents being most likely to have an opinion (see Table 73).

TABLE 73

AWARENESS OF EXTERNAL PROBLEMS

	Number of questions	Percent no opinions
Total external	78	19
Total independence	55	18
Commonwealth	9	6
Foreign resource development	2	16
United States	30	17
Great Britain	16	26
Total foreign commitments	23	21
Troops abroad	6	14
World organization	12	21
Other commitments	5	30

Accounting for these differences in awareness requires reference back to our earlier discussion of the conditions presumably affecting awareness. It would appear that issues debated most often in the past twenty years have referred to internal relations among groups and questions of independence. Symbols too have been the subject of continuous debate, but they have not received the same attention until recently. Since the 1940's, the role of government has been less debated except for some special instances. Finally, questions on foreign commitments have always had a specialized appeal.

In ranking the complexity of these issues, however, a somewhat different order emerges. Symbols would rank as least complex; so would activities of government, as long as technical questions relating to matters such as taxation were avoided. The issue of independence is relatively simple unless questions are raised about specific matters, particularly economic ones. Questions on the relations between groups can be highly complex where these involve alternative power arrangements. Foreign commitments are most difficult to classify, but probably are most remote to the ordinary voter.

It is difficult to separate the generality of issues from their complexity. The more specific questions are also likely to be more technical, and therefore more difficult to understand. But where specific questions do not at the same time require technical knowledge, as for example in the choice of a national flag, degree of awareness is probably not affected.

The evidence of the Gallup Poll surveys yields only limited indication of trends. An increasing tendency toward lessened awareness of the issues is present, for independence, only on questions pertaining to Britain. Foreign commitments generally also appear to be associated with an increasing proportion of "no opinions." But no uniform changes in the proportion of "no opinions" were apparent for any other issue areas.

Assuming that they are the critical dimensions of awareness, it is clear that neither constancy of debate, simplicity, or generality, in themselves insure a high degree of awareness (see Figure 3). It is especially noteworthy in this context that the issues which have most concerned politicians and the mass media over the past two decades have not necessarily been most important to the electorate. Yet the combination of the three conditions helps account at least partly for awareness.

Group characteristics and awareness.—In order to examine the extent to which different groups in the population saw the issues selected as significant, it was necessary to confine our analysis to 35

FIGURE 3

CONDITIONS AFFECTING AWARENESS, IN RANK ORDER,
COMPARED WITH ACTUAL AWARENESS

	Ranking of awareness-inducing conditions		
Actual awareness	Constancy of debate	Simplicity	Generality
Symbols	3	1	1
Role of government	4	2	2
Cleavages	1	4	5
Independence	2	3	3
Foreign commitments	5	5	4

questions for which complete information was available. (The resulting rank order is still the same whether we use 35 or the previous 227
questions, although the proportion of "no opinions" shifts in all cases.)
Of all available characteristics, education of respondents differentiated
most sharply among those able to offer an opinion. This finding has
been substantiated in numerous surveys. Differences between educational levels were pronounced for all issue areas except that of symbols. In the latter, the level of awareness was generally high so that
the scope for variation between educational groups was necessarily
limited. In addition, the simplicity of ideas and the emotionality
associated with problems of political symbols ensure that these are
readily grasped, regardless of years of schooling (see Table 74). An-

TABLE 74

"No Opinions" by Education and Problem Area
(in percent)

| | Educational level | | |
Problem area	Elementary	High school	University
External			
Independence (11)[a]	26	18	12
Foreign commitments (2)	26	18	14
Internal			
Cleavages (8)	28	20	13
Role of government (2)	14	10	5
Symbolic (6)	13	11	11

[a] Figures in parentheses indicate the number of questions used.

other indicator of social class, that of occupation, contributed little
in distinguishing between levels of awareness. The reasons why it
should be primarily eduation which distinguished between those with
or without opinions are largely self-evident. Increased education not
only results in increased information, but also sensitizes individuals to
available sources of knowledge and is associated with greater use of
communication media. Education, too, leads to skill in handling new
and difficult ideas. It also contributes to a greater feeling of com-
petence manifested in an increased willingness to participate in politics, a belief in the power of the citizen in democracy, and, in our case,
sufficient self-confidence to express an opinion.

Other characteristics associated with a relatively high proportion
of "no opinions" were French language, Catholicism, residence in

Quebec, and female sex. This was true for all categories of issues except symbols, where awareness was high for all groups, and foreign commitments, where the number of questions available made generalizations difficult. Looking at the lesser awareness of women, this again has been substantiated in other surveys.[9] One contributing factor is the characteristically lower level of education held by women. The more restricted exposure of women generally to a variety of social contacts, and their low level of interest in political events elaborated in Chapter X, could be expected to limit their knowledge of political issues. Sex-role expectations also discourage female assertiveness in an area which in North America, at least until the present, has been primarily a masculine domain.

French-Canadians and level of awareness.—More noteworthy was the high proportion of "no opinions" among the French-speaking, Catholics, and Quebec residents (see Table 75), perhaps because they have less education than the remainder of the population.[10] Another possibility is that these groups did not perceive themselves as affected by the issues in question since, as it had been hypothesized, "The more salient and clear-cut the issue, the more likely that a group will react in terms of its defined interests." [11] It hardly seems plausible, however, to accept such an explanation of why these origin groups were low on awareness. As we have demonstrated throughout the text, questions on education, immigration, ties with Britain, and the Commonwealth all have special relevance to those of French origin, and in many cases were significant in dividing opinions along a regional-ethnic axis.

The relatively high incidence of "no opinions" among those of French origin may be related to group values opposing openness to strangers. Such an explanation has been frequently offered in the face of the general resistance of French-speaking Canadians to participation in survey research. Some substantiation of this view comes from a study conducted at the Institute of Psychology at the University of Montreal, which used as subjects matched samples of male secondary-school students of the two official language groups. The two student bodies attended Catholic schools so that the findings were presumably not affected by religious affiliation. Respondents were

[9] Key, *op. cit.*, p. 186.

[10] Those in Quebec are more likely than the population as a whole to end their schooling at the elementary level, but it is difficult to evaluate this practice because educational standards vary considerably from province to province. Canada, Dominion Bureau of Statistics, *1961 Census of Canada*, Ottawa: Queen's Printer, 1963, Table 72.

[11] S. M. Lipset, P. F. Lazarsfeld, A. H. Barton, and J. J. Linz, "The Psychology of Voting: An Analysis of Political Behavior," in *Handbook of Social Psychology*, ed. by Gardner Lindzey, II, Cambridge: Addison-Wesley, p. 1170.

TABLE 75

PROPORTION OF "NO OPINIONS," BY REGION, LANGUAGE, RELIGION, AND PROBLEM AREA
(in percent)

Problem area	Region					Language		Religion	
	Maritimes	Quebec	Ontario	Prairies	British Columbia	English	French	Protestant	Roman Catholic
External									
Independence	18	26	14	13	11	18	32	18	30
Foreign commitments	26	23	18	23	23	29	14	20	23
Internal									
Cleavages	22	30	26	24	19	19	29	25	31
Role of government	10	16	8	8	8	12	26	9	15
Symbolic	13	15	13	14	17	14	18	12	15

NOTE: The number of questions on which this table is based varies for the characteristic and problem areas. For foreign commitments it is 1 or 2, and this is also the case for government and religion.

asked to evaluate the desirability of social traits from a list carefully matched for comparability in the two languages. The most noteworthy findings for our purposes were that 82 percent of the French considered "curious" undesirable compared with 50 percent of the English, while 90 percent of the former answered that "discrete" was desirable compared again with 50 percent of the English.[12] If these results have more general applicability, they may help account for our own findings with respect to French-English differences.

A fourth explanatory factor is related to the comparative position of different religious and linguistic groups in Canadian society. We know that the French-speaking and Roman Catholics have not achieved the same degree of power, especially on the economic scene, as English-speaking Protestants.[13] At the same time, as our surveys have demonstrated, these less powerful minorities often expressed views at variance with those of the majority. We would argue, then, that lesser power and contrary opinions combined in such a way as to result in the lessened participation of some minority-group members. In common-sense terms, it is easy to understand that even when a group supports its members in their unpopular views, some of them will still wish to avoid the possible complications and conflicts which would arise from openly challenging the majority. A group strong in power and upholding the majority viewpoint will be led to participate, to offer an opinion; a weak group characterized by an opposition viewpoint will tend to withdraw. Evidence for these statements is at least suggested by experimental studies of small groups. Most relevant is one which examined decision-making among air-force combat crews. The results suggested to the researcher that "the least powerful member of the group does not feel free to disagree with the more powerful members." [14] Less directly relevant, but still meaningful, are those small-group studies which find high-status persons to be

[12] "Significant Study of the Year Highlights Character Differences Between French, English Canadians," *Marketing*, October 13, 1961, pp. 54, 56, 72.

[13] John Porter, "The Economic Elite and the Social Structure in Canada," *Canadian Journal of Economics and Political Science*, 23, August, 1957, pp. 377–394; E. C. Hughes, *French Canada in Transition*, Chicago: University of Chicago Press, 1943, pp. 46–64; Bernard R. Blishen, "The Construction and Use of an Occupational Class Scale," *Canadian Journal of Economics and Political Science*, 24, November, 1958, p. 524; Yves de Jocas and Guy Rocher, "Intergeneration Mobility in the Province of Quebec," *Canadian Journal of Economics and Political Science*, 23, February, 1957, pp. 57–68.

[14] A. Paul Torrance, "Some Consequences of Power Differences on Decision Making in Permanent and Temporary Three-Man Groups," in *Small Groups: Studies in Social Interaction*, ed. by A. Paul Hare, Edgar F. Borgatta, Robert F. Bales, New York: Knopf, 1955, p. 491.

more active participants and to have more influence on the outcome of group decisions.[15]

The relationship between relative power, the nature of opinions, and the incidence of "no opinions" was examined for our own data. Looking at those questions where information was available on province of residence, official language, or religion, comparisons were made between majority and minority groups, with the less powerful minorities defined as Quebec resident, French-speaking, and Catholic. Our contention was: where members of these latter groups had a higher rate of "no opinions" than the majority, they would also be characterized by opinions deviating from the majority viewpoint. We found Quebec residents, Catholics, and the French-speaking most frequently to have both a higher proportion of "no opinions" and a lower proportion expressing the predominant viewpoint when the rate of "no opinions" was controlled, but the results were statistically not significant and could only be seen as suggestive.

There are then four possible explanations for the occurrence of a high level of unawareness among French-speaking, Catholic, and Quebec respondents. Of these, the possibility that they are personally unaffected by the issues at question seemed most remote. Their apparent unawareness was more likely related to some combination of low level of education, reluctance to reveal themselves to strangers, and minority-group status. The last two, in fact, suggest that if such restraining factors did not exist, there would likely be much more conflict in Canadian society than presently prevails.

Political party preference and awareness.—The effects of political party preference in relation to the distribution of "no opinions" yield results of special interest. CCF/NDP supporters were most aware, other party supporters were more similar to each other. The one instance where CCF/NDP supporters had a higher rate of "no opinions" than any of the other parties occurred in relation to questions on symbols, but the differences were slight and all parties had a low rate of "no opinions" (see Table 76). These findings were presumably

[15] R. F. Bales, F. L. Strodtbeck, T. M. Mills, and M. E. Roseborough, "Channels of Communication in Small Groups," *American Sociological Review,* 16, August, 1951, pp. 461–468; F. F. Stephan, "The Relative Rate of Communication Between Members of Small Groups," *American Sociological Review,* 17, August, 1952, pp. 482–486; F. F. Stephan and E. G. Mishler, "The Distribution of Participation in Small Groups: An Exponential Approximation," *American Sociological Review,* 17, October, 1952, pp. 598–608; F. L. Strodtbeck, R. M. James, and C. Hawkins, "Social Status in Jury Deliberations," *American Sociological Review,* 22, December, 1957, pp. 713–719; W. Vaughan and E. McGinnies, "Some Biographical Determiners of Participation in Group Discussion," *Journal of Applied Psychology,* 41, June, 1957, pp. 179–185.

TABLE 76

PROPORTION OF "NO OPINIONS," BY PARTY PREFERENCE AND PROBLEM AREA
(in percent)

	Conserv-ative	Liberal	CCF/NDP	Social Credit
External				
Independence (11)[a]	22	23	19	24
Foreign commitments (2)	20	21	17	20
Internal				
Cleavages (7)	15	15	15	16
Role of government (6)	12	12	7	10
Symbolic (9)	8	10	11	8

[a] Number of questions is given in parentheses.

a consequence of the nature of that party, mitigating the effects of its low power position. In particular, both its mass organization and appeal to principle contributed to a highly informed body of supporters. There is no reason to assume that this was a result of its social base, since it does not possess an unusually high proportion of well-educated supporters. The other parties, lacking the same form of organization or focus of appeal, were hence not able to induce the same high level of awareness among their supporters. But adherence to any political party in itself contributes to an awareness of issues, especially where party loyalties remain stable over time. For example, respondents who preferred the same party in a past and a forthcoming election had a lower level of "no opinions" than those who switched their party preference, while the highest proportion was found among those who, either through forgetfulness, concern with secrecy, failure to vote, or uncertainty, did not give a voting preference (see Table 77). Party loyalty in effect contributed to greater political awareness.

Summarizing the results for this one indicator of salience, there appeared a difference in awareness among problem areas. To account for these differences, problems were considered in terms of their currency, complexity, and specificity. A fuller analysis of the impact of issues will be reserved until we have had time to consider other indicators of salience. In respect to awareness, however, additional insight was gained by the discovery that the critical characteristics related to the degree of awareness were education, regional-ethnic factors, and party preference. Except for questions on political symbols, which appear to have been easily understood by all respondents, the social

TABLE 77

PROPORTION OF "NO OPINIONS," BY STABILITY OF PARTY PREFERENCE
AND PROBLEM AREA
(in percent)

	Favoured same party twice	Favoured different party	No preference given
External			
Independence (13)[a]	19	21	26
Foreign commitments (2)	20	22	23
Internal			
Cleavages (8)	21	27	29
Role of government (8)	12	13	19
Symbolic (9)	12	15	18

[a] Number of questions is given in parentheses.

characteristics mentioned were all more critical in determining the degree of awareness than were the issues themselves.

Urgency

Internal problems as the dominant concern.—From time to time the Gallup Poll has asked respondents unstructured questions on their personal evaluation of the main issues facing Canada. No attempt has been made to assemble all these, but two such questions were available for the surveys which we are intensively analyzing. In both of these, the first asked in 1957 and the second in 1960, the largest single majority mentioned unemployment as the main problem. In 1960, the threat of war rose to be of second importance. In both years, however, issues which we would consider relevant to internal problems were the dominant concern. Beginning with unemployment, these were mainly of an economic nature[16] (see Tables 78 and 79). It is noteworthy that none of the other national problems which we have considered in this study were spontaneously mentioned.

In two surveys conducted in 1961 and 1962, respondents were given structured questions listing issues and then asked to rank them in

[16] In 1957, the problems question was seventh in the questionnaire, following questions on leisure-time activities, advertising, working at two jobs, the Prime Minister, federal-provincial relations, and work preferences. In 1960, the problems question began the interview. It is unlikely in either case that respondents were directed into particular areas by the structure of the interview situation.

TABLE 78

MAIN ISSUES FACING CANADA,
DECEMBER, 1957
N = 2,105
(in percent)

Unemployment	41
War	8
Farm markets	6
Population problems	5
Cost of living	4
Personal faults	2
Housing	1
Social security	1
Education	1
Youth problems	1
Communism	1
Russia	1
Sputnik	1
Taxes	a
Other	6
Cannot say	17

a Less than 1 percent.

TABLE 79

MOST IMPORTANT PROBLEM FACING CANADA,
JULY, 1960
N = 717
(in percent)

Unemployment	40
Threat of war	24
Rising cost of living	6
Economic situation	5
Russia	4
National defense	3
Farm situation	2
Labour unions	2
Trade	2
Lack of religion	2
Immigration	1
Other	9
Do not know	5

order of importance.[17] In both years the four high-ranking issues were unemployment, medical insurance, taxation, and old-age benefits—all issues having some relevance to the role of government. Respondents were also asked about Canadian relations with the United States and Britain. In 1961, relations between the United States and Canada ranked tenth out of twelve issues. By the following year, this issue had risen somewhat in importance and was now midway in the twelve. Relations between Canada and Britain, however, were considered among the relatively least important. In 1961, questions were also asked about labour unions and immigration, and these ranked last.

Interest in a coming election also contributes a degree of urgency to the perception of political issues, at least to the extent of leading to a specific response. For example, several months before the 1962 general election respondents were asked to indicate their degree of interest in it; those with a greater degree of interest were more likely to express an opinion whether labour unions should participate as political parties (see Table 80).

TABLE 80

INTEREST IN COMING ELECTION AND OPINIONS ON HAVING
ORGANIZED LABOUR SUPPORT OWN PARTY, JANUARY, 1962
(in percent)

Opinion on support from labour	Interest in election			
	Very N = 152	Fairly N = 275	Not at all N = 60	Cannot say N = 211
Good thing	15	16	12	23
Bad thing	64	59	47	34
Undecided	20	25	42	44

Economic interests most urgent to Canadians.—The foregoing responses indicates that salience in respect to criticalness is greatest for issues pertaining to internal problems. On the basis of these, it appears that Canadians are most concerned about their economic interests, or what the authors of *Voting* call "position issues." The responses indicate the material interests of Canadians, and, even though, as our previous discussion revealed, awareness of these issues was only moderately high, except for social-welfare questions when it was consistently high, they nevertheless have been and continue to be of immediate urgency.

[17] The actual tabulations are not available for publication.

Political symbols represent style issues and therefore might be expected to have a more ephemeral though emotional impact. As we have seen, they produce a high degree of awareness, but in themselves they are not spontaneously seen as critical issues for the nation. The extent of awareness in itself, then, is not an adequate measure of salience. Given the social, economic, and sectional cleavages in Canada, matters of style or the working out of cultural interests are as much a problem to the nation as are position issues. Yet even while the conflicts and competing interests in Canada find a rallying point in emotion-laden, easily understood questions of political symbols, these questions do not get to the substance of the ordinary voter's concerns and perceptions. Relations between interest groups and questions of independence are examples of combined position and style issues, since they refer both to material interests and to the way these should be developed. According to Berelson, "in the broad sweep of political history Big Issues are those which combine Position and Style aspects, as, for example, slavery in this country [the United States] or the French Revolution." [18] But apparently, especially for the issue of independence, neither our indicators of awareness nor of urgency has revealed a high level of salience. Historically we cannot argue away the importance of these issues. Yet to the proverbial average man, in this case a Canadian, the significant concerns are those which relate to his economic well-being. Neither the symbols nor the substance of national independence have troubled him unduly.[19]

AN ASSESSMENT OF SALIENCY ✗

Each indicator used here gave a somewhat different perspective on saliency. The indicator of awareness emphasized the impact of political symbols, presumably through their simplicity and emotionality. An examination of awareness showed the importance of differences in access to information, ability to understand political ideas, and relative power position, which resulted in an advantage to those with more education, men, and the dominant English-speaking Protestants. Power position in itself was not, however, significant in its conse-

[18] Berelson, *et al., op. cit.* (see n. 1, above), p. 185.
[19] This does not deny the possibility that disaffected minorities, strongly committed to a point of view, can take drastic action to bring about political change. Even to the extent that such minorities may be able to arouse public controversy, this may be sufficient to mobilize more widespread public support or polarize public opinion. The activities of separatists and terrorists in French Canada are a case in point. What has disturbed many commentators is the relative silence of moderate voices in Quebec and the consequent growth of anti-French opinion among political leaders and the press outside Quebec.

quences for political parties. Their organizational character and the nature of their appeal had most bearing on whether their supporters would have opinions on issues. A mass type of organization and an appeal based on principle appeared to produce a greater awareness on the part of CCF/NDP supporters.

In making at least a partial attempt to determine importance of issues, symbols disappeared as a first-ranking issue, but issues pertaining to material interests emerged as paramount. This does not, of course, deny the potential importance of other issues, including those of symbols, but, from the evidence available, the impact of events over the past two decades has not led the average Canadian away from self-centred concerns.

There has been no unequivocal demonstration of the major saliency to rank and file citizens of the issues available to us for tapping the critical problems underlying the definition of national identity. But at the least, it is clear that they know about the national problems which Canada must face, although it is true that they are better acquainted with some than with others and that they are intensely concerned with only some of these issues.

XIII RESPONSES TO THE CHALLENGE OF NATIONAL VIABILITY

PROBLEMS AND SOLUTIONS: STABILITY AND CHANGE

AT THE OUTSET of this book we presented a number of challenges related to the emergence and continuity of nations: the development of a sense of unity, the overcoming of gross inequalities within the nation, the raising of standards generally, and the creation of a focus for national pride and for differentiation from other nations. In response to such challenges, a national identity takes shape.

We looked for the definition of national identity in the public conception of the major problems faced by a country and their solutions. The problems were classified under three headings: external, internal, and symbolic—a classification of widespread applicability. Within this general context it has been possible to explain the situation of Canada.

In our discussion of national problems, although the three problem areas obviously have a bearing on each other, we treated each of them as having some degree of independence. Assuming that they can be seen in this manner, it also seems likely that they can be ranked for particular countries and periods of time. To attempt such a ranking it is necessary to establish some criteria of evaluation. These could either be objective or subjective.

Objective criteria would be those which took into account the actual circumstances of the country under study. For example, the importance of external problems might be judged by the extent of military dependence on other nations for over-all defense, the need for safeguarding borders, or the nature of internal security measures. Military problems would also be intense where there was direct or implied threat to national integrity. External problems could also be seen in economic and political terms where, for instance, there was dependence on other nations for policy-making, markets, the development of resources, or the acquisition of resources and products.

Internal problems would be judged in terms of the existence of a heterogeneous population, especially where divisions in the population were associated with a regional locus, but more critically where these divisions were accompanied by an unequal distribution of rewards.

Finally, symbolic problems would be rated as important when unifying political symbols were absent. Theoretically at least, if such an evaluation were carried out systematically some ranking of national problems could probably be made.

No attempt is being made here to refine these categories for research purposes; rather, they are merely being suggested to indicate the kind of information that might be used in evaluating the seriousness of a country's problems.

Instead of, or in addition to, such objective criteria, more subjective ones could be employed. These would be concerned with citizens' perceptions of the seriousness of their country's problems. The effective use of such subjective criteria is affected by the varied nature of opinions and attitudes.[1] Our own discussion of salience in the preceding chapter considered that the important components of opinions were awareness and urgency. Awareness in turn was affected by the publicity, simplicity, and generality of the issues. Yet in attempting to use these components to arrive at a ranking for Canadian problems, the results were far from clear. While we attributed these equivocal findings at least partly to the incompleteness of our data and the use of varied indicators, the question remains whether a subjective or even an objective set of criteria would allow us to rank national problems. Even if we come up with a series of ideal types rather than pictures of concrete reality, these may still efficiently describe the essence of a nation's status at a given point in time.

Assuming for the moment that adequate criteria for ranking could be obtained, some interesting possibilities are suggested. Six orderings emerge. In two, external problems are uppermost in importance— situations where the struggle to attain or retain national integrity in the face of foreign control, either actual or threatened, commands the major part of a country's energies. Where external problems are followed in significance by internal ones we have a situation not unlike that of present-day Finland. In that country the threat of encroachment from Russia is always present. Internally the presence of an upper-status Swedish-speaking minority has resulted in linguistic problems as well as those relating to the general economic welfare of the country. Symbolic problems appear relatively insignificant. Under dif-

<hr />

[1] For example, Guttman, in his study of scalable attitudes, suggests that we take into account a number of components. These include intensity, or the strength with which the attitude is held; closure, or the finality of decision with respect to the attitude; and involution, or the extent to which the attitude is uppermost in the thoughts of its holders. Louis Guttman "An Outline of Some New Methodology for Social Research," *Public Opinion Quarterly*, 18, Winter, 1954–55, pp. 396–397.

ferent circumstances external problems may be succeeded by symbolic ones; the struggle for independence may be accompanied by a search for unifying symbols which will set the nation apart from foreign countries. The thirteen American colonies at the time of the War of Independence provide what is probably the best example of this ordering of problems.

Where a critical unevenness exists in the distribution of resources and rewards and a consequent conflict of interest between social groups, internal problems are most prominent. These may be followed by external problems, as is the case of present-day United States and Great Britain. A seemingly intractable level of unemployment and pockets of poverty and the struggle to secure civil rights for all citizens constitute critical internal problems for the United States today. At the same time major new external problems confront the United States in maintaining its position as a world power. The specific problems of Great Britain in the 1960's are different, but no less serious. Internally they involve the revamping of the social structure with respect to the production of goods and services, provision of adequate rewards, and the educational system—in effect, all components and conditions of the traditional social-class hierarchy. Externally they involve readjustments in status attendant on the loss of power as a colonial nation and the changing character of the Commonwealth.

Although symbol problems are not weighty in either the United States or Great Britain, in some countries they may be stimulated by major social cleavages. In Belgium, for instance, the division between Walloons and Flemish has been intensified by regional, linguistic, religious (in the sense of degree of observance of Catholicism) and economic differences. Some national symbols exist, most notably that of the king, but symbols attached to regions often command greater loyalty. Thus persons flying the national flag in a Flemish location have been subject to assault by their more particularistic neighbours. External problems also exist in Belgium, but they do not, at least since the withdrawal from the Congo, approach the magnitude of either internal or symbolic ones.

Finally, we have the situation in which symbolic problems rank first. It is likely to be the result of some discontinuity in the legitimately constituted political authority through insurrection, revolution, or foreign conquest. Rémond, for example, relates it in France to the position of the monarchy: "Each time an upheaval breaks the continuity of the regime, as in 1848 or 1871, royalism as a result enjoys the advantages of its relative permanency: faithful to the legitimate sovereign it will naturally survive the accidents of history." [2] In Belgium, the normally more critical internal problems were superseded by symbolic ones following World War II. Because of circumstances relevant to the behaviour of Leopold III during the war, parliament declared him "unable to reign." A 1950 referendum permitted his return, but when the king did so he was met with a general strike and abdicated in favour of his son. An examination of the results of the referendum showed that those favouring the king's return were concentrated among specific segments of the population. The issue then served to intensify party, regional, and religious divisions which are normally held in check by the unifying symbol of the king.

An additional illustration of the primacy of symbolic problems is that of France from 1871 to about 1875. At that time an end to the Franco-Prussian War was being negotiated, and while this was accompanied by major internal dissension centred in the Paris Commune, we have chosen to give second place to external problems. We have done so because of the significance of the Franco-Prussian War and, even after peace had been achieved in 1871, the continued threat from Germany to counter any attempt to retake Alsace-Lorraine. The Third Republic was established in 1875 partly in response to this latter threat. But between 1871 and 1875 the uppermost symbolic problem concerned the nature of the new state. Was it to be a republic or a monarchy, and, if a monarchy, which of the contending claims of the two pretenders, the Comte de Chambord or the Comte de Paris, were to be considered greatest? Although considerable sympathy for a monarchy existed at that time, and the Comte de Chambord became recognized as the legitimate claimant to the throne, the restoration was never achieved, mainly because he insisted on the adoption of the White Flag of the Bourbons before he would accept the crown.[3]

The selection and classification of the foregoing examples constitutes a degree of arbitrariness, especially since no clear-cut criteria for ranking were employed. Nevertheless, these examples indicate that an ordering of national problems is feasible for giving a condensed description of a country. By using illustrations from the same countries at different historical points we have emphasized again that the underlying problems and their assessment are not static. Whether or not the problems are ranked, each in itself refers to a critical aspect of a country's progress and each merits the analyst's attention.

On the basis of survey results, the various indicators of salience used

[2] René Rémond, *La Droite en France de 1815 à nos jour*, Paris: Aubier, 1954, p. 66 [My own translation].

[3] Samuel M. Osgood, *French Royalism Under the Third and Fourth Republic*, The Hague: Martinus Nijhoff, 1960, pp. 1–34.

here, and our assessment of present political conditions, Canada's problems may be ranked in order of importance from internal to symbolic to external. Public concern about internal issues is related to the major social changes currently taking place in French Canada, economic problems manifested in monetary crises and unemployment, and the questions which political leaders and commentators are asking about the state of Confederation. These complex problems have become focused into more comprehensible and emotional ones relating to political symbols. Even though many internal problems and problems related to symbols are closely connected with external issues of ties with Britain and especially the United States, the internal effects of these ties are more significant to the average Canadian than the ties themselves. For example, while the lack of uniquely Canadian political symbols is a result of Canada's beginnings as a British colony, present ties with Britain are scarcely strong enough to explain the current situation. American trade policies and ownership and control of Canadian resources and industries may cause some economic dislocations and incense elite groups in Canada, but the call for "maître chez nous" seems to be strong only in those places where it can be shown that there are obvious internal consequences for the economy.[4]

An examination of our Canadian data suggests two significant dimensions along which solutions to national problems can be ordered and which can probably be generalized to cover other situations. The first refers to the degree of innovation, which may be conceived of as a continuum going from old to new ways of doing things. The shifting nature of these definitions is apparent, since what is new at one point in time is old at another. While this undoubtedly increases the difficulty of using this dimension, it at the same time increases its utility as a tool for handling major social changes.

The second dimension is concerned with the nature of the orientation displayed through the choice of solutions. This orientation may be either inward looking, preferring solutions unique to the country, or outward looking—seeking guidance in solving problems from the experiences of others.

If each dimension is thought of for the moment as consisting of polar opposites, four characteristic types of solutions appear. A prefer-

[4] "Maître chez nous" was a slogan used by the Liberals in the Quebec provincial election of 1962, although it was directed more against ownership and control from English Canada than from outside the country. For an example of the consequences of close ties between the Canadian and American economies, see Peter C. Newman, "The Great Money Panic of 1963," *Maclean's*, May 16, 1964, pp. 20, 53–55.

ence for newness combined with an inward orientation is one possible response to national problems. It is well exemplified by the French Revolution. The Russian-inspired Chinese and Cuban revolutions better exemplify an innovative and outward orientation. Other countries have shown a preference for traditional ways of solving problems and an inward orientation. The institutions associated with the British Crown illustrate this. Those countries satisfied with continuing their colonial status represent our final category, that of a preference for old ways and an outward orientation. These examples then help to explain what is meant by the dimensions of innovation and orientation and the relation which these two have to each other.

In considering solutions situated along these two main dimensions, it also becomes possible to map our three problem areas in relation to them. Such graphic representation accompanied by the use of arrows can also indicate the direction of movement in the selection of solutions. We may illustrate in this fashion countries which select similar trends of responses to external, internal, and symbolic problems and those which take a different direction for each of the problem areas. The latter is exemplified by Canada (see Figure 4).

FIGURE 4

The Current Location of National Problems
and Solutions in Canada

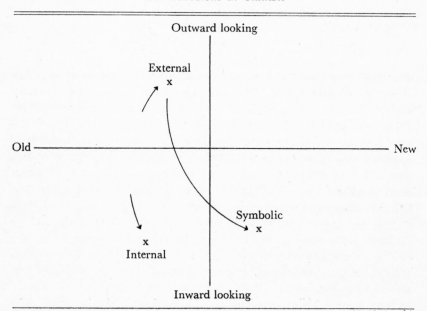

From data presented in Part II, we are able to identify the current dominant perspective on external problems as representing a high degree of outward orientation and a preference for old ties and loyalties. Although support for international agencies indicates some innovation, increasing support for the Commonwealth tends to keep the balance of solutions to external problems on the old side of the axis. The short arrow pointing to an increase in outward orientation attempts to take into account this shift in opinion. Internal problems are located in the old and inward segment of our graph. We are restricted in our judgments by the sample of questions available, but it may be fair to interpret increasing opposition to immigration as indicating a greater degree of inward orientation, and increased preference for bilingualism as indicating new responsiveness to internal innovations. The greatest changes in opinion trends are manifested in those relating to problems of symbols. The swing has been from a traditional, outward orientation to an innovative, inward one. In this respect, however, the search for specifically Canadian symbols has been greater than the concern with new ones. For example, while Canadians have become increasingly desirous of a Canadian Governor-General, this has not been accompanied by the feeling that some new form of symbolic head, rather than a Governor-General, would be preferable.

DEFINING AN IDENTITY

The Shaping of Opinions

The definition given by the public to its national identity is the result of social divisions within the society, roles and institutions associated with leadership and guidance on national objectives, and the shifting circumstances of social groups and the nation as a whole. The politically relevant social groupings are those which are, either singly or in combination, in positions differentially affected by social processes, and which are subjectively aware of differences in interests. Examinations conducted in a number of political settings have fairly consistently uncovered social characteristics most closely associated with, or best accounting for, particular forms of political opinions and behaviour. Some findings, such as the greater conservatism of women or the greater tendency of the working class to support social-welfare legislation, can even be generalized across national boundaries. But, as our Canadian Gallup Poll surveys have indicated, not all characteristics are equally meaningful in accounting for patterns of opinions.

Previous research provided a useful guide for the selection of our own materials and interpretation of our findings, but the existence of national differences makes it necessary to relate the social characteristics considered to the peculiar historical circumstances of each country.

Nations once rich and powerful may lose their wealth and power while those at one time an insignificant part of another nation may attain independence and great influence in the world. Internally, new economic and political philosophies may rise to importance in response to changing international conditions or to those closer to home. Technological change, shifts in population, the depletion of old or the discovery of new resources, the development of new value systems, all may contribute to changes in the internal distribution of perspectives and influences. Hence, influences on the shaping of opinions are no more static than are the relative rankings of national problems or their solutions.

There are many reasons for dealing with this whole complex of influences on opinions. We wish to know how opinions are formed, the degree of intensity with which different groups in the population hold their views, the integration of viewpoints on different issues, and the degree and nature of consensus. Though of great importance, opinion formation has been only incidentally discussed in this study because we neglected the agencies directly concerned with creating, disseminating, and making public, opinions. Intensity of opinions has been more directly tackled but here generalizations have had to be qualified because of the spottiness of our data. It is with consensus that we were most critically concerned, and because of the important questions it raises we shall leave this to a separate discussion.

Significance of Parties

In the preceding discussion and analysis we singled out national parties as having a unique potential for providing answers to the political problems posed by the formulation and clarification of a national identity. This potential lies in their function, either actual or possible, as agencies for the exercise of government through the attraction of popular support. Stated in this fashion, political parties play this role only in democratic states, although our earlier discussions conceived of the role of parties in sufficiently broad terms to include even one-party states. The pivotal position of parties is particularly well illustrated if we borrow the language of Parsons, Almond, or Easton and speak of "inputs" and "outputs." [5] Their terminology differs, but essentially the authors define inputs to the political system as demands for policies and general support from the public. The outputs from the political system represent decisions, policies, and leadership. In a democracy, political parties serve as the central mechanism for articulating these inputs and outputs. To attain power, parties are dependent on support; to retain it they must satisfy demands by the formulation of policies and the provision of leadership; by exercising their responsibilities they in turn affect the kinds of demands made on them and the polity in general. It does not matter who initially instigates demands relevant to the manner in which the nation's identity unfolds. Insofar as these have a bearing on the conduct of government and the external and internal integrity of the state, they will meet some response from national political parties. Consequently political parties are important and inevitable influences on the definition of identity, for the nation itself and for its citizens.

The effectiveness of parties has been seen as operating through three component features: the nature of support, the focus of appeal, and the type of organization. In other words, we have been concerned with the extent to which the electorate is involved in a party and in what fashion. The interaction of these three features produces eight party types, each of which has differing implications for the development of a national identity.[6] By viewing national identity from the perspective of the public definition of national problems and their solutions, a degree of consensus is implied. We have argued, then, that the three dimensions along which we have ordered parties have consequences for the homogeneity of viewpoint within parties. Our hypothesis is that the dimension with greatest significance for intraparty consensus is that relating to the focus of appeal. Parties which attract and hold supporters primarily on the basis of principles relating to, as we have said, "special interests, issues, groups, or ideologies" will be more likely to have supporters with similar viewpoints. Such a unifying framework for opinion is less likely to exist in parties mainly concerned with electoral success. Uniformity of outlook is

---

[5] Talcott Parsons, " 'Voting' and the Equilibrium of the American Political System," in *American Voting Behavior*, ed. by Eugene Burdick and Arthur J. Brodbeck, Glencoe: Free Press, 1959, pp. 80–120; David Easton, "An Approach to the Analysis of Political Systems," *World Politics*, 9, April, 1957, pp. 383–400; Gabriel A. Almond, "Introduction: A Functional Approach to Comparative Politics," in *The Politics of the Developing Areas*, ed. by Gabriel A. Almond and James S. Coleman, Princeton: Princeton University Press, 1960, pp. 9–17.

[6] See the discussion and examples in Chapter II.

further reinforced where mass organizations with a large body of participating supporters exist, and where support is restricted to relatively few groups in the population, rather than having a broad social base. Such parties permit the emergence of a high degree of consensus among supporters. This in turn reinforces divisions among parties, and may well mean that national integration is so hampered by the strength of partisan arguments that a party's definition of identity is presented as the only correct one. But in a system where the legitimacy of opposition parties has become institutionalized, some accommodation must be made to the claims of other parties. This comes about because all genuine political parties seek to attain office and assume the responsibilities of government. Parties which are not "majority bent" deserve to be characterized more as interest groups than as parties. In a democratic state the party forming the government must recognize that among the electorate are those of other political persuasions who must somehow be conciliated so that they will continue to acknowledge the legitimacy of the state. Unduly acrimonious partisan arguments would make such adjustments difficult if not impossible. Despite such slogans as "twenty years of treason," political arguments generally must be tempered in order not seriously to threaten the continuity of the political system. Because of these institutional requirements, political parties, though distinct in their orientations, may still be able to agree on some political values and even issues, and thus pave the way for some merging of viewpoints. This could be especially true of issues somewhat outside the realm of politics, or of problems which are basic to the unfolding of a national identity—issues which transcend party politics.

Returning to our typology of parties, we have suggested that parties able to appeal to a broad segment of the electorate have a greater potential for contributing to a national consensus than do those with a restricted social base. They can do this most effectively when their appeal is based on some unifying principle. Even where principle is lacking, however, and despite the fact that a major concern with getting elected tends to weaken internal party cohesion, the social diversity of supporters appears to promote some measure of national integration across party lines.

These generalizations about the nature of political parties with respect to their organization, bases of support, and type of appeal have been substantiated by an examination of Canadian public-opinion data. The Canadian data, however, only provided information about two types of parties: the broad-based cadre party of electoral success, and the narrow-based mass party of principle. In addition, public-opinion surveys used here were only able to indicate the social bases of support (and that imperfectly) whereas information about organization and type of appeal had to be derived from other published sources. Moreover, since our focus has been on public opinion, we have been more concerned with the effects of certain types of organization and party appeal on shaping opinions than with the organizations and appeals themselves. Hence empirical support for the typology of parties introduced in this study has been only partial, although the typology proved useful and gave promise of even greater usefulness with a more thorough-going comparative approach.

Consensus

The problem of consensus is central to our study. It arose as an issue whenever we discussed dominant opinions in the country as a whole, alterations in these, the relative homogeneity of various groupings, and the relationship between similarity in viewpoint and various social divisions. Unstated, however, have been a number of basic questions, among them, how much consensus is required for the continued existence of a society and on what matters. Although we intend to focus mainly on the total society, these problems may also be important for smaller groups.[7] Our main concern here, however, is with the total society.

Although consensus has been a traditional concern of sociological theory, surprisingly little guidance is provided by existing theory for relating empirical findings to general propositions about the nature of society.[8]

To see how consensus has been treated in sociological theory it is necessary to begin one step removed from the concept and look at the problem of social cohesion. The latter has generally been described in relation to two qualitatively different societies or principles of organization. Despite differences in terminology, Maine's status and contract, Spencer's military and industrial society, Durkheim's me-

---

[7] They obviously have no relevance to demographic characteristics such as age and sex, since these will continue to exist regardless of the degree of internal consistency of members' opinions. It is still of interest, however, to see what bearing shared experiences, for example, as a woman or an old person, have on opinions.

[8] When we speak here of empirical findings, we refer to them only in gross terms of majority points of view, rather than by such particular findings as that groups are distinguished by a 10 percent difference in viewpoint or that there is a 5 percent shift in opinions over time. Even if we had wished to emphasize such points, as we have often said, the survey data used for this study do not permit the treatment of individual findings with such a degree of precision.

chanical and organic solidarity, Tönnies' *Gemeinschaft* and *Gesell-schaft*, and Cooley's primary and secondary groups all bear on this theme. The first concept in these pairs relates the binding ties to similarities among group members, to an identity of interest, and to what Giddings first termed "consciousness of kind." The cohesiveness described by the polar opposites is derived instead from the functional interdependence of the differentiated parts.

According to those who used these concepts, consensus is a prominent feature of undifferentiated *Gemeinschaft*-type societies. The place of consensus in differentiated *Gesellschaft*-type societies is not as clear. In some views consensus is difficult to achieve in the latter societies because of the variety of interests represented. The relative lack of consensus presents a problem for their continuity and for the social well-being of their members. Exponents of this position include Tönnies and Durkheim.[9] Another viewpoint avoids posing the question of the place of consensus in differentiated societies because it sees social solidarity as a consequence of functional interdependence. This is a position which Durkheim takes at points.[10] A third view, while emphasizing both the potential and actual conflict associated with divergent interests existing within the same political society, also notes the presence of widespread consensus on certain basic values.[11] None of these assertions on the place of consensus in the maintenance of a social system is sufficiently specific to cope with the reality that consensus is neither an undifferentiated nor a static phenomenon. It is interesting and significant that Florence Kluckhohn, who has argued that the study of dominant values has been overemphasized and that variants have been neglected, and although she considers the latter

[9] See for example, Emile Durkheim, *The Division of Labor in Society*, trans. George Simpson, Glencoe: Free Press, 1960, pp. 353–395; Emile Durkheim, *Suicide*, trans. J. A. Spaulding and G. Simpson, Glencoe: Free Press, 1951, pp. 152–216, 241–276; Ferdinand Tönnies, "Gemeinschaft and Gesellschaft," in *Theories of Society*, ed. by Talcott Parsons, Edward Shils, Kaspar D. Naegele, and Jesse R. Pitts, New York: Glencoe, 1961, I, 191–201.

[10] Harry Alpert, *Emile Durkheim and His Sociology*, New York: Columbia University Press, 1939, p. 182.

[11] For example the work of Berelson, Linz, and Parsons stresses the importance of such agreement for the operation of the political system. De Tocqueville, Williams, and Eisenstadt speak of the need for accordance on more general social values in a plural society. B. Berelson, P. F. Lazarsfeld, and W. N. McPhee, *Voting*, Chicago: University of Chicago Press, 1954, pp. 313–321; Juan J. Linz, *The Social Bases of West German Politics*, unpublished doctoral dissertation, Faculty of Political Science, Columbia University, 1959, pp. 121–122; Parsons, *op. cit.* (see n. 5), pp. 80–120; Robin Williams, Jr., *American Society*, New York: Knopf, 1957, p. 209; S. N. Eisenstadt, *The Absorption of Immigrants*, London: Routledge & Kegan Paul, 1954, p. 137; Alexis de Tocqueville, *Democracy in America*, New York: Knopf, 1963, especially I, 254–330.

to be both required and permitted for the adequate functioning of all social systems,[12] is hard-pressed when dealing with empirical data to interpret variations within cultures as opposed to those between cultures.[13]

Granted that the cited writers confirm the necessity for a degree of consensus as well as for variations on critical issues, we have found empirical studies, often of small groups, of greater help in suggesting limits on the amount of variability permissible for the continuity of a social system. At the individual level these limiting conditions may be experienced as pressures to conform, but our concern here will be merely with listing their characteristics.

Observability of variations in opinions.—Not all those participating in a social system are necessarily aware that others in the same situation do not share their views on any specific or even general topic. Opinion polls have accustomed us to think of "public opinion," but opinions surveyed are often only public in the sense that the investigator has deliberately pursued techniques for making them manifest. Otherwise it is fair to say that there are normally many impediments to the dissemination of opinions. As a result the population may contain many variations in viewpoints without this ever being made known. Insofar as these variations are not made known this serves to protect their existence.[14] It is possible as well that the barriers to observability may lead persons to underestimate rather than overestimate the degree of conformity in their social setting. For example, in the study of value orientations already cited, members of one of the groups studied, the Rimrock Navaho, fairly consistently underestimated the degree of consensus in their group. While no prior theoretical provisions were made to account for discrepancies between actual and perceived consensus, in this case the authors suggest that it was a response to the transitional nature of the culture, by which members indicated their accompanying confusion.[15]

[12] Florence R. Kluckhohn and Fred L. Strodtbeck, *Variations in Value Orientations,* Evanston: Row, Peterson, 1961, p. 3.

[13] *Ibid,* p. 347; pp. 414–415. The latter citation is actually Strodtbeck's work.

[14] "Generally, the views expressed in public or with a possibility of being made public are more conforming." A. Paul Hare, *Handbook of Small Group Research,* New York: Free Press, 1962, p. 35. Hare supports his generalization by a number of studies, including the following: L. Festinger, "Laboratory Experiments: The Role of Group Belongingness," in *Experiments in Social Process,* ed. by J. G. Miller, New York: McGraw-Hill, 1950, pp. 31–46; H. H. Kelley and E. H. Volkhart, "The Resistance to Change of Group-Anchored Attitudes," *American Sociological Review,* 17, August, 1952, pp. 453–465; C. I. Hovland, I. L. Janis, and H. H. Kelley, *Communication and Persuasion: Psychological Studies of Opinion Change,* New Haven: Yale University Press, 1953.

[15] Kluckhohn and Strodtbeck, *op. cit.,* p. 336.

Common perspectives may be communicated by the mass media and by those in positions of leadership. The media, however, tend to emphasize the unusual rather than the common. Thus they may contribute less to a unified perspective and more to an awareness of lack of consensus.[16] Leaders, in performing their roles, while more likely than average group members to be aware of the relevant opinions of others,[17] are not necessarily concerned with passing on this information. But it seems likely that leaders would want to make the distribution of opinions in a group known to its members when this would serve as an indication of the internal weakness of the group vis-à-vis others. This need not be a technique restricted to the operation of small groups, but could be applicable to the national scene where political leaders could use their awareness of patterns of opinions to encourage greater unity of outlook.

Relative size of group holding opinions.—If the first limiting condition is based on the premise that "what you don't know won't hurt you," the second is derived from the fact that anonymity is more easily achieved in a large setting. The vastness of numbers may prove a cloak for nonconforming viewpoints. Yet once there is an awareness of differences in opinions, as experiments on small groups have frequently demonstrated, then those holding the majority viewpoint are at an advantage in persuading the minority to change their opinions. In situations, however, where differences in opinion are associated not with one or more individuals in a group but with entire groups, then awareness of majority views may only intensify the opposition of the minority. It may be as true in a total society as in a small group that it is difficult for nonconformists to hold out against the persuasiveness of overwhelming numbers, but in a total society nonconformists may be supported by cultural norms in their role as a beleaguered minority.[18]

Social status of opinion holders.—Public opinion on significant issues is the result of attempts by individuals and groups to formulate

[16] For example, after the Federal-Provincial Conference held in Quebec City in April, 1964, several provincial premiers complained that the mass media overemphasized areas of dissension, especially concerning Premier Lesage and Quebec, neglecting the accomplishments of the conference.

[17] Kamla Chowdhry and T. M. Newcomb, "The Relative Abilities of Leaders and Non-Leaders to Estimate Opinions of their Own Groups," *Journal of Abnormal and Social Psychology*, 47, January, 1952, pp. 51–57.

[18] The significance of cultural norms on nonconformity has not been overlooked by small group experimentalists. For example, in a study conducted in England, the presence of a nonconformist in a group appeared to strengthen the opinions of others. Cecily De Monchaux and Sylvia Shimmin, "Some Problems in Experimental Group Psychology: Considerations Arising From Cross-Cultural Experiments on Threat and Rejection," *Human Relations*, 8, 1955, pp. 53–60.

their own viewpoints and to propagate them. As we have already implied in the previous two points, not all individuals or groups have equal chance of success. The prestige and authority which accompany high-status positions also increase the likelihood of influencing opinions. This applies as much to groups as to individuals. To some extent, then, we must qualify our preceding discussion on the relative size of a group holding an opinion. In some cases majority status will be sufficient to intimidate those in the minority, in others it will not be enough unless it also goes along with some degree of dominance. From these observations we would infer that the strain imposed on the total society by a lack of consensus is greatest when opposition is between those groups or their leaders who enjoy high status. Lack of agreement between high and low status groups or among low status groups may preclude the development of a unified nation, but such situations are not as likely to lead to far-reaching consequences as when near-equals already in influential positions differ.

The relation between opinions and behaviour.—An opinion has serious implications for national consensus only when its expression leads to the possibility of action.[19] One way citizens can manifest their opinions is through voting, but this is often a limited means for bringing about changes. In Canada, elections normally take place once in every four or five years, although they have been much more frequent recently.

When elections do occur, they usually do not bring forth sharp party differences on issues since political parties have generally been reluctant to pursue distinctive policies or ideologies which would inevitably alienate some sections of the electorate. Despite the existence of splinter parties, no successful national party has coincided with the major opinion cleavages in the country. Thus East and West or English and French may often be far apart in viewpoint without, at the same time, having the opportunity of acting out their differences on the national scene. The restraints on political action which exist in Canada need not necessarily exist in other countries. Where more direct democracy is practised, or where political parties are more closely aligned with special interests, lack of consensus may be manifested in major political struggles.

The availability of alternatives.—When we raised the question of the amount of consensus a country needs, we did not conceive of it in narrowly empirical terms such as, for instance, that 75 percent agreement on an issue was preferable to 65 percent, or that conflict would

[19] Herbert McClosky, "Consensus and Ideology in American Politics," *American Political Science Review*, 58, June, 1964, p. 377.

be reduced in one area if 60 percent agreed while on another only 55 percent was required. It is doubtful, indeed, that such statements could ever be meaningfully made in the context of a constantly changing society. But to see in Canada specific categories of voters consistently differentiated by a large percentage margin could only be interpreted as indicating a lack of national consensus, at least on the issues surveyed. Yet Canada has existed in its present political form for almost one hundred years, and it is probably safe to assume that during most of that period consensus on similar issues has never been appreciably greater. We have explored the reasons why the major cleavages, the regional-economic and the regional-ethnic, have such a great impact on opinions and, correlatively, why political parties are restricted in their contributions to national integration. This investigation has suggested that countries such as Canada may provide alternatives to a general consensus. For example, Deutsch writes:

We know how much of a difference in language or culture has been bridged successfully in the emergence of such nations as the Swiss, the British, or the Canadians, provided that enough tangible and intangible rewards and opportunities were present, ranging from greater wealth, security, freedom, and prestige to the subtler attractions of new common symbols, dreams, and ways of life.[20]

It is debatable how successful an appeal to common symbols has been in Canada, but satisfaction of material needs and general political stability have usually been characteristic of the country. As general conditions related to the need for consensus, we would postulate that the satisfaction of material needs and the provision of political stability provide, as it were, alternatives to a high level of consensus. McClosky, who has compared the responses of the general electorate and those of political influentials to questions on democratic ideology, found that only influentials displayed a high degree of commitment to American political values and a high degree of ideological consistency. Yet we have the continued existence of American democracy despite a lack of widespread consensus.

The opinion has long prevailed that consensus is needed to achieve stability, but the converse may be the more correct formulation, i.e., that so long as conditions remain stable, consensus is not required; it becomes essential only when social conditions are disorganized. Consensus may strengthen democratic viability, but its absence in an otherwise stable society need not be fatal or even particularly damaging.[21]

[20] Karl W. Deutsch, "The Growth of Nations: Some Recurrent Patterns of Political and Social Integration," *World Politics*, 5, January, 1953, p. 177.

[21] McClosky, *op. cit.*, p. 377.

Perhaps the existence of a political culture which places a high premium on the orderly conduct of government may be a sufficient consensual element, despite lack of consensus on other crucial issues.

The existence of political stability as well as the satisfaction of material needs would lend themselves to empirical study. Indicators which could be used include the prevalence of general strikes, riots, assassinations, civil disobedience, and governmental turnover; the relation of emigration to immigration; the incidence of major economic dislocations such as depressions and inflations; the range of available rewards, especially income statistics; and the degree of "moral integration." [22] It is possible that other indicators could be developed but those mentioned here give a sufficient sampling of both significant and readily available data. According to our argument the utilization of such indicators should provide some objective criteria against which to evaluate satisfaction and stability and thus to judge the way in which the question of consensus is either sidetracked or accentuated.

The importance of consensus.—In this assessment of consensus we have considered the need to be more specific about its nature and implications than many previous sociologists, especially the early theorists. Whether it will ever be possible to deal with this problem in quantitative terms is a question which neither our data nor the state of our knowledge can answer. But we have begun with the assumption that perfect consensus is not a necessary nor even desirable state for any social system. Starting from this point we have sought from a variety of sources to delimit those factors which hold in check the divisive effects of a lack of consensus. Our conclusions have been that political strains are lessened when the following conditions exist: awareness of the distribution of opinions is low; groups conforming to the dominant viewpoints are themselves relatively large; conforming groups are of high status; the connection between opinions and behaviour is not direct; and there is provision for material wants and political stability. This is hardly an exhaustive treatment of the subject, and remaining questions would deal with the existence of other noteworthy conditions, the relative importance of the listed ones, and the effect of particular social contexts on their importance. Despite these qualifications, we hope our discussion will make some contribu-

[22] The concept of moral integration is used by Angell to refer to the relationship between normative standards and behaviour. He attempts to measure this relationship by using "welfare effort," ascertained in one case by expenditures on local welfare and in another by the amount raised for welfare, and by statistics on crime. Robert C. Angell, "The Computation of Indexes of Moral Integration," in *The Language of Social Research*, ed. by P. F. Lazarsfeld and M. Rosenberg, Glencoe: Free Press, 1955, pp. 58–62.

tion to a better understanding of the role of consensus for the emergence of a collective identity.

THE CASE OF CANADA

Public Opinion and the Image of Canada

It hardly seems necessary to reiterate, in the context of Canadian existence, the significance of the national problems and solutions upon which we have focused. It is possible to differ in evaluating their relative significance, but the evidence from this study leads to the judgment that, with some variations in respect to particular issues, internal problems continue to be the most pressing.

Even more important, however, are the directions of emerging consensus indicated by our data. For example, in perceptions of external problems, we have seen clearly the lessened significance of Britain, the increased importance of the Commonwealth, growing involvement with the United States, and continued commitment to foreign responsibilities. In total, Canadians appear satisfied with traditional alignments, but also increasingly tend to an outward orientation in external matters.

Innovativeness with regard to internal problems is not marked. Traditional divisions between the provincial and federal governments are favoured, with continuing and perhaps even growing support for provincial rights. The one field where some responsiveness to new approaches was apparent concerned French-English relations, but here our data were not sufficiently detailed to give an adequate picture of this most complex problem. Despite the part which the government has played in nation-building, Canadians are reluctant to see the government extend its economic activities except in social welfare. Social welfare, on the contrary, has become a widely accepted area for governmental activity.

It is on problems of symbols that the most dramatic shift in opinions has occurred over the past twenty years. From an acquiescence in the use of symbolic forms derived from another country, notably Britain, a desire has grown steadily for the new and uniquely Canadian. Yet the revolutionary impact of these opinion changes has been modest for a number of reasons. For one thing, up until the time of writing at least, no one has yet developed sufficiently dramatic symbols to unify even important segments of the population. For another, there appears to be more of a desire to modify or adapt existing symbols than to strike out in a completely new direction. This has meant, for example, in the case of the Governor-General, preference for having that office occupied by a Canadian rather than having it completely abolished. Yet it still can be concluded that there have been major changes in the opinions of Canadians on political symbols which yet remain to be mobilized.

It is apparent from the distribution of opinions reported in this study and from information and generalizations derived from other studies, that the major divisions in Canadian society, those based on region and origin and tied to economic factors, seriously weaken national consensus. Moreover, there are few signs of a reversal in this trend. This conclusion, however, should be qualified by the observation that views on symbolic problems are becoming less divergent between English and French-speaking Canadians. But granted the lack of a national consensus, our question is how serious this condition is for the stability and well-being of the country. The implications of a lack of consensus can be evaluated by the use of the criteria we previously developed. In terms of awareness of opinion differences, it is unlikely that Canadians are cognizant of the extent of regional differences. However, differences between French- and English-speaking Canadians are becoming increasingly more observable as a result of the actions of the mass media, separatist organizations, and political leaders in Quebec, and the responses of those in positions of leadership elsewhere in Canada.

We saw that the dominant views were most often expressed by the more prestigious groups in the society: the British-oriented, Protestant, those of high socioeconomic status, and those of central Canada. We suggested that when groups conforming to the majority opinion are of high status, the strain is less than if the opposite is the case, but the dominance of these groups in Canada has not been unchallenged. French-speaking Canadians, those of non-French, non-British ethnic origin, and those living in western Canada all have been concerned, and now more vocally than ever, with demonstrating their right to equal status and equal influence.

Again, although we suggested that strains are minimized when the confronting groups are relatively large, such majorities are difficult to achieve in Canada because of the fragmented nature of the country regionally and ethnically. In addition, a review of the tables contained in Part II will recall that while we considered the largest proportion expressing an opinion part of the dominant viewpoint on national problems, the dominant views often consisted of less than half of the sampled population because of the number of "no opinions" or the number of available alternatives. In essence, this means that in many cases the dominant viewpoint represents a feeble numerical plurality. Divergence in viewpoint is frequent, but the seriousness of this is often minimized because people are not called upon to act on their opinions. If they should, however, conflict could become manifest, as it has in the case of terrorist organizations in Quebec and in the threats of some western Canadians to refight the Battle of the Plains of Abraham.[23]

But for the most part the disintegrative potential inherent in the lack of consensus in Canada measured by our surveys, and the way in which this is associated with particular cleavages, is held in check by the relatively high level of material satisfaction and of political stability. In other words, the existing level of consensus could be a serious problem for the nation, as it has been on such occasions as the pre-Confederation rebellions in Upper and Lower Canada, the Red River Insurrection of 1869 and the Riel Rebellion of 1885, the two conscription crises of 1917 and 1944, and the Winnipeg general strike of 1919 which was treated by federal authorities as a prelude to revolution. To a lesser degree, the extent of emigration and the existence of inequality in rewards also indicate how close to the surface tensions are.

The Part Played by Political Parties

We have sought to find in national political parties one alternative to the existence of primordial ties based on common origin and territory. It is not suggested that political parties can ever replace such ties, but only that they have the potential for providing an additional focus for group loyalty. National political parties as representatives of civil ties cannot be expected to replace ties based on origin or region, but the continuity of the political state requires "an adjustment between them, an adjustment such that the processes of government can proceed freely without seriously threatening the cultural framework of personal identity, and such that whatever discontinuities in 'consciousness of kind' happen to exist in the general society do not radically distort political functioning." [24] If this is a problem for new states it is also one not yet completely solved in Canada.

According to the typology of parties previously developed, the Conservatives and Liberals could be described as broad-based cadre

[23] The latter view was expressed in an editorial in a Calgary community newspaper, The North Hill News, April 16, 1964.
[24] Clifford Geertz, "The Integrative Revolution, Primordial Sentiments and Civil Politics in the New States," in Old Societies and New States, ed. by Clifford Geertz, New York: Free Press, 1963, p. 155.

parties oriented toward electoral success. On the basis of those opinions of their supporters which we were able to examine, we found these two parties highly successful in controlling differences based on type of community and trade-union affiliation, and, in declining order, those associated with marital status, age, sex, and social class. Of the two major parties the Liberals have been better able than the Conservatives both to attract those of French origin and somehow to contribute to a greater unity of outlook among French- and English-speaking supporters.[25] In both parties, there was a suggestion that an opposition role, presumably when they were left with more committed supporters, was also associated with greater consensus among these supporters.

In our discussion at the outset of this study, we suggested that the greatest contribution to building sufficient national consensus for shaping a collective identity would come from broad-based parties of principle. These, however, are notably lacking in Canada.

All party systems function more easily when a common threat or a common enterprise binds the people together by reducing factional dissent and facilitating compromise. Canadian parties have, consequently, performed their tasks most easily when the country was engaged in some great national enterprise like the construction of railways, rapid economic development, or, of course, when exposed to a common external threat. Since the end of World War II the proportion of third party votes was lowest when the Conservative leader fired the country with his vision of northern development. This vision has faded, and at the present time, no external force or danger is felt keenly enough to impose a sense of national unity or emergency.[26]

At least one party based on principle, the CCF/NDP, exists, but its base of support is narrow. Its supporters possess a relatively unified outlook, but the restricted nature of its appeal has thus far prevented it from making a significant contribution to national integration. The Social Credit party is probably in the same position, as evident from its disintegration since the 1963 general election, although our own data were generally not sufficient to allow for generalizations. Whatever the future of the minor parties in Canada, they represent pri-

[25] According to an evaluation by John Meisel, "the Liberal party's immediate future looks brighter than that of any other party. It is not as much because the Liberals have the largest following and that they are only a few seats short of a Parliamentary majority. Of all the parties, they are strongest in the area where the present impact will be resolved if it is resolved at all: Quebec." John Meisel, "The Stalled Omnibus: Canadian Parties in the 1960's," *Social Research*, 30, Autumn, 1963, pp. 388–389.

[26] *Ibid.*, p. 379.

marily the centrifugal tendencies in the country. It is questionable if they can appreciably aid in the development of a unified national identity.

Omitted from detailed discussion have been such potentially integrative mechanisms as the educational system, the mass media, leadership in general, and political party leadership in particular, not because they are less important, but rather because they are outside the confines of this study. A more comprehensive analysis of the development of a national identity would clearly have to take them into account.

Perhaps least easy to justify in the light of our concentration on political parties is our neglect of party leadership. The complex of factors dividing Canada is perhaps better reconciled in the person or actions of party leaders. For example, such is an interpretation of Mr. Diefenbaker's electoral success in 1958.

His Dutch origin won favour among all the new Canadians assimilated into English Canada. His deep British convictions appealed to citizens of Anglo-Saxon origin. His modest beginnings were admired by the mass of little people. The veterans of two wars considered him as one of theirs. He had lived in Ontario, and he was a Westerner. His great vitality impressed youth. His passionate eloquence and his evangelical style awakened familiar echoes among many Protestants. They also permitted an effective resort to righteous indignation against his opponents' abuse of the rights of Parliament; the same argument met a cold response in French Canada, where there is not an equal reverence for parliamentary institutions.[27]

Some commentators have gone so far as to argue that, "In Canada more than anywhere else it is possible to define a party as being a body of supporters following a given leader. Parliamentary elections are primarily occasions on which the electors choose between party leaders and prospective prime ministers." [28]

If, in the face of these comments, some justification for our procedure is required, then it rests mainly on the historical continuity provided by focusing on parties themselves. We would argue as well that despite the effectiveness of some leaders, especially when they become prime ministers, others are not always able to attain the national significance which political parties do. Although arguing, then, for the validity of emphasizing party, we do not discount the importance of leaders. A study of leadership has been omitted for the

[27] J. M. Beck, "Quebec and the Canadian Election of 1958," *Parliamentary Affairs*, 12, 1958–59, p. 97. This interpretation is based on a similar one by the historian Michel Brunet in a communication with *Le Devoir*, March 27, 1958.

[28] H. M. Clokie, *Canadian Government and Politics*, Toronto: Longmans-Green, 1944, p. 91.

reasons cited here and because the issues upon which we focused could not be studied in relation to opinions of leaders as they could in relation to party preference.

Our contention has never been, despite our use of such terms as "homogeneous" and "consensus," that a completely united public opinion is a necessary condition for social stability, nor that group differences must be totally submerged.

It is neither important nor necessary that the component parts of a society coincide in their ideas and their desires; the important, the essential thing is that each should know, and to a certain extent incorporate in his own life, the ideas and desires of the others.[29]

We have been concerned with seeing how party loyalties in Canada have led to some identity of interest, and where they have been unsuccessful in compensating for more primordial loyalties. Whether parties themselves or other agencies can encourage greater empathy still remains to be answered. In writing about a contemporary situation where greater passions are aroused each day, predictions are foolhardy. Since we have seen during the past two decades the unfolding of views on national problems which bear on the formulation of a national identity, we may hope that the public and its leaders come to recognize that, since in some areas conflict of interest has become minor, these might be the basis on which a creative leadership could modify intransigence in others.

[29] José Ortega y Gasset, *Invertebrate Spain*, trans. Mildred Adams, London: George Allen and Unwin, 1937, p. 44.

INDEX

INDEX

259